GEOMETRY BY TRANSFORMATIONS

S.M.P. HANDBOOKS

Communicating With a Computer by
A. B. Bolt and M. E. Wardle

Practical Programming by
P. N. Corlett and J. D. Tinsley

Statistics and Probability by
J. H. Durran

SCHOOL MATHEMATICS PROJECT HANDBOOKS

GEOMETRY
BY
TRANSFORMATIONS

E. A. MAXWELL
Fellow of Queens' College, Cambridge

CAMBRIDGE UNIVERSITY PRESS
Cambridge
London · New York · Melbourne

Published by the Syndics of the Cambridge University Press
The Pitt Building, Trumpington Street, Cambridge CB2 1RP
Bentley House, 200 Euston Road, London NW1 2DB
32 East 57th Street, New York, NY 10022, USA
296 Beaconsfield Parade, Middle Park, Melbourne 3206, Australia

© Cambridge University Press 1975

Library of Congress catalogue card number: 74–76568

ISBN 0 521 20405 4

First published 1975

Printed in Great Britain
at the University Printing House, Cambridge
(Euan Phillips, University Printer)

CONTENTS

FOREWORD

'Elements of geometry carefully weeded of every proposition tending to demonstrate another; all lying so handy that you may pick and choose without ceremony. This is useful in fortification; you cannot play at billiards without this... And upon such terms, and with such inducements, who would not be a mathematician?'

These are not the words of some reactionary objecting to the approach to geometry found in the texts of the School Mathematics Project, but were, in fact, written in 1781 by James Williamson, a Fellow of Hertford College, Oxford, who felt compelled to challenge the methods of teaching geometry advanced by Clairaut.

Geometry in Williamson's view was no mere experimental science, but an unparalleled training ground for logical thought, precise argument and the cultivation of the art of proof. Writing some fifty years later, Augustus De Morgan observed that Williamson's remarks were not without force if directed against experimental geometry as 'an ultimate course of study', but that they 'lose their ironical character and become serious earnest when applied to the same as a preparatory method'. In De Morgan's opinion, once provided with such inducements the 'child of moderate powers' would not fail to be 'interested in the announcement that his separate truths are parts of one chain, and that it may be shown that one follows from another'.

Since De Morgan's time the teaching of geometry has undergone many changes, but one basic problem has remained: granted that geometry is introduced as an experimental science, how is the transition to geometry as a deductive study to be made? Indeed, should such a transition be attempted, and, if so, with which pupils?

Recently, such formal work has tended – in British schools at least – to be algebraic rather than synthetic. In traditional syllabuses, coordinate (analytic) geometry has usurped the place of pure geometry, while in the modern syllabuses formal geometry has come to be identified with linear algebra. Attempts by foreign mathematicians to produce formal treatments of geometry based on an approach through transformations have tended to be more attractive mathematically than pedagogically. If for no other reason, Dr Maxwell's book is especially welcome. In it, whilst not entirely abandoning an experimental approach, he aims to provide the reader with a coherent view of the geometry of the Euclidean plane, and to re-establish school geometry as a means to logical and deductive ends. The book could usefully be used in the classroom in conjunction with existing SMP texts, and is also most suitable for the purposes of teacher education – both pre-service and in-service (of which the most important component is, of course, self-education). As Dr Maxwell remarks, not all the material is easy; we can, however, be assured that, in his hands, it will be presented clearly!

The SMP is pleased that this work should be published in its series of Handbooks. It is a welcome contribution towards the improvement of geometry teaching in schools.

A. G. HOWSON

PREFACE

Although interest at school level in the geometry of transformations is comparatively recent, there is already a literature too large to be quoted usefully here. I have consulted, to my considerable benefit, all the following:

1. *Synopses for modern secondary school mathematics* (O.E.E.C.)
   Following the seminar at Royaumont, whence much of the impetus to modernisation derived.
2. *Some lessons in mathematics* (Cambridge, 1964)
   Mathematical reflections (Cambridge, 1970)
   Two excellent books prepared by the Association of Teachers of Mathematics. Both deal with subjects other than geometry, and give references to other publications. The former, in particular, has a very detailed and useful bibliography.
3. *Geometric transformations*, by I. M. Yaglom (Random House, The L. W. Singer Company)
   Vol. 1 (displacements and symmetry) 1962
   Vol. 2 (similarity transformations, etc.) 1968
   Two outstanding volumes, translated from the Russian of 1955 by Allen Shields.
4. *Transformation geometry*, by Max Jeger (George Allen and Unwin, 1966)
   Another outstanding volume, translated from the German of 1964 by A. N. Deicke and A. G. Howson.
5. *Introduction to geometry*, by H. S. M. Coxeter (Wiley, 1961)
   A masterly and far-ranging survey of many aspects of geometry.
6. *Geometry revisited*, by H. S. M. Coxeter and S. L. Greitzer (Random House, The L. W. Singer Company, 1967)
   What was for the authors a re-visit will be for most people a new and exciting journey.
7. *A course of geometry for colleges and universities*, by D. Pedoe (Cambridge, 1970)
   Another wide-ranging survey. In particular, there is a vivid account of transformations using the technique of complex numbers.
8. *Beginners' book of geometry*, by G. C. Young and W. H. Young (Chelsea reprint)
   First published in 1905, and now reprinted in 1970. This book

was some 50 years ahead of its time, and it is hard to see, in retrospect, why its influence was not much more decisive. The subject matter is, essentially, the first stage of a school geometry course.

9. *Motion geometry and vectors*, by J. B. Wordsworth (Warne, 1969) A very useful elementary introduction.

10. *Deductive transformation geometry*, by R. P. Burn (Cambridge, 1975). This book, not published at the time of writing, gives a thorough and detailed account of the abstract bases of the theory.

11. The various 'projects' have produced texts of their own, and these are of great value. Special mention may be made of

   (i) *School Mathematics Project* (Cambridge)
   Geometry is a recurring theme throughout the many volumes. In particular, there is in the Further Mathematics Series an excellent volume (Draft Edition) on *Linear algebra and geometry*.

   (ii) *The Scottish Mathematics Group, Modern mathematics for schools* (Blackie and Chambers) has valuable chapters on geometry.

The miscellaneous examples at the end are taken from a number of public examinations, and I am grateful for permission to use them. The references are:

C.: Cambridge Local Examinations Syndicate.

C.J.E.: Cambridge Scholarship Examinations.

C.I.E.: Cambridge Institute of Education.

S.I.E.: Sheffield Institute of Education.

M.A.: Teaching Diploma of the Mathematical Association.

S.M.P.: School Mathematics Project.

I am deeply indebted to my pupil Dr N. G. Lloyd who read the manuscript and made a number of valuable corrections and suggestions, and to Dr R. P. Burn, of Homerton College, who not only helped with the correcting of the proofs but, in doing so, earned the reader's gratitude by removing ambiguities and errors.

I have on several former occasions paid tribute to the Staff of the Cambridge University Press, and it is a pleasure to record once again my sincerest thanks.

Cambridge 1975   E.A.M

INTRODUCTION

The upheaval in mathematical education has been particularly severe in geometry, and there seems little means at present of assessing a course that can prove generally satisfactory.

This book is less the result of a plan than of a growth that, I should like to think, has gradually become organic. Part I is an account of Basic Geometry, with continual appeals to experience. The axioms are, essentially, what the eye sees when it folds paper and pricks figures from one sheet to another; and who nowadays will be more conscious of logical gaps than the author, brought up in Scotland over half a century ago? But one consistent aim, however unsuccessfully fulfilled, has been to envisage the argument through (if the language is not too confused) the eye of the pupil; I want him to understand what it is all about rather than to get lost in niceties that more mature experience will later, rightly, judge to be vital.

Part II is a lengthy and fairly detailed account of the fundamental transformations from which so much of interest in geometry derives. I have tried to knit Parts I and II together so that a thread of argument runs continuously along; for example, the circle appears later than usual, after the isometries have been studied and just before similarities throw their shadows.

Part III gives a brief account of the use of matrices to solve problems in transformations.

The book is, I suppose, aimed basically at middle and upper school, though its exact placing in a mathematics course will depend on the surrounding context – parts of the book would probably stretch (and, I believe, interest) many undergraduates.

I have tried to make the text as clear as I can, but there is little doubt that some of the work just *is* difficult. For this I make no apology: clarity and difficulty are quite distinct features, and much of the fascination of mathematics comes from grappling with the latter. But I hope that there is plenty of material at all levels to give adequate satisfaction to all readers.

I find it quite impossible to give sources for my own education in the subject. A list of books is appended, and I have profited from most of them. Much of the material I worked out for myself, to find later that other authors had already been there. In particular, notation that I 'invented' kept reappearing in earlier writings – a tribute, perhaps, to the inevitability of mathematical symbolism.

In brief, nothing new is claimed, but it is hoped that the gathering together of threads will prove helpful to mathematicians at a variety of stages of development.

It is not easy to decide just how many examples the reader should be given to solve in a book of this kind. But perhaps I might add two related suggestions: the teacher will find his command of the subject growing if he makes up for himself examples to illustrate points that are causing difficulty; and the reader without a teacher will learn much if he follows that same course and also pushes some of the existing examples beyond their stated limits. The fascination of geometry comes with the urge to discover new facts (however trivial) *for oneself*.

PART I
BASIC GEOMETRY

1
FIRST IDEAS

The science of geometry deals with shapes, measurements and displacements. Its basis is the experience of these properties in the natural world, supplemented by deductions from that experience by the normal processes of logical thought. The starting-point is a search for *primitive elements* so simple (or seemingly so simple) that they cannot be described in terms of anything simpler.

The essential material of geometry is threefold:

(i) the *geometrical objects*, such as point, straight line and plane;

(ii) the means of *measurement*, such as length and angle;

(iii) the *relationships*, such as equality, parallelism and perpendicularity.

This threefold material is closely inter-connected. For example, it is often through considerations of measurement that relationships between geometrical objects are best exhibited.

The three terms just named are familiar as words. A first task is to review them with an eye to greater precision.

1. The method of folding

Much introductory work can be based on a simple technique of paper-folding.

Take any sheet of flat paper: the shape does not matter, but flatness is essential.

Note that when we speak of a plane we mean precisely a flat surface of this type.

Fold the paper by laying one part across the other and pressing carefully to make a *crease*, indicated by the dotted line in Figure 1.

Definition. The word *folding* will be used for this process. An instruction, 'Fold the paper' according to some particular rule will mean, without further elaboration of statement, that a *crease* (such as that marked *XY* in the diagram) is required to be made.

The crease is in the shape commonly called a *straight line*. Such a straight line is not to be defined in terms of any conception simpler than itself. The examination of a crease shows exactly what is intended.

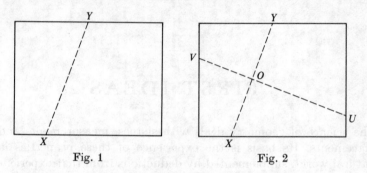

Fig. 1   Fig. 2

2. The method of pricking

A second process, to be called *pricking*, must be described next. To mark a position from the front of a sheet of paper to the back, or from one sheet of paper to another in contact with it, the paper is pricked in the obvious way by a pin or similar sharp object. The aim is to transfer a geometrical figure (for example, a triangle – of which we speak later) in its exact detail from one position to another.

The purist will, rightly, note the looseness of the phrase at the end of the preceding sentence. Until the sheets are separated, the details are indeed exact, if we neglect the thickness of the paper; but the process of separation necessarily removes the exactness of *position*. It is an act of faith, based on reasonable experience, that figures which agree when in contact continue, after separation, to do so in all respects except position. This is a basic assumption, hardly expressed (perhaps hardly expressible), about the nature of space itself, and we make it freely.

Definition. Two figures which can be brought into contact in this way, either being a pricking of the other, are said to be *congruent*.

3. Perpendicular lines

Take a sheet of paper and fold it to give the line *XY* (Figure 2). Fold it again so that *X* falls exactly over *Y* [transparent paper may help] and so obtain a second crease UV. Denote by the letter O the inter-section of the two creases.

Definition. The position O indicates precisely what is meant by a *point*. Euclid's well-known definition of a point as having 'position but no magnitude' describes adequately what we have in mind. Indeed, pricking was said in Section 2 to mark a *position* when the word *point* would have been equally appropriate.

Points on a straight line are said to be *collinear*; straight lines having a point in common are said to be *concurrent*.

Notation. The point of intersection of two straight lines such as XY, UV is denoted by the symbol

$$XY \cap UV$$

or, equivalently, by

$$UV \cap XY,$$

the alternative forms emphasising that the roles of XY and UV are interchangeable. The intersection is said accordingly to be *symmetrical* in XY and UV.

It is convenient to write

$$XY \cap UV \equiv O,$$

though those accustomed to the notation of sets may prefer to see $\{O\}$ on the right-hand side, emphasising that the intersection of the set of points of XY with the set of points of UV is the set of points consisting of the single element O.

Definition. The crease UV obtained as above, by folding with X upon Y, is said to be *perpendicular* to XY.
We write

$$UV \perp XY.$$

The common process of 'doubling' a sheet of paper by folding about XY and then 're-doubling' by folding about OU (now lying in contact with OV) – the effect is that of 'a corner with four sheets super-posed' – shows that the sheet can also be folded in reverse order, first about UV and then about XY, to give the same creases (Figure 3). Thus not only is UV perpen-

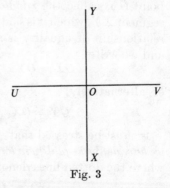

Fig. 3

dicular to XY, but also XY is perpendicular to UV, and we may equally well write

$$XY \perp UV.$$

The relationship of perpendicularity between XY and UV is, in fact, another example of one that is symmetrical.

4. Segments

A straight line may be imagined, possibly with some difficulty, as extending indefinitely in both directions. A part of such a line (for example, XY or UV in the cases considered) is called a *segment*. As we have implied, a segment XY is named in terms of its *end points* X and Y.

There is an ambiguity of usage here: the indefinitely extended straight line through X and Y is also given the name XY. Thus the symbol XY may mean *either* the whole line *or* that part of it whose end points are X and Y. In practice, the context usually makes the meaning perfectly clear. Precision of notation is possible, but rather cumbersome.

For example, the construction of the crease UV in Section 3 divided the segment XY into two smaller segments OX, OY, both being parts of the straight line XY.

5. Equality of segments

Two segments that can be superposed exactly by folding are said to be *equal*, the phrase *equal in length* of normal language being implicit. Thus equality is a particular case of the congruence of figures to which we referred in Section 2.

For example (Figure 4), a crease UV which causes a point X to fall upon a point Y meets the segment XY in a point O for which OX and OY are equal. The point O is called the *middle point* of the segment XY, which it is said to *bisect*. The relationship of equality is symmetrical, and we write

$$OX = OY$$

or, alternatively,

$$OY = OX.$$

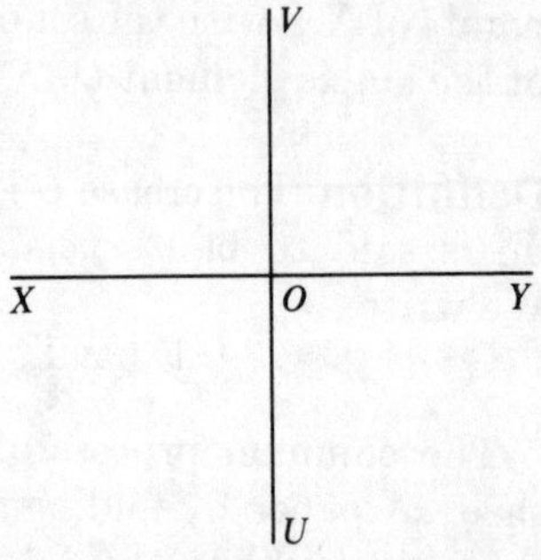

Fig. 4

It must be stressed that, with the only means at present available, *we have defined equality in terms of superposition by folding*. In Figure 5, where the dotted lines denote creases,

$$XY = UV \quad \text{and} \quad UV = PQ.$$

But we cannot make, as a deduction, the natural conclusion $XY = PQ$, since *there is no crease by which we can fold XY upon PQ*.

It is true that we have no doubt about what we think we mean when we say that '$XY = UV$ and $UV = PQ$ implies $XY = PQ$', but it must be realised that *this is one more basic assumption about the nature of space*. What we are, in fact, implying is that two rods are assumed to be equal in length if they can be moved to any one place where they are found to be 'equal', and we shall make the assumption of equality, usually without comment.

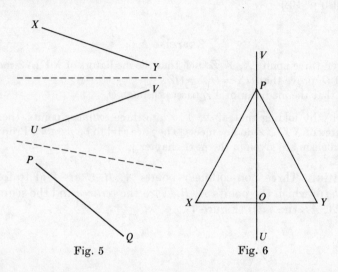

Fig. 5　　　　　　　　　　Fig. 6

Notation. This is a convenient point at which to introduce a useful piece of symbolism. The symbol $\Rightarrow$ is used to denote *implication* in the sense just used, that the statement

$$\left. \begin{array}{l} 'XY = UV \\ UV = PQ \end{array} \right\} \Rightarrow XY = PQ'$$

means, '$XY = UV$ and $UV = PQ$ implies $XY = PQ$'.

The symbol $\Leftrightarrow$ is used similarly to denote 'two-way implication' in the sense that the symmetrical relationships of perpendicularity and equality can be written

$$XY \perp UV \Leftrightarrow UV \perp XY \quad \text{and} \quad XY = UV \Leftrightarrow UV = XY.$$

6. The mediator, or perpendicular bisector

Let X, Y be two given points (Figure 6). Fold X upon Y so that a crease UV is obtained meeting XY in O. Then, as we have seen,

$$OX = OY, \quad UV \perp XY.$$

The line UV, through the middle point of XY and perpendicular to it, is called the *mediator* or *perpendicular bisector* of XY.

Let P be any point whatever on UV. Then, in the folding, X falls upon Y, and P is unaffected. Hence, by the definition,

$$PX = PY.$$

In the language of normal conversation, P is *equidistant* from X and Y. [See also p. 10.]

Exercise A

1. Given three points X, Y, Z such that the mediators of XY, XZ meet in a point O, prove that $OX = OY = OZ$.
Verify that the mediator of YZ passes through O.

2. Verify by folding that, if X, Y, Z are three *collinear* points, then the mediators of XY, XZ do not meet. [They are said to be *parallel*. Properties of parallelism are given in the next chapter.]

Definition. Three non-collinear points A, B, C are said to form a *triangle*, of which the points A, B, C are the *vertices* and the segments BC, CA, AB the *sides* (Figure 7).

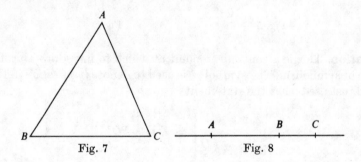

Fig. 7   Fig. 8

7. Order

The concept of order introduces another of those basic ideas that are easier to comprehend than to explain.

Let A, B, C be three given points on a line (Figure 8). Consider first the notion of *sense*: a pencil travelling from a point A *towards* (itself an undefined, instinctive concept) a point B is said to traverse the line *in the sense* $\overrightarrow{AB}$. If it continues beyond B to a point C, the new journey is $\overrightarrow{BC}$ and the total journey is $\overrightarrow{AC}$. It is natural symbolism to write

$$\overrightarrow{AB} + \overrightarrow{BC} = \overrightarrow{AC}.$$

When, as in Figure 8, $\overrightarrow{BC}$ is the immediate continuation of $\overrightarrow{AB}$, the points A, B, C are said to be *in order* on the line. Alternative language is that B is *between* A and C; the segment AC, indeed, consists of those points that lie between A and C, and of those points only. It is also said that A and C are on *opposite sides* of B.

The idea of *between-ness* can be demonstrated dramatically. Draw the line through B perpendicular to AC (Figure 9) and cut the paper along that line into two parts. If B is between A and C, then each part contains one, and only one, of the points A and C.

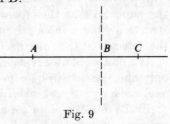

Fig. 9

The symbol $\overrightarrow{BA}$ is used to denote that sense has been *reversed*, so that the pencil describing the line passes from B to A. Taking advantage of the normal language of algebra, we agree to write

$$\overrightarrow{AB} = -\overrightarrow{BA}.$$

The relation $\qquad \overrightarrow{AB} + \overrightarrow{BC} = \overrightarrow{AC} \qquad$ (A, B, C collinear)

holds with complete generality, stating, in effect, that the journey from A to B and on to C is the same in its result as a journey from A to C.

The particular case

$$\overrightarrow{AB} + \overrightarrow{BA} = \overrightarrow{AA}$$

agrees with the convention $\overrightarrow{AB} = -\overrightarrow{BA}$ on the understanding that $\overrightarrow{AA}$, being no journey in total, is interpreted as zero.

Other uses of the language of order will be incorporated as we go, often without comment. Suppose, for example, that OA, OB, OC are three segments with a common point O (Figure 10), and imagine a thin rod to turn about O through the positions OA, OB, OC in succession. Then OB lies *between* OA and OC.

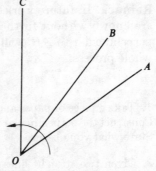

Definition. The *sense of rotation* shown in Figure 10, being opposite to that of the hands of a clock, is called *counterclockwise*, as indicated by the arrow. When sign is involved, it is conventional to take the *counterclockwise* sense as *positive* and the clockwise sense as negative.

Fig. 10

8. Constructions

Implicit in what has been done are *constructions* for performing certain geometrical operations:

(i) *To construct the straight line joining two given points A, B:* Fold the paper so that the crease passes through A and B. The simpler instruction, 'Use a ruler', though more popular in practice, suffers from the defect that the ruler itself has to obtain a straight edge somehow.

As a matter of observation, it is in the nature of space that one, and only one, crease can be constructed though A and B, so that *there is one, and only one, straight line through two given points.*

(ii) *To bisect a given segment AB and to find its mediator:* Fold the paper so that A lies exactly on top of B, and then crease.

(iii) *To draw the straight line perpendicular to a given straight line and passing through a given point not on it:* Let AB be the given line and P the given point not on it (Figure 11). Fold the paper about AB and prick P through to Q. Then PQ is the required line.

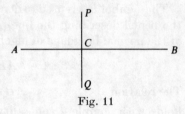

Fig. 11

There is one, and only one, straight line through P perpendicular to AB.

Definition. The point
$$C = PQ \cap AB$$
is called the *foot* of the perpendicular PC from P to AB.

Remark. In future work it will be assumed that these constructions are known without further description. A phrase such as, 'Draw PC perpendicular to AB' will be used without explanation to cover the whole process.

Exercise B

1. Take a piece of paper and on it mark three points A, B, C. Construct the perpendicular from A to BC, from B to CA, and from C to AB. State what you observe.

2. Given two straight lines AB, AC meeting in A, obtain a construction to find a point X on AC such that $AX = AB$.

3. Given two straight lines AB, AC meeting in A, obtain a construction to find a point P such that $PB \perp AB$ and $PC \perp AC$.

State why you can expect from Question 1 that, if $X = AB \cap PC$ and $Y = AC \cap PB$, then $PA \perp XY$.

4. Confirm by folding that if, in Question 3, $AB = AC$, then $PB = PC$.

9. Rays

A *ray* issuing from a point A is that part of a straight line through A which lies on one definite side of A. If A lies on a line segment XY, as in Figure 12, then there are through A two *opposite* rays $\overrightarrow{AX}$, $\overrightarrow{AY}$.

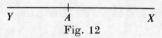

Y   A   X

Fig. 12

Notation. The *symbol of inclusion* $\in$ is used in the sense that

$$A \in XY$$

means that A is one of that set of points constituting the line segment XY.

It will often be convenient to name a line, regarded as an entity, by a single symbol in lower case italics such as l. Then the statement

$$`A \in l\text{'}$$

means that the point A is on the line l. By natural extension, the statement

$$`A \notin l\text{'}$$

means that the point A is not on l.

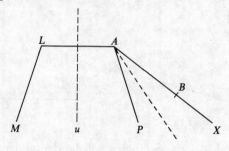

Fig. 13

10. Transfer of a segment

Let LM be a given segment and $\overrightarrow{AX}$ a given ray (Figure 13). It is required *to transfer LM to $\overrightarrow{AX}$ by finding a point B on $\overrightarrow{AX}$ such that $AB = LM$.*

This can be done by two foldings:

(i) Fold L onto A, by the crease marked u, and prick M through to P, so that

$$AP = LM.$$

(ii) Fold the line AP onto AX, by the crease marked v, and prick P through to B so that $AB = AP.$

Then $AB = AP = LM,$

as required. (See the remarks in Section 5 and the further discussion in Sections 14 and 15 at the end of of this Chapter.)

Exercise C

1. Confirm by folding that the sequence (Figure 13) (i) fold A onto L and prick B through to C, (ii) fold the ray $\overrightarrow{LC}$ onto the ray $\overrightarrow{LM}$, places the point B upon M.

2. *An important result* (compare Section 6). Prove that, *if a point P has the property $PX = PY$, then P is necessarily on the mediator of XY.* [Fold the ray PX on to the ray PY.]

11. Angle

Let $\overrightarrow{OA}$, $\overrightarrow{OB}$ be two rays issuing from a point O (Figure 14). Taken together, they define an *angle*, of which they are individually the *arms* and for which the notation is $\angle AOB$. We are assuming that the reader will accept the word 'angle' in its natural sense, while admitting that exact specification is by no means simple.

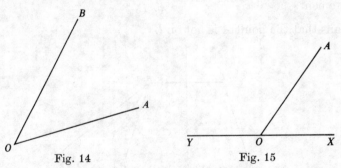

Fig. 14   Fig. 15

Unless stated otherwise, angles will be denoted using the *counter-clockwise convention* that $\angle AOB$ is so named that the hands of a clock turn *against* the sense from $\overrightarrow{OA}$ to $\overrightarrow{OB}$. The convention is sometimes emphasised by the notation $\angle AOB$. The distinction between counter-clockwise and clockwise is described as the *sense* of an angle. Equality of angle is defined by superposition (analogous to length in Section 5).

Definitions. When $O \in XY$, then $\angle XOY$, with arms $\overrightarrow{OX}, \overrightarrow{OY}$, is called a *straight angle*.

If $\overrightarrow{OA}$ is a ray through O as shown in Figure 15, then the two angles

$\angle XOA$, $\angle AOY$ are *supplementary*. Adding the angles, in the obvious sense of the phrase,

$$\angle XOA + \angle AOY = \text{a straight angle.}$$

It is assumed as sufficiently self-evident that *all straight angles are equal*, and that $\angle XOY$ *cannot be equal to a straight angle unless the points X, O, Y are collinear in that order*.

Let two straight lines AB, CD meet in O, as in Figure 16. Four angles are formed,

$$\angle AOC, \ \angle COB, \ \angle BOD, \ \angle DOA.$$

The angles $\angle AOC$, $\angle BOD$ are called *vertically opposite*, as are the angles $\angle COB$, $\angle DOA$.

Then *vertically opposite angles are equal*, since, for example,

$$\left. \begin{array}{l} \angle AOC + \angle COB = \text{a straight angle} \\ \angle COB + \angle BOD = \text{a straight angle} \end{array} \right\} \Rightarrow \angle AOC = \angle BOD.$$

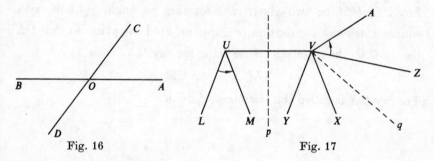

Fig. 16   Fig. 17

Definition. We have seen that

$$AB \perp CD$$

$$\Rightarrow \angle AOC = \angle COB = \angle BOD = \angle DOA,$$

in that the four angles can be folded to coincidence. Each angle is then called a *right angle*.

Since two right angles, suitably placed, make a straight angle, it follows that *all right angles are equal*.

12. Transfer of an angle

Let $\angle LUM$ be a given angle, V a given point and $\overrightarrow{VZ}$ a given ray (Figure 17). It is required *to transfer* $\angle LUM$ *to a position* $\angle ZVA$ *by finding a ray* $\overrightarrow{VA}$ *such that* $\angle ZVA = \angle LUM$.

This can be done by two foldings:

(i) Fold U onto V by the crease marked p, and prick UL, UM onto VX, VY respectively. Note that *the sense of* $\triangle LUM$ *is reversed in the process*, so that
$$\triangle YVX = \triangle LUM.$$

(ii) Fold the line VX onto VZ, by the crease marked q, and prick VY onto VA. Once again sense is reversed, so that
$$\triangle ZVA = \triangle YVX.$$
Hence
$$\triangle ZVA = \triangle YVX$$
$$= \triangle LUM.$$

The transfer of equality of angle is subject to the same difficulties as were mentioned earlier for length. The work of Sections 14 and 15 will again afford a convenient reference.

13. The bisector of an angle

Let $\overrightarrow{UL}$, $\overrightarrow{UM}$ be two given rays forming an angle $\triangle LUM$ with counterclockwise convention (Figure 18). Fold the plane so that $\overrightarrow{UL}$ lies on $\overrightarrow{UM}$, the resulting crease being the ray $\overrightarrow{UX}$. Then
$$\triangle LUX = \triangle XUM.$$
The ray $\overrightarrow{UX}$ is called the *bisector* of $\triangle LUM$.

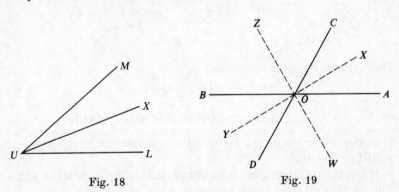

Fig. 18   Fig. 19

Suppose now that AB, CD are two straight lines meeting in O (Figure 19). Let $\overrightarrow{OX}$, $\overrightarrow{OY}$, $\overrightarrow{OZ}$, $\overrightarrow{OW}$ be the bisectors of, respectively, $\triangle AOC$, $\triangle BOD$, $\triangle COB$, $\triangle DOA$. Then
$$\triangle AOC = \triangle BOD$$
$$\Rightarrow \triangle AOX = \triangle XOC = \triangle BOY = \triangle YOD;$$

and $\triangle COB = \triangle DOA$

$\Rightarrow \triangle COZ = \triangle ZOB = \triangle DOW = \triangle WOA.$

It follows that

$$\triangle XOY = \triangle XOC + \triangle COB + \triangle BOY$$
$$= \triangle AOX + \triangle XOC + \triangle COB \quad (\triangle BOY = \triangle AOX)$$
$$= \triangle AOC + \triangle COB$$
$$= \text{a straight angle.}$$

Hence XOY *is a straight line* and, similarly, ZOW *is a straight line.*
Also
$$\triangle XOC + \triangle COZ = \tfrac{1}{2}(\triangle AOC + \triangle COB) = \tfrac{1}{2}\triangle AOB$$
$$= \text{right angle,}$$
so that $$XY \perp ZW.$$

We therefore have the result: *the bisectors of the angles between two straight lines meeting in O form two perpendicular straight lines also meeting in O.*

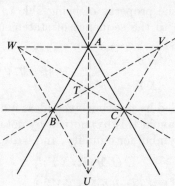

Fig. 20

Exercise D

1. On a sheet of paper mark three points A, B, C and the three lines BC CA, AB, extended in both directions. Obtain, by folding, the six angle bisectors (two at each of A, B, C) shown as dotted lines in Figure 20 and verify that they meet in threes at the points T, U, V, W indicated.

Prove from the results of this section that

$$AU \perp VW, \quad BV \perp WU, \quad CW \perp UV.$$

2. Given two rays $\overrightarrow{AX}$, $\overrightarrow{AY}$, give a construction for the points P, Q, R taken in order on $\overrightarrow{AX}$ such that
$$AP = PQ = QR = AY.$$

3. Let P be any point on the bisector of the angle $\angle XOY$ between two rays $\overrightarrow{OX}$, $\overrightarrow{OY}$. Using the construction given in Section 8, draw $PA \perp OX$, $PB \perp OY$, where $A \in OX$ and $B \in OY$. By folding OX onto OY, confirm that $PA = PB$.

Prove also that $\overrightarrow{PO}$ is the bisector of the angle between $\overrightarrow{PA}$ and $\overrightarrow{PB}$.

14. Equivalence relations

[This section and the next may be postponed should that seem more convenient.]

Two related concepts have caused trouble in the preceding exposition: equality of length, and equality of angle. This is not unreasonable in an argument which, on the one hand, tries to be self-contained and which, on the other, draws its nourishment from the world of human experience. The similarity of these troubles with others that arise in this book (and more so in mathematics generally) suggests a short digression into problems that are closely connected.

The statement, '$LM = XY$' expresses a *relationship* between LM and XY, namely the property of being able to be brought to coincidence. Reactions to the sequence of statements expressed by the language (Section 5)

$$\left. \begin{array}{l} `LM = XY \\ XY = UV \end{array} \right\} \Rightarrow LM = UV'$$

are, however, clouded by pre-conceived ideas induced by the notation of equality; so, to avoid this hypnotism by notation, we temporarily replace the usual symbol for equality, and write, instead,

$$`(LM)\,\mathbf{R}\,(XY)`,$$

which we read as, 'LM *is related to* XY'.

The particular relationship $\mathbf{R}$ under review has three characteristics which we isolate as important for more general discussion in other contexts:

(i) $(LM)\,\mathbf{R}\,(LM),$

since LM automatically is in coincidence with itself.

Definition. A relationship with this 'self-corresponding' property is said to be *reflexive*.

Exercise E

1. Verify that, if, alternatively, $\mathbf{R}$ is used to denote the relationship of perpendicularity between straight lines, then $\mathbf{R}$ is not reflexive.

(ii) $(LM)\,\mathbf{R}\,(XY) \Leftrightarrow (XY)\,\mathbf{R}\,(LM),$

or, in words, LM is related to XY in the same way that XY is related to LM. This is true in the present case, since bringing LM to coincidence with XY also brings XY to coincidence with LM.

Definition. A relationship with this property is said to be *symmetric*.

2. Prove that, if **R** is used to denote the relationship of perpendicularity between straight lines, then **R** is symmetric.

$$
\text{(iii)} \qquad \left.\begin{array}{l} (LM)\,\mathbf{R}\,(XY) \\[2mm] (XY)\,\mathbf{R}\,(PQ) \end{array}\right\} \Rightarrow (LM)\,\mathbf{R}\,(PQ),
$$

and

or, in words, 'LM is related to XY, while XY itself is related to PQ' leads to, 'LM is also related to PQ'.

Definition. A relation which 'follows through' in this way is said to be *transitive*.

This is the troublesome relation for equality of length and equality of angle, since for each of them it comes from an observation of the properties of space that has to be made explicitly. The transitivity here is a consequence of experimental evidence.

3. Two perpendicular lines XY, PQ meet in A (Figure 21). By considering the two facts (i) $PA \perp XY$ and (ii) $XY \perp AQ$, prove that, if **R** is used to denote the relationship of perpendicularity between straight lines, then **R** is not transitive.

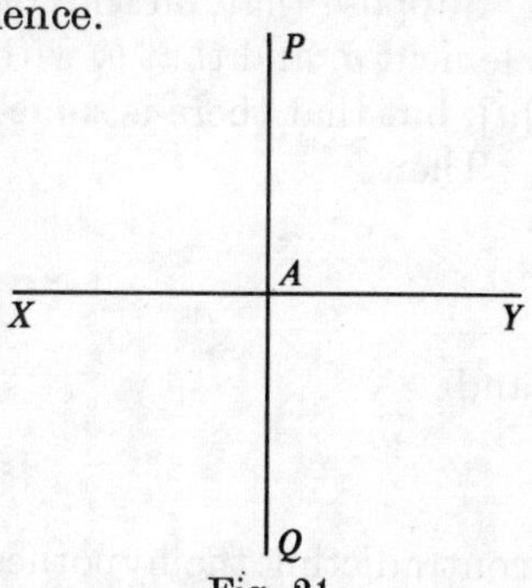

Definition. An *equivalence relation* is one that is all three of reflexive, symmetric and transitive.

Fig. 21

4. A set of points $A, B, C, \ldots$ is taken on a given line and O is an assigned point of that line. The relation $A\,\mathbf{R}\,B$ means that A lies between O and B (strictly *between*, coincidence between A and B being excluded). Prove that the relation is (i) not reflexive, (ii) not symmetrical, but (iii) transitive.

15. Equivalence classes

Let S be a given set of elements (points, lines, etc.) and let **R** be a given equivalence relation. Select any one of the elements, giving it for convenience the name a, and then choose all the elements related to a, say $a_1, a_2, a_3, \ldots$; thus

$$
a\,\mathbf{R}\,a_1, \quad a\,\mathbf{R}\,a_2, \quad a\,\mathbf{R}\,a_3, \quad \ldots.
$$

These elements are said to constitute *the equivalence class of a for the relation* **R**.

In the same way, starting from an element $b \in S$ we obtain the equivalence class of b as the elements $b_1, b_2, b_3, \ldots$ such that

$$b \, \mathbf{R} \, b_1, \quad b \, \mathbf{R} \, b_2, \quad b \, \mathbf{R} \, b_3, \quad \ldots$$

and so for any sequences with initial elements c, d, ...

Denote by $[a]$ the class of all elements equivalent to a, by $[b]$ the class of all elements equivalent to b, and so on.

Certain properties come quickly:

(i) *Every element of S is in its own equivalence class.*

This is an immediate consequence of the reflexive property $a \, \mathbf{R} \, a$.

(ii) *If a is in the equivalence class of b, then b is in the equivalence class of a.*

This is an immediate consequence of the symmetric property $a \, \mathbf{R} \, b \Leftrightarrow b \, \mathbf{R} \, a$.

(iii) *The set S of elements is split by* **R** *into a number of disjoint equivalence classes, no two having any element in common.*

Suppose that, on the contrary, $[a]$ is the equivalence class of some element a, and that b, with equivalence class $[b]$, is an element not in $[a]$; but that there is some element b_1 of $[b]$ that does belong to $[a]$.

Then
$$b_1 \in [a] \implies b_1 \, \mathbf{R} \, a,$$

$$b_1 \in [b] \implies b \, \mathbf{R} \, b_1$$

and
$$\left. \begin{matrix} b \, \mathbf{R} \, b_1 \\ b_1 \, \mathbf{R} \, a \end{matrix} \right\} \implies b \, \mathbf{R} \, a,$$

contradicting the hypothesis that b is not an element of $[a]$.

The upshot of these three properties is that *the relation* **R** *divides the set S into a number of distinct classes with the properties that any two elements of the same class are related but that no two elements are related if they belong to different classes.*

Note that a class may be named in terms of any one of its elements, so that
$$[a] = [a_1] = [a_2] = \ldots.$$

Exercise F

1. Let a set S be partitioned in any way, so that each of its elements occurs in one and only one partition. Prove that the relation $a \, \mathbf{R} \, b$, meaning that a is in the same partition as b, is an equivalence relation.

2. A relation among the integers is defined by the property $a \, \mathbf{R} \, b$ when $a - b$

is a multiple of 3 (possibly zero). Prove that **R** is an equivalence relation, the corresponding classes being

$$\{\ldots, -3, 0, 3, 6, \ldots\},$$
$$\{\ldots, -2, 1, 4, 7, \ldots\},$$
$$\{\ldots, -1, 2, 5, 8, \ldots\}.$$

3. Seven points A, B, C, D, E, F, G are given in order on a line. A relation **R** is set up between the points of the segment AG such that $P\,\mathbf{R}\,Q$ means that P, Q lie in the same one of the six subdividing segments of AG. Prove that **R** is an equivalence relation.

In the particular cases with which we have been concerned, in Sections 10 and 12, *the relation of equality* divides segments into classes, which we describe as of equal length; and the *relation of equality* divides angles into classes, of equal magnitude. It is familiar that length is measured by units such as centimetre or inch; and that angle is measured by units such as degree or radian. Equality of length and of angle is expressed by the equality of these measurements.

The justification for treating the transfer of length and angle as transitive is firmly based on observation, and it is to observation that we appeal.

16. Note on measurement of angle

It is assumed familiar that angles are measured in *degrees*, and that

a right angle contains 90°,
a straight angle contains 180°,
one complete revolution contains 360°.

For radian measure, a text-book on trigonometry should be consulted. For our purposes, the standard formula is

$$\pi \text{ radians} = 180°.$$

Thus a right angle has measure $\frac{1}{2}\pi$ and a complete revolution has measure 2π.

2

PARALLEL LINES

1. Definition

Several treatments of parallelism are available. All involve at some stage a further assumption about the nature of space, and the present version seeks to make the assumption one that will appear to give reasonable agreement with experience.

Let XY be a given line and D a given point not on it (Figure 22). Draw through D the line perpendicular to XY, meeting XY in A; draw through D the line UV perpendicular to AD.

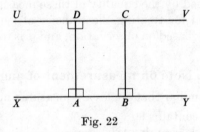

Fig. 22

The line UV so defined will, as a temporary measure, be called *parallel to XY with respect to D*, written

$$UV \parallel XY.$$
$$(D)$$

The special part played by D in this definition is awkward, and steps must be taken to eliminate it. For this we shall need the spatial assumption just mentioned, and, as a preliminary, a definition.

Definition. A *quadrilateral* is a figure defined by four points A, B, C, D and the segments AB, BC, CD, DA joining them. The four points are the *vertices* and the four segments are the *sides*. The two other segments, AC and BD, are called the *diagonals* of the quadrilateral.

Unless the contrary is stated, it is assumed that (apart from A, B, C, D) no two of the segments AB, BC, CD, DA have a point in common. Thus the quadrilateral $ABCD$ in Figure 23 (*a*) is typical in this respect, whereas the case shown in Figure 23 (*b*) is excluded.

[18]

The *assumption to be made is*:

*If three of the angles at the vertices of a quadrilateral are right angles, so is
the fourth.*

A glance at a sheet of writing-paper will confirm this as reasonable.

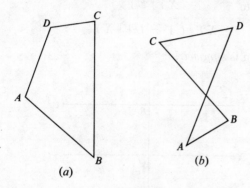

(a)   (b)

Fig. 23

Now take any point C on UV; draw CB perpendicular to XY,
meeting it in B. Then the quadrilateral $ABCD$ has right angles at
A, B, D, and therefore, by the assumption, at C. Hence

$$UV \| XY.$$
$$(C)$$

That is, UV is parallel to XY with respect to *any* point C on UV. We
may therefore drop the suffix and write, simply,

$$UV \| XY,$$

or, in words, UV is parallel to XY.

2. Parallelism as an equivalence relation

The relationship of parallelism has the three properties required for an
equivalence relation:

(i) For the *reflexive* property we regard a straight line as parallel to
itself; this is the particular case arising when D in Section 1 is taken
to be on XY.

(ii) The first use of Figure 22 was to exhibit the relationship

$$UV \| XY,$$
$$(D)$$

leading to the form $UV \| XY.$

Interchange of the roles of the lines XY, UV and of the points D, A gives correspondingly the relationship

$$XY \parallel UV,$$
$$(A)$$

leading to the form $\qquad XY \parallel UV.$

Hence $\qquad\qquad XY \parallel UV \Leftrightarrow UV \parallel XY,$

so that parallelism is *symmetric*.

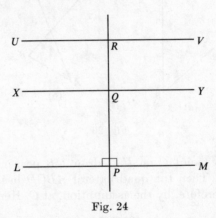

Fig. 24

(iii) Now take three straight lines XY, UV, LM (Figure 24) so that

$$XY \parallel LM, \quad UV \parallel LM.$$

Let P be any point on LM and draw the line through P perpendicular to LM. By comparison with Figure 22, this line meets XY in Q, where

$$PQ \perp XY$$

and also meets UV in R, where

$$PR \perp XY.$$

Hence QR (being the line PQR) is perpendicular to each of XY and UV, and so $\qquad\qquad XY \parallel UV.$

To summarise,

$$\left.\begin{array}{l} XY \parallel LM \\ LM \parallel UV \end{array}\right\} \Rightarrow XY \parallel UV,$$

so that parallelism is *transitive*.

It follows that *parallelism is an equivalence relation, the equivalence classes being the sets of mutually parallel lines.*

Corollary 1. *If LM, XY are two parallel lines, and P is any point of LM, then the line through P perpendicular to LM does meet the line XY* (at the point which is, uniquely, the foot of the perpendicular from *P* to *XY*).

[We show immediately that there are lines in the plane which do *not* meet; i.e. the parallel lines. Hence this remark.]

3. Some properties of parallelism

(i) *Parallel lines (excluding the case of complete coincidence) have no points in common:* In Figure 22, fold the plane about AD, so that, by the right angles, $\overrightarrow{AX}$ lies on $\overrightarrow{AY}$ and $\overrightarrow{DU}$ lies on $\overrightarrow{DV}$. If XY, UV did have a point K in common, they would, by the folding, have to have a second point L. The result of this, however, would be *two* distinct straight lines joining K and L, contradicting the uniqueness postulated in Chapter 1, Section 8. [See the Appendix, p. 268.]

(ii) *Through a given point D, precisely one straight line UV can be drawn parallel to a given line XY:* Let A be the foot of the perpendicular from D to XY, and draw the line through D perpendicular to AD. This is the unique line parallel to XY.

This property is one that is often taken as the basic assumption for the theory of parallel lines, when it is known as *Playfair's axiom*.

4. The rectangle; the square

In Section 1 we used a quadrilateral $ABCD$, all of whose angles are right angles. Such a quadrilateral is called a *rectangle*.

By definition of parallelism in Section 1,

$$AB \parallel CD \quad \text{and} \quad AD \parallel BC,$$

so that *the opposite sides of a rectangle are parallel.*

We interject here the definition: *any quadrilateral whose opposite sides are parallel is called a parallelogram.* The rectangle is a particular case.

The fundamental properties of rectangles, now to be proved, are:

(i) *opposite sides are equal;*

(ii) *the diagonals AC, BD are equal and bisect each other.*

Let u be the mediator of AB (Figure 25) and write

$$u \cap AB = P, \quad u \cap CD = Q,$$

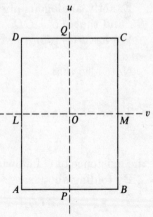

Fig. 25

where Q exists by virtue of Corollary 1. Then

$$AP = PB, \quad u \perp AB.$$

Since the quadrilateral $APQD$ has right angles at A, P, D, it is a rectangle, and so

$$u \perp CD,$$

agreeing with the observation that the quadrilateral $BPQC$ also has a right angle at each vertex.

Fold the rectangle $ABCD$ about u:

$$\left.\begin{array}{c} u \perp AB \\ PA = PB \end{array}\right\} \Rightarrow A \text{ falls on } B;$$

$$\left.\begin{array}{c} AD \perp AP \\ BC \perp BP \end{array}\right\} \Rightarrow AD \text{ falls on } BC;$$

$$u \perp CD \Rightarrow QD \text{ falls on } QC;$$

$$\left.\begin{array}{c} QD \text{ falls on } QC \\ AD \text{ falls on } BC \end{array}\right\} \Rightarrow D \text{ falls on } C$$

$$\Rightarrow QD = QC$$

$$\Rightarrow u \text{ is also the mediator of } CD.$$

Further, $\left.\begin{array}{c} A \text{ falls on } B \\ D \text{ falls on } C \end{array}\right\} \Rightarrow AD = BC.$

Now let v be the mediator of AD, meeting AD in L and BC in M.

Exactly analogous argument shows that v is also the mediator of BC and that $AB = CD$.

We have therefore proved that *the opposite sides of a rectangle are equal*.

Note also that

$$u \parallel AD \parallel BC \quad \text{and} \quad v \parallel AB \parallel CD.$$

To prove that second general property, let

$$u \cap v = O,$$

the existence of O following from Corollary 1.

By folding about u,

$$\angle LOA = \angle MOB, \quad \angle LOD = \angle MOC,$$

where angles are named from the superpositions and not by counter-clockwise sense.

Similarly, by folding about v,

$$\angle LOA = \angle LOD, \quad \angle MOB = \angle MOC.$$

Hence $\angle LOA = \angle MOB = \angle MOC = \angle LOD.$

Similarly, $\angle POA = \angle POB = \angle QOC = \angle QOD.$

The sum total of the eight angles just named is four right angles, so that the sum of two angles, one from each set, is a right angle. Hence, immediately, $PQ \perp LM,$

so that $OPAL, OPBM, OQCM, OQDL$ are all rectangles, as was otherwise clear anyway.

Further,

$$\angle AOB + \angle BOC = (\angle AOP + \angle POB) + (\angle BOM + \angle MOC)$$

$$= 2 \text{ right angles,}$$

so that *AOC is a straight line*; in the same way *BOD is a straight line.*
Finally, the foldings show that

$$OA = OB = OC = OD,$$

so that *AC and BD are equal and bisect each other.*

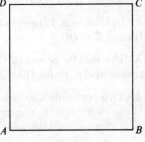

Definition. A *square* is a rectangle whose sides are equal (Figure 26).

The following properties are important, and should be proved as an exercise.

Fig. 26

Exercise A
The square

1. It is, in fact, sufficient that *two adjacent sides* of a rectangle should be equal in order that it may be a square.

2. The diagonals of a square are equal in length.

3. Each diagonal of a square bisects the angles at the vertices through which it passes.

4. The diagonals of a square are perpendicular.

For future reference, note the following two *corollaries* of the rectangle properties.

2-2

Corollary 2. $\qquad \angle PAO = \angle PBO \quad$ (*fold about u*)

$$= \angle QCO \quad (\textit{fold about } v)$$

$$\Rightarrow \angle BAC = \angle ACD.$$

Thus the diagonal AC makes with AB the same angle that it makes with CD.

Corresponding results hold for the other diagonal and the other pair of parallel sides.

Corollary 3. *Let u, v be two given perpendicular lines meeting in O. Take any point A not on u or v. Fold about u so that A gives a point B, and then about v so that A gives a point C. Then O is the middle point of AC.*

The same point C would have been obtained by folding first about v and then about u.

Exercise B

1. Points P and Q are taken on the side AD of a rectangle $ABCD$, and the lines through P, Q perpendicular to AD meet BC in points X, Y respectively. By means of the assumption in Section 1, prove that $ABXP$ and $CDQY$ are rectangles and that $PXYQ$ is also a rectangle.

2. In Question 1, prove that, if P, Q are chosen so that $AP = PQ = QD$, then $AX = QC$.

3. The middle points of the sides AD, BC of a rectangle $ABCD$ are P, X respectively. Prove that $AX = PC$.

4. Two perpendicular lines u, v are given, and P is a point not on either of them. Show how to construct a segment AB, with A on u and B on v, such that P is the middle point of AB.

5. The transversal theorems

Let XY, UV be two given parallel straight lines (Figure 27). A straight line t meeting each of them is called a *transversal*. Write

$$t \cap XY = A, \quad t \cap UV = C.$$

There are four angles at A and four at C. Of these, two have been marked at A and two at C. (The reader should refer to the diagram; words become tedious.) It is to be proved that, UV being parallel to XY, *the four marked angles are equal and the four unmarked angles are equal, the angles of either set being supplementary* (cf. Chapter 1, Section 11) *to those of the other*.

It is immediate that these properties all follow once it is proved that

$$\angle YAC = \angle UCA.$$

Let B be the foot of the perpendicular from C to XY, and D the foot of the perpendicular from A to UV. The configuration is precisely that of the rectangle $ABCD$ in Figure 25. Hence, by Corollary 2,

$$\angle BAC = \angle ACD,$$

or $\angle YAC = \angle UCA.$

With counterclockwise notation,

$$\triangle YAC = \triangle UCA.$$

Similarly, $\triangle CAX = \triangle ACV.$

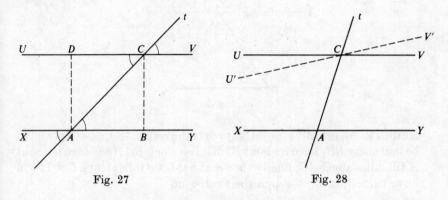

Fig. 27   Fig. 28

6. The converse transversal results

Let XY, UV be two straight lines (Figure 28) crossed by a transversal t at points A, C in such a way that

$$\triangle YAC = \triangle UCA.$$

To prove that

$$\triangle YAC = \triangle UCA \Rightarrow UV \parallel XY.$$

Suppose that $U'V'$ is the line through C parallel to XY. Then

$$\triangle YAC = \triangle U'CA,$$

so that $\triangle U'CA = \triangle YAC = \triangle UCA.$

The two equal angles $\triangle U'CA$, $\triangle UCA$ have the arm CA in common, and so the arms CU, CU' coincide. Hence UCV is precisely the line through C that is parallel to XY.

7. The angles of a triangle

Let ABC be a given triangle. It is required to prove that *the sum of its angles is equal to two right angles.*

Draw through A the straight line XAY parallel to BC (Figure 29). Then, from the transversals AB, AC respectively,

$$\angle CBA = \angle XAB, \quad \angle ACB = \angle CAY.$$

Hence

$$\angle CBA + \angle BAC + \angle ACB = \angle XAB + \angle BAC + \angle CAY$$

$$= \angle XAY$$

$$= \text{a straight angle.}$$

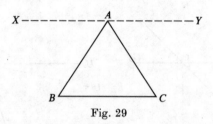

Fig. 29

Remark. An intuitive 'proof' supports the result. 'Suppose a pencil to be laid along BC. Turn it about B till it lies along BA; then turn it about A till it lies along AC; finally turn it about C till it lies along CB. It will have turned, in all, through the angle-sum

$$\angle CBA + \angle BAC + \angle ACB,$$

and also, by observation, through a straight angle.'

But the fact that the three turnings are about *different* vertices makes the 'proof' less satisfactory than appears at first sight.

Corollary 4. *The sum of the angles of a quadrilateral is equal to four right angles.*

Divide the quadrilateral $ABCD$ into two triangles ABD, CBD (see Figure 30). The sum of the angles of the quadrilateral is, in either case, equal to the sum of the angles of the component triangles, and this sum is four right angles.

Comment. There is a curiosity of logic here. In dealing with parallel lines we assumed (observing, say, a sheet of note-paper) that a quadrilateral with three right angles (a very special case) has its fourth angle a right angle too. From this, via the transversal theorems, we have deduced the result that the sum of the angles of a triangle is two right angles and hence the extended result that the sum of the angles of *any* quadrilateral is four right angles.

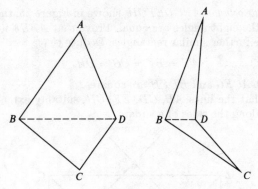

Fig. 30

Exercise C†

1. Given that, in Figure 31, BI bisects the angle at B and CI bisects the angle at C, prove that $\angle BIC$ exceeds $\frac{1}{2}\angle BAC$ by one right angle.

2. Given that, in Figure 32, BX, BU trisect the angle at B (dividing it, that is, into three equal parts) and that CX, CU trisect the angle at C, prove that $\angle BXC$ exceeds $\angle BUC$ by one third of the supplement (Chapter 1, Section 11) of $\angle BAC$.

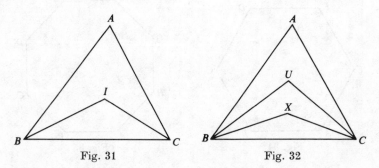

Fig. 31   Fig. 32

3. Given that, in Figure 33, $ABCD$ is a rectangle and that PA, PB, RC, RD bisect the angles at A, B, C, D respectively, prove that $PQRS$ is a rectangle and (using an argument by folding if you wish) that its sides are equal, so that it is a square. Check (again by an argument based on folding if you wish) that $PR \perp QS$ and that $AD \parallel RP \parallel BC$ and $AB \parallel QS \parallel DC$.

4. In the *hexagon $ABCDEF$*, shown in Figure 34, the six sides are equal and the six angles are equal. (Such a hexagon is called *regular*.) Prove that $ABDE$ and $BCEF$ are rectangles, and deduce that $AD = BE = CF$.

† The fact that a right angle is measured by 90° (ninety degrees) is not essential, but eases calculations.

5. In the regular *octagon ABCDEFGH*, shown in Figure 35, the eight sides are equal and the eight angles are equal. Prove that *ABEF* is a rectangle and name three further similar rectangles. Deduce that

$$AE = BF = CG = DH.$$

Prove also that *ACEG* and *BDFH* are squares.

Prove also that the lines *AB, CD, EF, GH*, suitably extended in both directions, lie along the sides of a square.

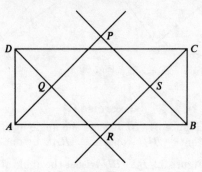

Fig. 33

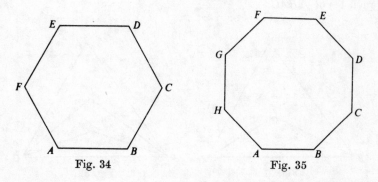

Fig. 34   Fig. 35

6. *ABCD* is a rectangle in which the length *AB* is twice the length of *AD* (Figure 36). The line $\overrightarrow{DA}$ is produced to *P* so that *AP* = *DA*; *R* is the middle point of *CD*, and the rectangle *PQRD* is completed. Prove that the quadrilaterals *AURD, BURC, AUQP* are congruent squares and that *AQBR* is a square.

8. The isosceles triangle

A triangle is called *isosceles* when two of its sides are equal, and *equilateral* when all its sides are equal.

The main result is that *the angles opposite the equal sides are equal:* In △*ABC*, let *AB* = *AC* (Figure 37).

Fold the triangle (about the line u through A) so that $\overrightarrow{AB}$ falls along $\overrightarrow{AC}$. Since $AB = AC$, the point B falls on C, so that $\angle ABC$ is folded on to $\angle ACB$. The two angles are therefore equal.

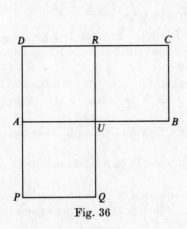

Fig. 36

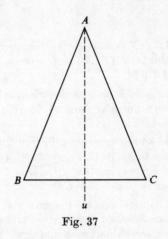

Fig. 37

Note that, when sense is taken into account,

$$\triangle CBA = \triangle ACB.$$

The *converse* result is also true: *if two angles are equal, then the sides opposite them are equal:*

Suppose that $\angle ABC = \angle ACB$ (Figure 38). Fold the triangle about that line p through A which is such that C falls on some point D of the the line BC. [In fact, $p \perp BC$.] Then

$$\angle ADC = \angle ACD \text{ (folded)}$$
$$= \angle ACB \text{ (re-named)}$$
$$= \angle ABC \text{ (given)}.$$

But $\angle ABC = \angle ADC$
$$\Rightarrow AB \parallel AD,$$

which is impossible (since the two lines have a common point A) unless the two lines coincide. Thus C falls on B, and so

$$AB = AC.$$

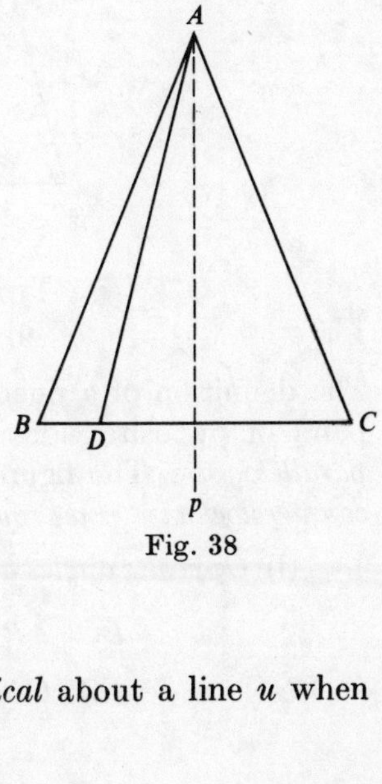

Fig. 38

Definition. A figure is said to be *symmetrical* about a line u when folding about u places one half of the figure exactly in contact with the other half; u is called an *axis of symmetry*.

For example, the isosceles triangle ABC is symmetrical about the *axis u*.

Exercise D

1. ABC is an isosceles triangle in which $AB = AC$, and X, Y are the middle points of AB, AC respectively. Prove that $\angle AXY = \angle AYX$ and also that $XY \parallel BC$.

2. ABC is an isosceles triangle in which $AB = AC$, and D is the foot of the perpendicular from A to BC. A point X is taken on AD. Prove that $\angle ABX = \angle ACX$.

3. In the figure described in Question 2, the line through D parallel to AB meets AC in U. Prove that $UD = UC$.

By proving that $\angle UAD = \angle UDA$ (each being a right angle less $\angle ACB$), prove that $UA = UD$.

4. Prove that the diagonal AC of a square $ABCD$ divides the square into two isosceles right-angled triangles. Hence prove that the square is symmetrical about each diagonal.

5. Prove that there are four lines about which a square is symmetrical and two about which a rectangle is symmetrical.

6. In Figures 34, 35, prove that the regular hexagon has six axes of symmetry and that the regular octagon has eight.

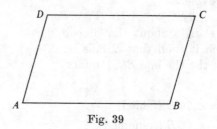

Fig. 39

9. The parallelogram

The definition of a quadrilateral was given in Section 1. When the pairs of opposite sides are parallel, the quadrilateral is called a *parallelogram*. The figure will be named *by taking the vertices in the counterclockwise sense round it*; for example, $ABCD$ in Figure 39.

(i) *Opposite angles are equal:* By the transversal results,

$$DC \parallel AB \Rightarrow \hat{A} + \hat{D} = 2 \text{ right angles,}$$

$$DA \parallel CB \Rightarrow \hat{C} + \hat{D} = 2 \text{ right angles.}$$

Hence $$\hat{A} = \hat{C}.$$

Similarly, $$\hat{B} = \hat{D}.$$

(ii) *Opposite sides are equal:* Fold A onto B by the crease u (Figure 40). Then

$$u \perp AB.$$

But $$DC \parallel AB$$

$$\Rightarrow u \perp DC$$

$$\Rightarrow D \text{ folds onto a point } P \text{ lying on } BC.$$

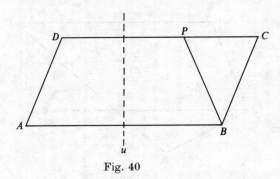

Fig. 40

Hence $\quad \angle BCP = \text{supplement } \angle ADP \quad (AD \parallel BC)$

$$= \text{supplement } \angle DPB \text{ (folding)}$$

$$= \angle BPC.$$

The triangle BPC thus has equal angles at P and C, so that

$$BC = BP$$

$$= AD \text{ (folding)},$$

as required.

Similarly $AB = CD$.

(iii) *The diagonals bisect each other:* Fold $\triangle ADC$ about AC to give $\angle AD_1 C$ (Figure 41). Then

$$AD_1 = AD \text{ (folding)}$$

$$= BC \text{ (parallelogram)};$$

and $\quad \angle CAD_1 = \angle CAD \text{ (folding)}$

$$= \angle ACB \ (AD \parallel BC).$$

Now fold A onto C, with crease u. Then

$$\angle CAD_1 = \angle ACB \Rightarrow AD_1 \text{ lies on } CB;$$

$$AD_1 = CB \Rightarrow D_1 \text{ lies on } B.$$

But $u \perp AC$, since A is folded onto C, and the foldings give, respectively

D_1 coincident with D,

D_1 coincident with B.

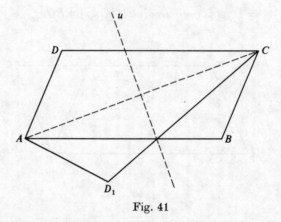

Fig. 41

Hence, using Corollary 3, the line DB passes through the point $u \cap AC$, which is the middle point of AC. Similarly AC passes through the middle point of DB.

The diagonals AC, BD thus bisect each other at their common point.

Exercise E

Questions 1–4 are standard results

The vertices of the quadrilaterals are to be named in the counterclockwise sense.

1. Prove that $\left.\begin{array}{l} AB = DC \\ AB \parallel DC \end{array}\right\} \Rightarrow ABCD$ is a parallelogram.

2. Prove that $\left.\begin{array}{l} AB = DC \\ AD = BC \end{array}\right\} \Rightarrow ABCD$ is a parallelogram.

3. Prove that AC, BD bisect each other at their common point $\Rightarrow ABCD$ is a parallelogram.

4. Prove that $ABCD$ is a parallelogram $\left.\right\}$ $\Rightarrow$ D, C, E, F are the vertices of
$ABEF$ is a parallelogram $\left.\right\}$ a parallelogram.

5. Prove that, if X, Y are the middle points of the sides AB, CD respectively of a parallelogram $ABCD$, then $AXYD$ is a parallelogram.

6. The diagonals AC, BD of a parallelogram $ABCD$ meet in O, and P, Q, R, S are the respective middle points of OA, OB, OC, OD. Prove that $PQRS$ is a parallelogram.

7. The middle points of the sides AB, BC, CD, DA of a parallelogram $ABCD$ are X, Y, Z, U respectively. Prove that $XYZU$ is a parallelogram.

8. $ABCD$ is a parallelogram; a line through A meets CD in P, and the line through B parallel to AP meets CD in Q. Prove that $DP = CQ$ and that $\angle DAP = \angle CBQ$.

9. The parallelograms $ABCD$, $APCQ$ have the diagonal AC in common. Prove that $BPDQ$ is also a parallelogram, or B, P, D, Q are collinear.

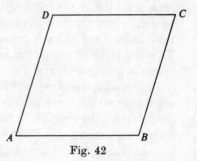

Fig. 42

Definition. A *rhombus* is a parallelogram whose sides are equal (Figure 42).

The following properties are important and should be proved as an exercise.

Exercise F

The rhombus

1. It is, in fact, sufficient that two adjacent sides of a parallelogram should be equal in order that it may be a rhombus.

2. Each diagonal of a rhombus bisects the angles at the vertices through which it passes.

3. The diagonals of a rhombus are perpendicular.

4. A rhombus is a square if one of its angles is a right angle.

5. A parallelogram is a rhombus if its diagonals are perpendicular.

6. A rhombus has two axes of symmetry.

7. Given a triangle ABC, find a point P on AB and a point Q on AC such that $BP + CQ = PQ$. [Let the bisector of the angle $\angle ABC$ meet the bisector of the angle $\angle ACB$ at U. Consider rhombi with BU and CU respectively as diagonals.]

3

THE MEASUREMENT OF
DISTANCE AND ANGLE:
AREA

(a) MEASUREMENT

1. The problem

Since childhood we have all become so accustomed to processes of measurement that we can hardly realise that difficulties are involved in so far as the theory is concerned – accuracy in practice is different. This is a state of mind that one would not wish to change, but some remarks seem necessary.

Essentially, measurement consists in selecting a unit and seeing how often that unit is contained in the thing being measured. Consider, for definiteness, the length of a line AB. Suppose that XY is a given unit: metre, centimetre, ... By the method given in Chapter 1, Section 10, we can transfer the segment XY to the segment AB so that X lies at A while Y lies at a point C of AB on the same side of A as B is. Then further transfer can place X at C so that Y falls on D, then X on D so that Y falls on E, ...

It may happen that after, say, 7 such steps the end Y falls exactly on B. In that case, we say that the measure of AB is 7 units of length; and so for any other whole number. The problems begin when the end Y never falls on B. We take it as obvious that Y then will ultimately 'go beyond B', giving a measurement which, in ordinary use of language, is a whole number of units together with a (proper) fraction.

A glance at an ordinary graduated ruler indicates the next step; the unit is divided into 2, 4, 8, 10, ... equal parts according to convenience (equality being checked, in theory at least, by superposition) and the fraction is measured against the *sub-units*. In this way there appear measurements such as $3\frac{1}{2}$, $4\frac{7}{10}$, $2\cdot75$.

For normal purposes this suffices. The real problem arrives with measurements that cannot be expressed as fractions of the type p/q, where p and q are integers: in other words, when the unit cannot be subdivided into any whole number of parts in such a way that the segment being measured consists of a whole number of them.

Exactly analogous considerations apply to the measurement of angle, and need not be repeated. By means of a protractor an angle can be measured in degrees and fractions of a degree (minutes, seconds) with considerable, but not necessarily complete, accuracy.

The formulae

$$1 \text{ right angle} = 90 \text{ degrees},$$

$$1 \text{ degree} = 60 \text{ minutes},$$

$$1 \text{ minute} = 60 \text{ seconds},$$

will be familiar.

The dilemma in measurement cannot be resolved simply. There is required, in some form or other, a theory of *rational* and *irrational* numbers. Broadly, rational numbers are those which, expressed in decimal form, *either* terminate *or* recur indefinitely; for instance,

$$\tfrac{3}{8} = 0 \cdot 375,$$

$$\tfrac{1}{7} = 0 \cdot 142857 \ 142857 \ 142857 \ 142 \ldots,$$

the blocks 142857 repeating endlessly. By contrast, irrational numbers cannot be so expressed; their decimal forms go on indefinitely without such recurrent repetitions. For example,

$$\sqrt{7} = 2 \cdot 645751 \ldots,$$

$$\pi = 3 \cdot 141592 \ldots,$$

$$\log_{10} 3 = 0 \cdot 477121 \ldots,$$

the decimal parts continuing endlessly and without falling into repetitive pattern.

The decimal form of statement does, however, form a basis for progress: *an irrational number can be approximated very closely by a finite decimal, and can, indeed, be contained within two such decimals arbitrarily close to each other*. For example:

$\sqrt{7}$ is approximated by $2 \cdot 64576$ and lies between the rational numbers $2 \cdot 6457$, $2 \cdot 64576$;

π is approximated by $3 \cdot 14159$ and lies between the rational numbers $3 \cdot 14159$, $3 \cdot 141593$;

$\log_{10} 3$ is approximated by $0 \cdot 477$ and lies between the rational numbers $0 \cdot 477$, $0 \cdot 4772$.

The plan is clear, but details are hard, and we leave the matter there.

(b) AREA

2. The idea of area

Consider any *closed* figure such as a triangle ABC or a rectangle $PQRS$ (Figure 43). A portion of the plane enclosed by such a figure is called a *region*, so that the diagram represents a triangle ABC with *perimeter* $AB + BC + CA$ and a region within it; and a rectangle $PQRS$ with perimeter $PQ + QR + RS + SP$ and a region within it.

The aim is to set up a machinery for comparing regions and hence for attaching numerical values. The word *area* is used here to denote the measure of a region.

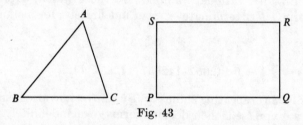

Fig. 43

The following basic assumptions are abstracted from experience of day-to-day measurement:

(i) It is assumed that regions that can be exactly superposed have equal area.

(ii) It is assumed that the areas of regions can be added and subtracted according to the normal laws of computation in the sense of the examples that follow. (For convenience, write 'area $ABCD$' for the area of the region $ABCD$.)

In Figure 44,

$$\text{area } ABCD = \text{area } ABC + \text{area } ACD,$$

$$\text{area } ABCD = \text{area } ABCDE - \text{area } ADE,$$

$$\text{area } ABCDE = \text{area } ABCD + \text{area } ACDE - \text{area } ACD.$$

We start by comparing parallelograms.

3. Parallelograms

Let $ABPQ$, $ABXY$ be two parallelograms (Figure 45) so related that they have the side AB in common while the sides PQ, XY opposite to AB lie along a straight line parallel to AB. It is to be proved that the two parallelograms are equal in area.

The triangle AYQ is 'translated' to the position BXP† through a distance AB parallel to the line AB. This is an immediate consequence of two facts:

(i) $QYPX \parallel AB$ (the directions $\overrightarrow{QYPX}$, $\overrightarrow{AB}$ are the same);

(ii) $QP = YX = AB$ (the distances moved by the vertices Q, Y, A as they go to P, X, B are the same).

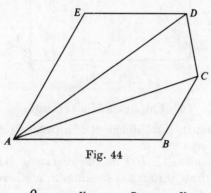

Fig. 44

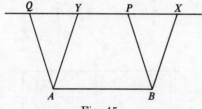

Fig. 45

Thus the triangles AYQ, BXP, being brought to superposition by the translation, are equal in area.

Subtract each triangle from the quadrilateral $ABXQ$. The resulting areas have the relationship

$$\text{area } ABXQ - \text{area } BXP = \text{area } ABXQ - \text{area } AYQ,$$

or $$\text{area } ABPQ = \text{area } ABXY.$$

This result is often stated, succinctly but not very accurately, in the form, *parallelograms on the same base and between the same parallels have equal areas.*

Corollary 1. *A parallelogram $ABCD$ is equal in area to the rectangle having AB as one side and its other vertices U, V on the line CD* (Figure 46).

† *Translations* will be considered later. For the moment, the idea that AYQ is moved across to the position BXP is sufficient.

This corollary is a particular case of the main theorem (Section 4). Its usefulness appears when we come to seek a measure for the area of a parallelogram.

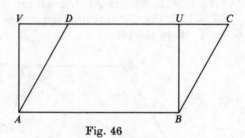

Fig. 46

4. The area of a triangle

Preliminary result. *Each diagonal of a rectangle divides it into two triangles of equal area.*

Let the diagonals AC, BD of the rectangle $ABCD$ meet in O (Figure 47), and draw through O the lines u, v, where

$$u \parallel AD \parallel BC, \quad v \parallel AB \parallel DC.$$

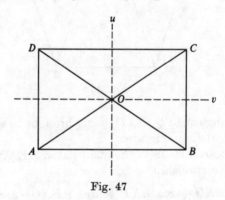

Fig. 47

Then, by Chapter 2, Section 4, folding about u places A, D on B, C respectively, so that $\triangle OCB$ coincides with $\triangle ODA$, giving

$$\text{area } OCB = \text{area } ODA.$$

Similarly, by folding about v,

$$\text{area } OCD = \text{area } OBA.$$

Adding,

$$\text{area } OCB + \text{area } OCD = \text{area } ODA + \text{area } OBA$$

$$\Rightarrow \text{area } BDC = \text{area } BDA.$$

Hence each of these areas is equal to one half of the area of the rectangle $ABCD$.

In the same way,

$$\text{area } ACD = \text{area } ACB = \tfrac{1}{2} \text{ area } ABCD.$$

Theorem 1 (The main theorem). *The area of a triangle is equal to one half the area of a rectangle having the same base and with its opposite side passing through the third vertex of the triangle.*

Let $ABXY$ be a rectangle and ABC a triangle whose vertex C lies on the line XY (Figure 48).

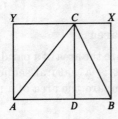 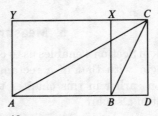

Fig. 48

Let D be the foot of the perpendicular from C to the line AB. Then $ADCY$, $BDCX$ are rectangles, and

$$\text{area } ADC = \tfrac{1}{2} \text{ area } ADCY,$$
$$\text{area } BDC = \tfrac{1}{2} \text{ area } BDCX.$$

Now *either* C lies between X and Y, in which case

$$\text{area } ABC = \text{area } ADC + \text{area } BDC$$
$$= \tfrac{1}{2}\{\text{area } ADCY + \text{area } BDCX\}$$
$$= \tfrac{1}{2} \text{ area } ABXY;$$

or C is not between X and Y; say C lies on the side of X opposite to Y, in which case

$$\text{area } ABC = \text{area } ADC - \text{area } BDC$$
$$= \tfrac{1}{2}\{\text{area } ADCY - \text{area } BDCX\}$$
$$= \tfrac{1}{2} \text{ area } ABXY.$$

In either case, the area of the triangle is one half of that of the rectangle.

Exercise A

1. $ABCD$ is a rectangle and P, Q, R, S are the middle points of the sides AB, BC, CD, DA respectively. Prove that

$$\text{area } PQRS = \tfrac{1}{2} \text{ area } ABCD.$$

2. Prove that each diagonal of a parallelogram divides it into two triangles of equal area.

3. P, Q are the middle points of the sides AD, BC of a rectangle $ABCD$; points X, Y are taken on AB, CD respectively. Prove that

$$\text{area } PQX = \text{area } PQY.$$

4. $ABCD$ is a quadrilateral in which $AB \parallel DC$ and the angles at A and D are right angles, but BC is not parallel to AD. The middle points of AD and BC are P and Q. Prove (for example, by an argument based on folding) that area $PQCD$ cannot be equal to area $PQBA$.

5. Measure of area

The work of Section 4 enables us to compare the area of a parallelogram or triangle with that of a rectangle. It is a natural sequel to the discussion earlier in this chapter to compare the area of a rectangle with that of a square.

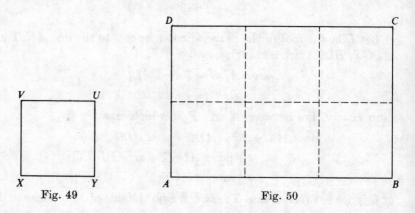

Fig. 49   Fig. 50

Let XY be a segment whose length is one unit, and draw the square $XYUV$ – a rectangle all of whose sides are equal to the unit of measurement (Figure 49).

Just as the length of a segment AB is measured by the 'number of times' that it contains XY, so the area of a rectangle $ABCD$ is measured by the 'number of times' that it contains $XYUV$.

When the lengths of the sides of the rectangle are whole numbers there is no problem. Figure 50 illustrates a rectangle in which AB is 3 units and AD is 2 units. Division of AB into 3 equal parts and of AD into 2 equal parts leads to the six unit squares indicated in the diagram. The area is thus 6 (= 3 × 2) square units.

Exactly similar argument shows that, if AB is of length m units and AD is of length n units, where m, n are integers, then

$$\text{area } ABCD = mn \text{ square units.}$$

The extension to the case when the lengths of AB and AD are rational numbers is comparatively simple. Suppose that the lengths are p/q and r/s, where p, q, r, s are integers. Divide the given unit XY into qs equal parts and take one of these as sub-unit. Then the length of AB is ps sub-units and the length of AD is rq sub-units. Hence the rectangle contains $(ps) \times (rq)$ sub-squares and its area is $psrq$ square sub-units. But the square $XYUV$ contains $(qs)^2$ square sub-units, and so the 'number' of units in the rectangle $ABCD$ is $(psrq) \div (qs)^2$, or $(pr)/(qs)$. Hence

$$\text{area } ABCD = (p/q) \times (r/s)$$
$$= (\text{length } AB) \times (\text{length } AD).$$

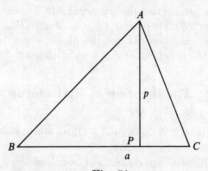

Fig. 51

When the lengths of AB and AD are (one or both) *irrational numbers*, we fall back on the earlier considerations: each length can be approximated by a rational number, and the area evaluated via these rational numbers is a close approximation to the area of the rectangle.

To summarise: it is reasonable to use the formula

area of rectangle = product of lengths of sides,

and we now assume that this result is adequately established for our purposes.

Corollary 2. *Let ABC be a triangle whose side BC is of length a* (*Figure 51*). *Draw the line through A perpendicular to BC, meeting it in P, where AP has length p. Then*

$$\text{area of triangle } ABC = \tfrac{1}{2}BC \times AP = \tfrac{1}{2}ap.$$

The line AP is called the *altitude* through A, and the formula is often expressed in the form

$$\text{area of triangle} = \tfrac{1}{2}\,\text{base} \times \text{altitude}.$$

Exercise B

1. A parallelogram (*rhombus*) $ABCD$ has all its sides equal. Prove that $AC \perp BD$ and that
$$\text{area } ABCD = \tfrac{1}{2}AC \times BD.$$

2. Prove that, if AP is the altitude through A of a triangle ABC in which the angle at A is a right angle, then the length of AP is equal to

$$(AB \times AC)/BC.$$

3. Through a point P on the diagonal AC of a rectangle $ABCD$ are drawn lines XPY, UPV parallel to AB, AD respectively, where $X \in AD$, $Y \in BC$, $U \in AB$, $V \in DC$. Prove that area $BUPY = $ area $DVPX$.

4. The diagonals AC, BD of the quadrilateral $ABCD$ meet in U. Prove that, if area $ABD = $ area CBD, then area $ADU = $ area CDU.

Prove that if each diagonal divides the quadrilateral into two triangles equal in area, then the quadrilateral is a parallelogram.

6. The theorem of Pythagoras

(See also Chapter 5, Section 2.)

Let ABC be a given triangle with a right angle at A (Figure 52).

Definition. The side BC opposite to A is called the *hypotenuse* of the right-angled triangle.

To prove that, *if squares $ABPQ$, $ACXY$ are drawn on the sides AB, AC, then the sum of their areas is equal to the area of a square drawn on the hypotenuse BC.*

For convenience, denote the lengths AB, AC by c, b respectively.

By producing the lines XC, XY, PB, PQ, obtain the quadrilateral $LXMP$ as shown in Figure 53.

Exercise C

Questions 1–4 refer to Figure 53

1. Prove that $XCL \parallel YAB \parallel MQB$ and that $XYM \parallel CAQ \parallel LBP$, and that these sets of lines are perpendicular.

2. Prove that
$$XC = YA = MQ = XY = LB = AC \; (= b),$$
$$YM = AQ = BP = QP = CL = AB \, (= c).$$

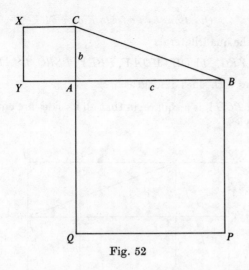

Fig. 52

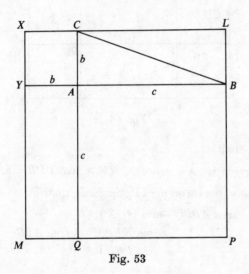

Fig. 53

3. Deduce that $LXMP$ is a square.

4. By folding about XAP (to be proved a straight line), deduce that area $ACLB$ = area $AYMQ$ = 2 area ABC.

Next fold the figure so that X, L lie on M, P and the line YB gives the line marked US. Then fold it so that X, M lie on L, P and the line CQ gives the line marked GV. The further intersections, F, D, R are shown in Figure 54. The ultimate aim is *to prove that $BCUV$ is a square.*

Questions 5–8 refer to Figure 54

5. Prove that the quadrilaterals

$$XURC, \; XYFG, \; MVDU, \; MQAY, \; PBFV, \; PSRQ, \; LCAB, \; LGDS$$

are all rectangles with sides of lengths b, c.

6. Deduce that $BCUV$ is a square, in that all its sides are equal and all its angles right angles.

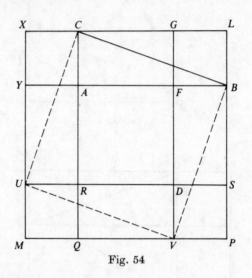

Fig. 54

7. Deduce also that

$$\text{area } BLC = \text{area } CXU = \text{area } UMV = \text{area } VPB = \text{area } ABC.$$

8. Deduce, finally, the theorem of Pythagoras, that

$$\text{area } ABPQ + \text{area } ACXY$$
$$= \text{area } XLPM - 4 \text{ area } ABC$$
$$= \text{area } BCUV.$$

7. The triangle inequality

One other fundamental property, familiar by observation, should be mentioned here:

The shortest distance between two points is the length of the straight line joining them.

If, indeed, a taut string has its ends fixed at two points B, C, then it cannot be made to pass through any other point unless its length is increased. (See the *comment* below.)

Corollary 3. *The sum of the lengths of any two sides of a triangle is greater than the length of the third side.*

Thus, if we write

$$'>'\text{ to denote 'is greater than'},$$

$$'<'\text{ to denote 'is less than'},$$

then (see Figure 55)

$$AB + AC > BC, \quad BC + BA > CA, \quad CA + CB > AB.$$

Corollary 4. *If* $PB + PC = BC$, *then* P *lies in the segment* BC *and, conversely, if* P *lies in the segment* BC, *then* $PB + PC = BC$.

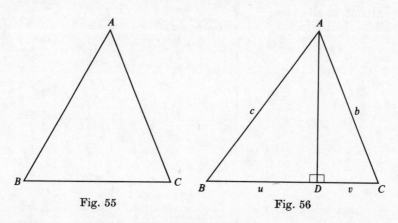

Fig. 55   Fig. 56

Comment. This statement of the property, though going back to fundamental experience, is really too glib. We are, in fact, using *two* definitions of a straight line: the result of folding a sheet of paper, and the result of stretching a piece of string. Each is experimentally very reasonable, but their juxtaposition highlights the difficulties inherent in moving between experience and logic.

An argument for the truth of the property, based on the theorem of Pythagoras may be of interest. Let D be the foot of the perpendicular from the vertex A of a triangle ABC to the base BC (Figure 56). Denote lengths as follows:

$$BC = a, \quad CA = b, \quad AB = c, \quad BD = u, \quad CD = v.$$

Now the square on the hypotenuse of a right-angled triangle, being equal to the sum of the squares on the other two sides, is greater than the square on either of them. In particular, from the triangles ADB, ADC respectively,

$$c > u, \quad b > v,$$

so that

$$b + c > u + v.$$

If D lies between B and C, then

$$u + v = a,$$

so that
$$b + c > a;$$

and if D is not between B and C but, say, to the right of C, then

$$u - v = a$$

and so, since necessarily

$$u + v > u - v,$$

there is still the inequality

$$u + v > a.$$

Hence, in all cases,

$$b + c > a.$$

PART II
TRANSFORMATIONS AND THEIR ALGEBRA

4

REFLECTIONS

Introductory remarks on transformations. The work to follow concerns the problems that arise when a given figure (say, for this introduction, a triangle *ABC*) is moved from one position to some other position in its plane, possibly being turned over or enlarged in the process. Such a movement is called a *transformation* or *mapping* and we are to deal in particular with *similarity transformations*, under which given figures retain their shapes, and (a special case of these) *isometries*, under which given figures retain their shapes and their sizes.

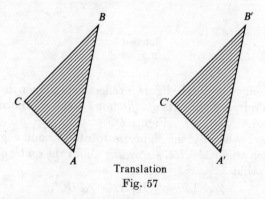

Translation
Fig. 57

So that we may use the names freely, we give at once a list of basic isometries and illustrate them by transforming a triangle *ABC* to a triangle *A'B'C'*:

(i) *Translation*, whereby the figure is moved bodily through a given distance in a given direction; in Figure 57, the lines *AA'*, *BB'*, *CC'* are equal and parallel.

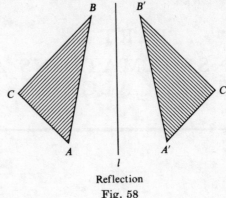

Reflection

Fig. 58

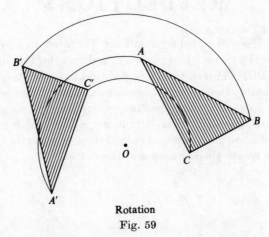

Rotation

Fig. 59

(ii) *Reflection*, whereby the figure is reflected in a given line (compare reflection in a mirror); the *axis of reflection l* is the mediator of each of the segments AA', BB', CC' (Figure 58).

(iii) *Rotation*, whereby the figure is rotated about a given point through a given angle; A, B, C are swung about the *centre of rotation O* (Figure 59) so that

$$\triangle AOA' = \triangle BOB' = \triangle COC',$$

and $\qquad OA = OA', \quad OB = OB', \quad OC = OC'.$

(iv) *Glide reflection*, whereby the figure is first reflected in a given line and then translated a given distance parallel to that line (the order of the two operations can be interchanged without affecting the end result); ABC is reflected in the line l to PQR and then translated so that

$PA' = QB' = RC'$, each being parallel to l (Figure 60). This isometry does not come immediately to mind, but its importance appears later.

Notation. Symbolism such as

$$\triangle ABC \to \triangle A'B'C'$$

will denote that the triangle ABC is transformed to the position $A'B'C'$. The vertices A', B', C' are named in the order of the vertices A, B, C from which they arise.

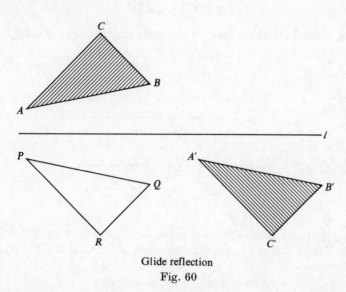

Glide reflection

Fig. 60

Definition. The definition of congruence given in Chapter 1, Section 2, is now extended to define two figures as *congruent* when *they can be brought into coincidence by a succession of isometries.*

Notation such as

$$\triangle ABC \equiv \triangle A'B'C'$$

denotes the congruence of the two triangles.

Transformation by isometry has four important properties:

(i) *Straight lines* → *straight lines:* Let AB be a given line and C any point on it, say between A and B. Then (see Chapter 3, Section 7)

$$AC + CB = AB.$$

By the isometry

$$A \to A', \quad B \to B', \quad C \to C',$$

we have

$$AC = A'C', \quad CB = C'B', \quad AB = A'B'$$

$$\Rightarrow A'C' + C'B' = A'B'$$

$$\Rightarrow C' \text{ is on } A'B' \text{ (and between } A' \text{ and } B').$$

Similar argument holds for the other positions of C relative to A and B.

(ii) *Angles → angles of the same magnitude:* Let $\angle ABC$ be a given angle and suppose that, under the isometry, $A \to A'$, $B \to B'$, $C \to C'$. Then

$$\triangle ABC \equiv \triangle A'B'C',$$

being capable of being brought to coincidence by the given isometry. Hence, in particular,

$$\angle A'B'C' = \angle ABC.$$

Note, though, that *the sense of the angle may not be retained.*

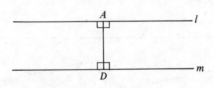

Fig. 61

(iii) *Parallel lines → parallel lines.* Let l, m be two parallel lines (Figure 61). Take $A \in l$, $D \in m$ such that $AD \perp l$, $AD \perp m$. By the isometry,

$$A \in l \to A' \in l', \quad D \in m \to D' \in m',$$

where, by (ii), $A'D' \perp l, \quad A'D' \perp m'.$

Hence $l' \parallel m'.$

(iv) *Given two triplets A, B, C and A', B', C' of non-collinear points, such that $B'C' = BC$, $C'A' = CA$, $A'B' = AB$, there is a unique isometry under which $A \to A'$, $B \to B'$, $C \to C'$.*

Take *any* point P and let $Q = AP \cap BC$. (If $AP \parallel BC$, take $Q = BP \cap CA$ and modify accordingly.) Let $Q' \in B'C'$ be such that $B'Q' = BQ$, $Q'C' = QC$; then $A'Q' = AQ$. Let $P' \in A'Q'$ be such that $A'P' = AP$, $P'Q' = PQ$. Then a transformation $P \to P'$ is defined uniquely, and it is easily proved to be the required isometry.

In studying transformations, there are, among others, three features which merit attention:

(i) *fixed points,* unchanged by the transformation;
(ii) *fixed lines,* unchanged though possibly not point for point;

(iii) *orientation*, the property that discriminates between the relations $\underset{\wedge}{ABC} = \underset{\wedge}{A'B'C'}$ and $\underset{\wedge}{ABC} = \underset{\wedge}{C'B'A'}$; informally, orientation 'determines which way round a figure lies'.

We might, under (i), talk of *invariant points* and, under (ii), talk of *invariant lines* or, more restrictedly, *lines of invariant points*.

Exercise A

1. Prove that, if $\angle ABC$ is a right angle, there is no isometry such that $A \to B$, $B \to C$, $C \to A$.

2. Prove that, if there is an isometry under which $A \to A$, $B \to B$, $C \to C'$ (where C' is different from C), then $C'C \perp AB$.

3. Three points A, B, C lie on a straight line, and there is an isometry $A \to C$, $C \to A$, $B \to B$. Prove that B is the middle point of AC.

1. Reflection

(The transformation known as reflection is chosen as a starting point since it is richer in properties than the more obvious translation.)

Let l be a given line and P a point in arbitrary position (Figure 62). The *reflection* of P in l is the point P' obtained when the plane through l and P is folded about l, and P is then pricked through. The line l is the mediator of the segment PP'.

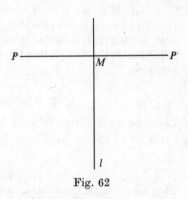

Fig. 62

The line l, known as the *axis of reflection*, is a *line of self-corresponding points*. There are no other self-corresponding points, but *every line perpendicular to l is self-corresponding, though not point for point.*

The process $P \to P'$ of reflecting P to P' in the line l is an *operation* conveniently denoted by the symbol $\mathbf{l}$. We write

$$P' = P\mathbf{l},$$

for 'P under the operation $\mathbf{l}$'. The point P' may also be called the *image* of P under $\mathbf{l}$.

There is considerable variety of usage covering this notation; in particular, many writers would say '$P' = \mathbf{l}P$'. On balance the order selected seems the more convenient for the manipulations that are to follow.

Exercise B

1. Prove that $m\mathbf{l}$ is a self-corresponding line $\Rightarrow m \perp l$ or $m = l$.

2. Prove that
$$P' = P\mathbf{l} \quad (P \notin l)$$
$$\Rightarrow PP' \text{ is a self-corresponding line.}$$

3. Prove that
$$P' = P\mathbf{l} \Rightarrow P = P'\mathbf{l}.$$

4. Let l, m be two perpendicular lines meeting in U. Take a point P not on l or m, and let $P' = P\mathbf{l}, P'' = P'\mathbf{m}$. Prove that U is the middle point of PP''.

5. ABC is a given triangle, P, Q are the middle points of AB, AC and l is the line PQ. Prove that $A\mathbf{l} \in BC$.

6. UA, UB are two given rays and l is the bisector of the angle AUB. Prove that $P \in UA \Rightarrow P\mathbf{l} \in UB$.

7. ABC is an isosceles triangle. Points P, Q are taken on the equal sides AB, AC respectively, so that $AP = AQ$. Prove that, if $BQ \cap CP = U$, then AU bisects the angle BAC.

8. A parallelogram $ABCD$ is reflected upon itself $(A \to A, B \to D, C \to C, D \to B)$ by reflection in the diagonal AC. Prove that it is a rhombus.

If, further, it is reflected upon itself $(A \to D, B \to C, C \to B, D \to A)$ by reflection in the line joining the middle points of AD, BC, prove that it is a square.

2. The reflection of a line

Let u be a given line (Figure 63). The result of reflecting its points in l is *a set of points lying on a line u'*, where it is now natural to write

$$u' = u\mathbf{l}.$$

This result is an immediate consequence of folding about l, or, better, to include the *whole* line u (with parts on either side of l), it is an immediate consequence of rotating the plane of the paper, in space, round l till u falls upon u'.

If $P, Q \in u$, so that $P', Q' \in u'$, then the *segment* PQ is folded on (or rotated to) the segment $P'Q'$. The two segments are congruent, written

$$P'Q' \equiv PQ,$$

corresponding to the statement in everyday language that $PQ, P'Q'$ are equal in length.

Since $u \to u'$ and, from folding, $u' \to u$, the common point U is self-corresponding and therefore U is on l. Thus

$$u \cap u' \in l.$$

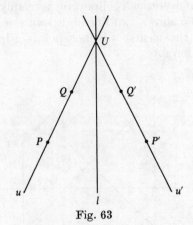

Fig. 63

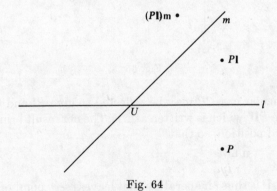

Fig. 64

3. An algebra for reflections

Let l, m be two given intersecting lines and P an arbitrary point (Figure 64). The reflection of P in l is the point Pl, and the further reflection of this point in m is the point $(Pl)\,\mathbf{m}$. The brackets may be removed without ambiguity on the understanding that the notation

$$Plm$$

means that P *is first operated upon by the reflection* l *and the result then operated upon by* $\mathbf{m}$.

3

This idea of *product operator* can be extended in the obvious way to sequences of reflections; for example,

$$P\mathbf{lmnp} = (P\mathbf{l})\,\mathbf{mnp} = \{(P\mathbf{l})\,\mathbf{m}\}\,\mathbf{np} = [(P\mathbf{l})\,\mathbf{mn}]\,\mathbf{p}.$$

That the *order of operation* is important is readily appreciated by an example. Figure 65 shows two lines *l*, *m* and the 'paths' whereby a point *P* reaches the clearly distinct points *P***lm** and *P***ml**. (See Exercise C, Question 2.)

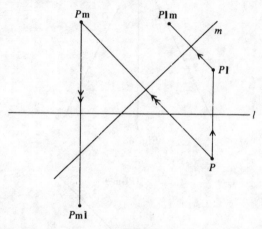

Fig. 65

As a particular case, *P* may be reflected to give *P***l** and then back again to give *P***ll**, which is written as $P\mathbf{l}^2$. The net result brings *P* back to its original position, so that

$$P\mathbf{l}^2 = P.$$

The product $\mathbf{l}^2$ is thus an operation that leaves *every* point of the plane unchanged. Such an operation is called the *identity* operation, denoted by the symbol **I**. The two operations $\mathbf{l}^2$ and **I** therefore give the same transform for an *arbitrary* point *P*, and so we may reasonably write

$$\mathbf{l}^2 = \mathbf{I}.$$

Two features of operators in general (not necessarily reflections) may conveniently be made here:

(i) If **a** is any operator, then further operation by **I** follows the 'unit' property of elementary algebra,

$$\mathbf{aI} = \mathbf{Ia} = \mathbf{a}.$$

(ii) If **a**, **b**, **c** are any three operations, then their successive action is subject to the *associative law* of elementary algebra

$$(\mathbf{ab})\,\mathbf{c} = \mathbf{a}(\mathbf{bc}),$$

each side denoting operation by **a**, followed by operation by **b**, followed by operation by **c**.

From this point onwards, *manipulations involving the associative law will be performed without further comment.*

Illustration 1. To prove that, if **l**, **m**, **n** *are reflections such that* **nl** = **ml**, *then* **n** = **m**.

$$\mathbf{nl} = \mathbf{ml}$$
$$\Rightarrow (\mathbf{nl})\,\mathbf{l} = (\mathbf{ml})\,\mathbf{l}$$
$$\Rightarrow \mathbf{n}(\mathbf{l}^2) = \mathbf{m}(\mathbf{l}^2)$$
$$\Rightarrow \mathbf{nI} = \mathbf{mI}$$
$$\Rightarrow \mathbf{n} = \mathbf{m}.$$

Exercise C

1. Use a geometrical argument to verify the result just stated, that **nl** = **ml** $\Rightarrow$ **n** = **m**.

2. To prove the result stated in the text, that **lm** need not be the same as **ml**:

(i) Let l be a given axis of reflection, u a given line, and $u' = u l$. Prove that, if u' coincides with u, then either u is l (the coincidence being point for point) or $u \perp l$ (the coincidence not being point for point).

(ii) Let m be a line such that l is the bisector of an angle between m and u. Prove that

$$u\mathbf{l} = m, \quad u\mathbf{lm} = m, \quad u\mathbf{lml} = u.$$

(iii) Prove that **lm** = **ml** $\Leftrightarrow$ **lml** = **m**.

(iv) Deduce that **lm** $\neq$ **ml** when l, m are different, except in the special case $l \perp m$.

3. Prove that, if l, m are distinct non-parallel lines, then **lm** has precisely one self-corresponding point.

4. Lines l, m, n meet in a point O, and P is an arbitrary point. Prove that the points P, $P\mathbf{l}$, $P\mathbf{lm}$, $P\mathbf{lmn}$ are equidistant from O.

5. Prove that, if l, m are two parallel lines, the length of the segment joining P and $P\mathbf{lm}$ is independent of the position of P.

6. The lines l, m are perpendicular, Prove that the points P, $P\mathbf{l}$, $P\mathbf{m}$, $P\mathbf{lm}$ are at the vertices of a rectangle.

7. The lines l, m are the diagonals PR, QS of a square $PQRS$. Examine the effect on the vertices of each of the reflections **l**, **m**, **lm**, **ml**, **lml**.

4. Inverse operations

Let $\mathbf{a}$ be a given operation, not necessarily a reflection. Take an arbitrary point P and write

$$P\mathbf{a} = P'.$$

In the cases with which we are concerned, there is an operation $\mathbf{b}$, say, taking P' back to P, so that

$$P'\mathbf{b} = P.$$

Then, *for all P*,

$$P\mathbf{ab} = (P\mathbf{a})\,\mathbf{b} = P'\mathbf{b} = P = P\mathbf{I}$$

$$\Rightarrow \mathbf{ab} = \mathbf{I}.$$

Similarly

$$P'\mathbf{ba} = (P'\mathbf{b})\,\mathbf{a} = P\mathbf{a} = P' = P'\mathbf{I}$$

$$\Rightarrow \mathbf{ba} = \mathbf{I}.$$

Hence

$$\mathbf{ab} = \mathbf{ba} = \mathbf{I}.$$

It is now natural to follow the idea of $\mathbf{I}$ as a unit operation by the idea of $\mathbf{b}$ as an operation *inverse* to $\mathbf{a}$ and to use the symbolism of elementary algebra by writing $\mathbf{a}^{-1}$ for $\mathbf{b}$. Then

$$\mathbf{a}(\mathbf{a}^{-1}) = (\mathbf{a}^{-1})\,\mathbf{a} = \mathbf{I}.$$

Corollary 1. *Reversal of the roles of $\mathbf{a}$, $\mathbf{a}^{-1}$ in the last relation shows that $\mathbf{a}$ is the operation inverse to $\mathbf{a}^{-1}$, thus*

$$(\mathbf{a}^{-1})^{-1} = \mathbf{a}.$$

Four remarks.

(i) Notation such as $\mathbf{a}^{-2}$ is occasionally used to denote $(\mathbf{a}^{-1})^2$, the successive operation of $\mathbf{a}^{-1}$ followed by $\mathbf{a}^{-1}$.

(ii) It will always be assumed that an operation $\mathbf{a}$ has an inverse $\mathbf{a}^{-1}$ unless the contrary is stated explicitly.

(iii) It ought perhaps to be emphasised that there is no implication of division in the use of the symbol $\mathbf{a}^{-1}$. That symbol stands for what has been defined, and nothing more.

(iv) Attention should be drawn to the step in the argument,

$$P(\mathbf{ab}) = P\mathbf{I}$$

$$\Rightarrow \mathbf{ab} = \mathbf{I}$$

for all P. Without the proviso, that deduction could not be made. Suppose, for example, that $\mathbf{l}$ is a reflection and P a point of the line l. Then

$$P\mathbf{l} = P = P\mathbf{I};$$

but the deduction $1 = I$ is manifestly absurd. There are, in fact, many points P in the plane (all the points not on l) for which the relation $P1 = PI$ does *not* hold.

The algebraic symbolism of inverses, once started, is useful in many ways. As an easy illustration, consider the argument:

$$1^2 = I$$
$$\Rightarrow 1^2 1^{-1} = I 1^{-1}$$
$$\Rightarrow 1(11^{-1}) = 1^{-1}$$
$$\Rightarrow 1I = 1^{-1}$$
$$\Rightarrow 1 = 1^{-1},$$

agreeing with the immediate observation that *a reflection is its own inverse*.

Illustration 2. To prove that *the inverse of the product operation* **ab** *is the product operation* $\mathbf{b^{-1}a^{-1}}$.

Suppose that **x** is the operation inverse to **ab**. Then

$$(\mathbf{ab})\,\mathbf{x} = \mathbf{I}$$
$$\Rightarrow \mathbf{a^{-1}abx} = \mathbf{a^{-1}I} = \mathbf{a^{-1}}$$
$$\Rightarrow \mathbf{bx} = \mathbf{a^{-1}} \qquad\qquad (\mathbf{a^{-1}a = I})$$
$$\Rightarrow \mathbf{b^{-1}bx} = \mathbf{b^{-1}a^{-1}}$$
$$\Rightarrow \mathbf{x} = \mathbf{b^{-1}a^{-1}} \qquad\qquad (\mathbf{b^{-1}b = I})$$

so that if there is an inverse, it can only be $\mathbf{b^{-1}a^{-1}}$. Substitution shows at once that

$$(\mathbf{ab})\,(\mathbf{b^{-1}a^{-1}}) = (\mathbf{b^{-1}a^{-1}})\,(\mathbf{ab}) = \mathbf{I}.$$

[The sequence of argument ending at $\mathbf{x} = \mathbf{b^{-1}a^{-1}}$ does not of itself prove that **ab** has an inverse even when **a** and **b** have inverses severally. It merely tells us what such an inverse can be. Hence the need for the final line.]

Exercise D

1. Prove that $(\mathbf{abc})^{-1} = \mathbf{c^{-1}b^{-1}a^{-1}}$.

2. Let **a**, **b** be two operations (not necessarily satisfying the relations $\mathbf{a}^2 = \mathbf{I}$, $\mathbf{b}^2 = \mathbf{I}$) having inverses, and let

$$\mathbf{u} = \mathbf{a^{-1}ba}.$$

Prove that $\qquad\qquad \mathbf{u}^2 = \mathbf{a^{-1}b^2a}, \quad \mathbf{u}^3 = \mathbf{a^{-1}b^3a}.$

Prove also that $\qquad \mathbf{u^{-1}} = \mathbf{a^{-1}b^{-1}a}, \quad \mathbf{u^{-2}} = \mathbf{a^{-1}b^{-2}a}.$

5. Orientation

Brief mention was made at the start of this chapter to the characteristic of *orientation*, which, in its turn, was foreshadowed in Chapter 1 by the concept of the *sense* of an angle.

Let ABC be a given triangle and suppose that the sides are traversed in the senses $\overrightarrow{AB}$, $\overrightarrow{BC}$, $\overrightarrow{CA}$, so that the vertices appear in the order $A \to B \to C \to A$. If this sequence goes against the hands of a clock, the sense is *counterclockwise* and if it goes with the hands, the sense is clockwise. This distinction, illustrated in Figure 66, gives the two possible *orientations* of the triangle.

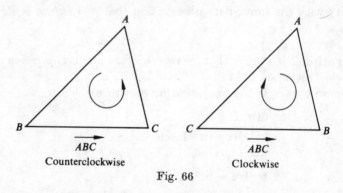

ABC
Counterclockwise

ABC
Clockwise

Fig. 66

Note that counterclockwise has been stated first. Long tradition in mathematics has established the convention that, when sign is attached (as in trigonometry), counterclockwise is to be taken as positive.

A transformation which retains orientation is called *direct*; one which reverses orientation is called *opposite*.

It is useful at times to indicate orientation by symbolic notation. If an operation **a** transforms a triangle ABC by direct orientation, we write

$$(\overrightarrow{ABC})\,\mathbf{a} = \overrightarrow{A'B'C'}.$$

For a reversal, we write

$$(\overrightarrow{ABC})\,\mathbf{a} = \overleftarrow{A'B'C'}.$$

Exercise E

1. Prove that, if **a** is a direct transformation and **b** opposite, then $\mathbf{a}^2$ and $\mathbf{b}^2$ are both direct but $\mathbf{ab}$ is opposite.

2. Prove that the inverse $\mathbf{a}^{-1}$ has the same orientation as **a**.

3. By starting first with a quadrilateral $ABCD$ divided into two triangles ABC, ACD, extend the idea of orientation to a quadrilateral and show that (all triangles being assumed to transform similarly) a direct transformation retains orientation round a quadrilateral while an opposite orientation reverses it. [Note the convention on p. 18.]

Extend this idea to a *pentagon* defined by five vertices A, B, C, D, E with sides AB, BC, CD, DE, EA.

6. Orientation under reflection

Let $A'B'C'$ be the reflection of a given triangle ABC in a line l, (Figure 67), so that

$$A' = Al, \quad B' = Bl, \quad C' = Cl.$$

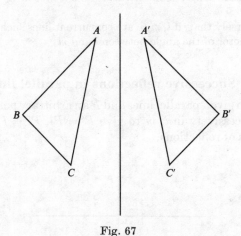

Fig. 67

Since the two triangles can be brought into coincidence by folding, they are congruent:

$$\triangle A'B'C' \equiv \triangle ABC.$$

The process of reflection, however, *reverses the orientation*, so that

$$(\triangle \overrightarrow{ABC})l = \triangle \overleftarrow{A'B'C'}.$$

This is readily seen by the folding, which brings the faces into contact. The two triangles 'lie on top of each other', point for point, so that a pencil, traversing $\triangle ABC$, simultaneously traverses $\triangle A'B'C'$ '*on the wrong side of the paper*', which leads to reversal when the paper is unfolded to its initial condition.

Hence *reflection is an operation which reverses orientation*.

Exercise F

1. Prove that the product of two reflections cannot be a reflection.

2. Let l, m be two given lines meeting in a point U, and take two points P, Q collinear with U. Prove that there is a line n through U such that

$$P\mathbf{n} = P\mathbf{lm}, \quad Q\mathbf{n} = Q\mathbf{lm}.$$

3. Comment on the relevance of Question 2 to Question 1.

4. By considering the intersection of mediators, prove that the three points P, $P\mathbf{l}$, $P\mathbf{lm}$ are equidistant from the point of intersection $l \cap m$.

5. Three concurrent lines l, m, n are so related that n bisects the angle between l and m. Prove by geometrical argument that $\mathbf{lnm} = \mathbf{n}$, and deduce that $\mathbf{nln} = \mathbf{m}$.

Prove conversely that, if l, m, n are concurrent lines such that $\mathbf{m} = \mathbf{nln}$, then n is a bisector of the angle between l and m.

7. Successive reflections in parallel lines

Let l, m be two given parallel lines and P an arbitrary point (Figure 68). Reflect P successively in l, m to give $P' = P\mathbf{l}$, $P'' = P\mathbf{lm}$. Then, by the properties of reflections,

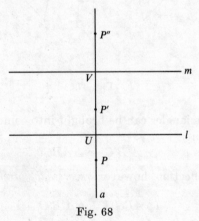

Fig. 68

(i) P, P', P'' lie on a line a perpendicular to l and m, meeting l in U and m in V;

(ii) $\overrightarrow{PU} = \overrightarrow{UP'}$, $\overrightarrow{P'V} = \overrightarrow{VP''}$.

Hence
$$\overrightarrow{PP''} = 2\overrightarrow{UP'} + 2\overrightarrow{P'V}$$
$$= 2\overrightarrow{UV}.$$

The transformation **lm** is thus a *translation* in the direction perpendicular to l and m, through a distance double that between l and m, and in the sense from l to m.

Exercise G

1. Prove the *converse result*, that a translation through a distance d in a given direction can be obtained as a product of two reflections.

2. Given two parallel lines u, v and two points P, Q in general position, prove that, if $P' = \mathbf{P}\mathbf{uv}$, $Q' = \mathbf{Q}\mathbf{uv}$, then $PP'Q'Q$ is a parallelogram.

How could you place P, Q for the parallelogram to be (i) a rectangle, (ii) a square, (iii) a rhombus?

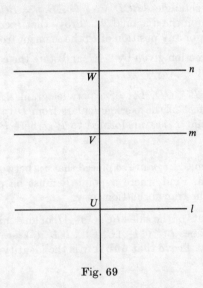

Fig. 69

Now let l, m, n be three given parallel lines, and let a line perpendicular to them meet them in U, V, W respectively (Figure 69). By what we have just done, the product **lm** is equivalent to the translation $2\overrightarrow{UV}$, with similar notation for other products.

It follows that *the triple product* **lmn** *has the property*

$$(\mathbf{lmn})^2 = \mathbf{I}.$$

To prove this, write the left-hand side in the form

$$\mathbf{lmnlmn}$$

$$= (\mathbf{lm}).(\mathbf{nl}).(\mathbf{mn}).$$

The product is the result of the successive transformations $2\overrightarrow{UV}$, $2\overrightarrow{WU}$,

$2\overrightarrow{VW}$, the result of which is to bring any point P of the plane back to its original position. Hence, as required,

$$(\mathbf{lmn})^2 = \mathbf{I}.$$

An alternative equivalent form is

$$\mathbf{lmn} = \mathbf{nml}.$$

This result, with its converse, is given in a little more detail in Chapter 6, Section 6.

Exercise H

1. The sides of a rectangle $ABCD$ are $x = AB$, $y = BC$, $z = CD$, $w = DA$. A point P is taken on the diagonal AC. Prove that $P\mathbf{xzwy}$ is also on AC.

Prove also that, for any position of P, the segment from P to $P\mathbf{xzwy}$ has magnitude and direction given by $2\overrightarrow{AC}$, and state the corresponding result if $\mathbf{xzwy}$ is replaced by $\mathbf{xzyw}$.

2. The sides AB, BC, CD, DA of a parallelogram $ABCD$ are x, y, z, w respectively. The feet of the perpendiculars from D to AB, BC are X, Y respectively. A point P is transformed to P', where $P' = P\mathbf{xzwy}$. Prove that $\overrightarrow{PP'} = 2\overrightarrow{XY}$.

3. Three parallel lines u, v, w are so placed that v is between u, w and equally distant from them. Find where a point P must be placed if it is self-corresponding in the transformation $\mathbf{uvw}$.

4. The middle points of the sides BC, CA, AB of an equilateral triangle are U, V, W, and the lines BC, CA, AB, VW, WU, UV are denoted by a, b, c, u, v, w respectively. Prove that $\mathbf{aubvcw}$ is the identity $\mathbf{I}$.

5

ROTATIONS

1. Definitions

Let U be a given point and α a given (magnitude of) angle. Take a point P in arbitrary position, and rotate the *ray* $\overrightarrow{UP}$ through an angle α in the counterclockwise sense to the position $\overrightarrow{UP'}$ (Figure 70).

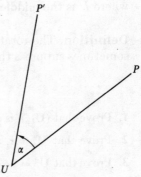

The operation from P to P' is called a *rotation* and is denoted by the symbol $\mathbf{U}_\alpha$. Then

$$P' = P\mathbf{U}_\alpha.$$

The point P' is called the *image* of P.

The point U is the *unique self-corresponding point* of the rotation, every other point being rotated elsewhere.

Fig. 70

There is, however, one formal exception: when α is a multiple of 2π, every point is rotated round to itself. Thus

$$\mathbf{U}_{2k\pi} = \mathbf{I}$$

for every integer k.

Though there are no lines of self-corresponding points for any non-identity rotation, the rotation $\mathbf{U}_\pi$ (or $\mathbf{U}_{(2k+1)\pi}$ for arbitrary integer k) brings rays through U into a position where they lie along their original straight lines but pointing in the opposite direction. Thus $\mathbf{U}_{(2k+1)\pi}$ *has an infinity of lines which self-correspond, but not point for point.*

The inverse $\mathbf{U}_\alpha^{-1}$ of a given rotation $\mathbf{U}_\alpha$ is that operation which restores every point to its original position. The definitive relation in terms of corresponding points is

$$P'\mathbf{U}_\alpha^{-1} = P \Leftrightarrow P' = P\mathbf{U}_\alpha;$$

and, as in the case of a general transformation,

$$\mathbf{U}_\alpha \mathbf{U}_\alpha^{-1} = \mathbf{U}_\alpha^{-1}\mathbf{U}_\alpha = \mathbf{I}.$$

The return of the ray UP to its original position shows that

$$\mathbf{U}_\alpha^{-1} = \mathbf{U}_{(-\alpha)},$$

[63]

being a rotation through an angle α in the *clockwise* sense and therefore a rotation through $(-\alpha)$ in the *counterclockwise* sense.

The following properties are immediate, and should be verified:

(i) $\mathbf{U}_0 = \mathbf{I}$;

(ii) $\mathbf{U}_\alpha \mathbf{U}_\beta = \mathbf{U}_{\alpha+\beta}$,

where $\mathbf{U}_\alpha \mathbf{U}_\beta$ means, 'Perform $\mathbf{U}_\alpha$, *then* $\mathbf{U}_\beta$';

(iii) $\mathbf{U}_\alpha \mathbf{U}_\beta \mathbf{U}_\gamma = \mathbf{U}_{\alpha+\beta+\gamma}$;

(iv) $PU_\pi = P'$,

where U is the middle point of PP'.

Definition. The rotation $\mathbf{U}_\pi$ is called a *half-turn* about U. We shall sometimes suppress the suffix and use the simpler notation $\mathbf{U}$.

Exercise A

1. Prove that $(\mathbf{U}_{\frac{1}{2}\pi})^2$ is a half-turn about U.

2. Prove that $\mathbf{U}_\pi^2 = \mathbf{I}$, and that $\mathbf{U}_\pi^{-1} = \mathbf{U}_\pi$.

3. Prove that $\mathbf{U}_\alpha^2 = \mathbf{I} \Leftrightarrow \alpha$ is an integral multiple of π.

4. Given an equilateral triangle ABC, named with counterclockwise orientation, prove that B is a self-corresponding point of the transformation

$$\mathbf{A}_{\frac{1}{3}\pi} \mathbf{B}_{\frac{1}{3}\pi} \mathbf{C}_{\frac{1}{3}\pi},$$

and that the transformation is, in fact, a half-turn about B.

Deduce that

$$\mathbf{A}_{\frac{1}{3}\pi} \mathbf{B}_{\frac{1}{3}\pi} \mathbf{C}_{\frac{1}{3}\pi} \mathbf{A}_{\frac{1}{3}\pi} \mathbf{B}_{\frac{1}{3}\pi} \mathbf{C}_{\frac{1}{3}\pi} = \mathbf{I}.$$

2. The image of a line under rotation

Let U be a given centre of rotation and α a given angle (Figure 71). Take an arbitrary line l with a point P upon it, and apply the rotation $\mathbf{U}_\alpha$ so that

$$l' = l\mathbf{U}_\alpha, \quad P' = P\mathbf{U}_\alpha,$$

where $P' \in l'$.

As a result of the rotation (regarded, for example, as given by rotating the page about U and then tracing the lines UP and l onto a sheet of paper below),

$$\angle PUP' = \alpha \text{ (counterclockwise)}$$

and

$$(l, l') = \alpha,$$

where the symbol (l, l') denotes the angle of a counterclockwise rotation from l to l'. Thus *the counterclockwise angle from a line to its image is equal to the angle of rotation* α.

A little more precision is sometimes useful. Suppose that $\alpha \neq \pi$ or 2π, so that l does meet l', and write

$$A = l \cap l'.$$

Let $M \in l$ be the point (Figure 72) such that

$$A = M\mathbf{U}_\alpha,$$

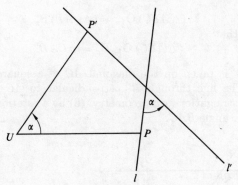

Fig. 71

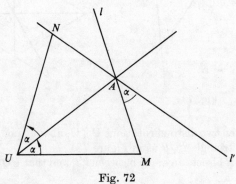

Fig. 72

while $N \in l'$ is such that

$$N = A\mathbf{U}_\alpha.$$

Then $$(AM)\mathbf{U}_\alpha = (NA),$$

so that $$AM \equiv NA,$$

the two segments being congruent through being brought to coincidence by $\mathbf{U}_\alpha$. Also, by definition of rotation,

$$UM \equiv UA \equiv UN.$$

The triangles NUA, MUA therefore correspond by reflection in the line UA. In particular, UA *bisects the angle (counterclockwise)* $\measuredangle NAM$ *from l' to l.*

Exercise B

1. The altitude AP of an equilateral triangle ABC is produced its own length to O, so that $\overrightarrow{PO} = \overrightarrow{AP}$. Prove that

$$(\triangle ABC)\, \mathbf{O}_{\frac{1}{3}\pi} = (\triangle CAB)\, \mathbf{B}_{\pi}.$$

Prove also that

$$(\triangle ABC)\, \mathbf{O}_{\frac{1}{3}\pi}\, \mathbf{B}_{\pi} = \triangle CAB.$$

2. A point B' is taken on the diagonal AC of a square $ABCD$ so that $AB' = AB$. The line through B' perpendicular to AC meets BC in P. Prove (i) by 'straightforward' geometry, (ii) by a rotation argument, that AP bisects the angle BAC.

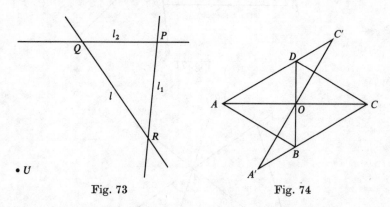

Fig. 73   Fig. 74

3. A line l is given two distinct rotations $\mathbf{U}_{\alpha}$, $\mathbf{U}_{\beta}$ about a point U to positions l_1, l_2, forming a triangle PQR as in Figure 73.

Prove that UR bisects an angle between l, l_1 and that UQ bisects an angle between l, l_2.

4. A rhombus $ABCD$ (Figure 74) is rotated about the point O which is the intersection of the diagonals to the position $A'B'C'D'$ such that A' is on BC and C' is on AD. Prove that B' is on BC and D' on AD.

Illustration 1. *The theorem of Pythagoras.* [It is perhaps of interest to state the standard Euclidean proof of the theorem of Pythagoras in terms of rotation. See also Chapter 3, Section 6.]

Let ABC be a triangle whose angle at A is a right angle (Figure 75). Draw the squares

$$BCMN, CAXY, ABQR.$$

Also draw the line from A perpendicular to BC and MN, meeting them in U and V respectively. [The three lines BY, CQ, AV can be proved to intersect, but that must not be assumed.]

It is to be proved that

$$\text{area } BCMN = \text{area } CAXY + \text{area } ABQR.$$

(i) Subject $\triangle ABN$ to the rotation $\mathbf{B}_{\frac{1}{2}\pi}$. Then

$$(ABN)\,\mathbf{B}_{\frac{1}{2}\pi} = QBC,$$

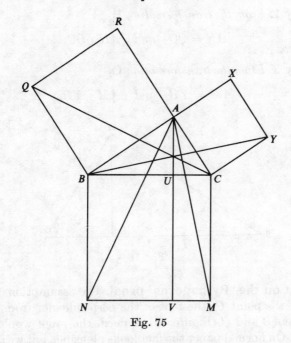

Fig. 75

so that $\qquad\qquad \triangle ABN \equiv \triangle QBC$

and, in particular,

$$\text{area } ABN = \text{area } QBC.$$

But, by the standard theorem for the area of a triangle (Chapter 3, Section 4),

$$\text{area } ABN = \tfrac{1}{2}\text{ area } NVUB, \qquad \text{area } QBC = \tfrac{1}{2}\text{ area } ABQR,$$

and so $\qquad\qquad\qquad \text{area } NVUB = \text{area } ABQR.$

(ii) Subject $\triangle BCY$ to the rotation $\mathbf{C}_{\frac{1}{2}\pi}$. Then

$$(BCY)\,\mathbf{C}_{\frac{1}{2}\pi} = MCA,$$

so that, as before,

$$\text{area } CAXY = \text{area } VMCU.$$

(iii) Adding the results of (i) and (ii),

$$\text{area } CAXY + \text{area } ABQR = \text{area } VMCU + \text{area } NVUB$$
$$= \text{area } BCMN,$$

as required.

The theorem is usually stated in the form: *The area of the square on the hypotenuse of a right-angled triangle is equal to the sum of areas of the squares on the other two sides.*

Corollary 1. *From the transformation* $\mathbf{B}_{\frac{1}{2}\pi}$,

$$AN = QC \quad and \quad AN \perp QC.$$

Corollary 2. *From the transformation* $\mathbf{C}_{\frac{1}{2}\pi}$,

$$AM = YB \quad and \quad AM \perp YB.$$

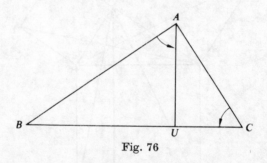

Fig. 76

Comment on the 'Pythagoras' proof. The assumption is usually made that the point U, the foot of the perpendicular from A to BC, lies between B and C (Figure 76). Indeed, the proof would collapse without it. On normal paper the fact looks plausible, but we need some sort of assurance that appearances may not at times be deceptive. Essentially, we need some appeal to *order*, which 'Euclid' as such does not give.

[Note that salvage via trigonometry (e.g. $\sin \theta \leqslant 1$) will not do if trigonometrical results used are themselves based on the theorem of Pythagoras.]

Within the framework of this text we can provide an answer (though detailed scrutiny of foundations might prove more disturbing). We have proved that the sum of the angles of a triangle is two right angles, so that, if one angle is itself a right angle, each of the others must be less. In particular, $\triangle ACB$ is less than a right angle. Let a ray start at position AB and rotate about A until $\triangle BAU = \triangle ACB$. Then $\triangle BAU < \triangle BAC$, so that, with the meaning indicated in Chapter 1,

Section 7, AU lies *between* AB and AC. This gives us confidence, admittedly short of firm proof, that U, on AU, lies between B, on AB, and C, on AC. It is immediate that $AU \perp BC$, since

$$\angle UBA + \angle BAU = \angle UBA + \angle ACU = \text{right angle}$$

$$\Rightarrow \angle AUB = \text{right angle}.$$

Hence the point U is the foot of the perpendicular from A to BC, and it does lie between B and C.

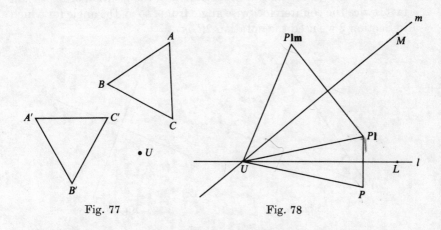

Fig. 77   Fig. 78

3. The rotation of a triangle

Let ABC be a triangle subjected to a rotation $\mathbf{U}_\alpha$. The image is a triangle $A'B'C'$ which is congruent to ABC (Figure 77). The *process of rotation, however, preserves orientation*, so that

$$(\overrightarrow{ABC})\,\mathbf{U}_\alpha = \overrightarrow{A'B'C'}.$$

This can be verified by imagining a slow rotation from ABC to $A'B'C'$. At no place is there a step which can cause reversal of orientation.

4. Rotation as a product of reflections

Let l, m be two given lines meeting in a point U (Figure 78). For convenience of reference take a point $L \in l$ and a point $M \in m$, as shown. Let P be an arbitrary point; reflect it in l to give $P\mathbf{l}$, and then reflect $P\mathbf{l}$ in m to give $P\mathbf{lm}$. It is to be shown that *the transformation from P to $P\mathbf{lm}$ can be obtained (for all P) by a rotation through an angle $2 \angle LUM$ about U.*

In the first place, the reflections give

$$UP = U(P\mathbf{l}) = U(P\mathbf{lm}).$$

Also, from the reflections,

$$\angle PU(P\mathbf{l})\dagger = 2 \angle LU(P\mathbf{l}),$$

$$\angle (P\mathbf{l}) U(P\mathbf{lm}) = 2 \angle (P\mathbf{l}) UM,$$

so that, by addition,

$$\angle PU(P\mathbf{lm}) = 2 \angle (LUM).$$

But the angle on the right is independent of the position of P; it is, in fact, twice the counterclockwise angle from l to m, the angle for which in Section 2 we used the notation $2(l, m)$.

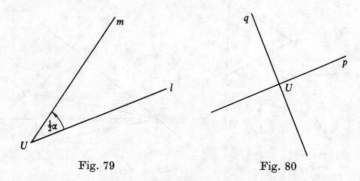

Fig. 79   Fig. 80

Hence, *the product transformation* $\mathbf{lm}$ *is equivalent to a rotation* $\mathbf{U}_{2(l, m)}$ *through an angle* $2(l, m)$ *about the point* $U = l \cap m$.

The *converse result* is also true, and very important.

Let U be a given point and α a given angle. Take an *arbitrary* line l through U (Figure 79), and let m be the line, also through U, such that

$$(l, m) = \tfrac{1}{2}\alpha.$$

Then, by the result just proved,

$$\mathbf{lm} = \mathbf{U}_{2(l, m)} = \mathbf{U}_\alpha.$$

Corollary 3. *A half-turn* $\mathbf{U}_\pi$ *is equivalent to successive reflection in two perpendicular lines, selected arbitrarily through* U *and taken in either order.*

In fact, if p, q are two such lines (Figure 80),

$$\mathbf{pq} = \mathbf{U}_{2(p, q)} = \mathbf{U}_\pi,$$

and $$\mathbf{qp} = \mathbf{U}_{2(q, p)} = \mathbf{U}_\pi.$$

† That is, the counterclockwise angle between the lines joining U to P and U to $P\mathbf{l}$.

Illustration 2. To prove that, *if p and q are distinct intersecting lines,*

$$\mathbf{pq} = \mathbf{qp} \Leftrightarrow p \perp q.$$

(i) Suppose that $p \perp q$. We have just proved that

$$\mathbf{pq} = \mathbf{qp}(= \mathbf{U}_\pi).$$

(ii) Suppose that

$$\mathbf{pq} = \mathbf{qp}.$$

Then the angle θ from p to q is equal to the angle ϕ from q to p, and so each is a right angle (Figure 81).

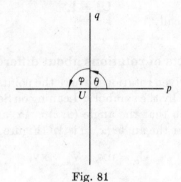

Fig. 81

Exercise C

1. The altitudes AP, CR of a triangle ABC are produced to A' and C' so that $\overrightarrow{PA'} = \overrightarrow{AP}$, $\overrightarrow{RC'} = \overrightarrow{CR}$. The sides BC, CA, AB are named a, b, c. Identify the points $A'\mathbf{a}$, $A'\mathbf{ac}$, $C\mathbf{a}$, $C\mathbf{ac}$, assuming that $\overrightarrow{ABC}$ is counterclockwise.

Verify by geometrical argument that A is obtained from A', and C' from C, by a rotation about B of $2 \measuredangle CBA$, and prove that $A'C = C'A$.

2. A triangle ABC with a right angle at A is reflected in AC followed by reflection in AB to position AB_2C_2. Prove that BCB_2C_2 is a rhombus.

3. The sides BC, CA, AB of a triangle ABC are named a, b, c. Successive reflection in c followed by b gives the triangle $A_2B_2C_2$ ($A_2 \equiv A$), where $(A, B, C)\,\mathbf{cb} = (A_2, B_2, C_2)$. Prove that the figure $BCB_2C_2C_1$ is symmetrical about the line CA.

Prove also that, if $\hat{A} > \hat{B}$, the angle between B_2C_2 and the axis of symmetry is $\hat{A} - \hat{B}$. What happens if the sides CA, CB are equal?

4. The angle at A of a triangle ABC (named in the counterclockwise sense) is $\tfrac{1}{3}\pi$. The triangle is given a rotation $\mathbf{A}_{\frac{1}{3}\pi}$ to the position $AB'C'$ and it is found that $B'C'$ passes through C. Calculate the angles of the triangle ABC.

Prove also that $BB' = B'C$.

5. Products of rotations about a given point U

Let U be a given point and $\mathbf{U}_\alpha$, $\mathbf{U}_\beta$ two rotations. Then it is immediate that

$$\mathbf{U}_\alpha \mathbf{U}_\beta = \mathbf{U}_{\alpha+\beta}.$$

In particular, $\qquad\qquad \mathbf{U}_\alpha \mathbf{U}_{-\alpha} = \mathbf{I},$

the two successive rotations being equal in magnitude and opposite in sense.

Note also that

$$\mathbf{U}_\pi^2 = \mathbf{I},$$

as is clear geometrically.

6. Products of rotations about different points

Let $\mathbf{U}_\alpha$, $\mathbf{V}_\beta$ be two given rotations, where the points U, V are different. Denote the line UV by the symbol x. Leaning on Section 4, let u be the line through U such that the angle (u, x) is $\frac{1}{2}\alpha$, and let v be the line through V such that the angle (x, v) is $\frac{1}{2}\beta$ (Figure 82). Then

$$\mathbf{U}_\alpha = \mathbf{ux}, \quad \mathbf{V}_\beta = \mathbf{xv},$$

so that

$$\mathbf{U}_\alpha \mathbf{V}_\beta = (\mathbf{ux})(\mathbf{xv}) = \mathbf{u}(\mathbf{x}^2)\mathbf{v} = \mathbf{u}(\mathbf{I})\mathbf{v}$$

$$= \mathbf{uv}.$$

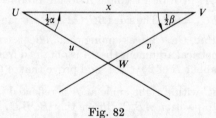

Fig. 82

(i) *Suppose that the lines u, v are not parallel, so that $\alpha + \beta \neq 2\pi$:* Let $W = u \cap v$. Then $\mathbf{uv}$ is the rotation about W through an angle $2(u, v)$; and this, being twice the counterclockwise angle from u to v, is (taken in two stages) twice the angle from u to x *plus* twice the angle from x to v. Thus

$$2(u, v) = 2(\tfrac{1}{2}\alpha + \tfrac{1}{2}\beta) = \alpha + \beta,$$

so that

$$\mathbf{U}_\alpha \mathbf{U}_\beta = \mathbf{W}_{\alpha+\beta},$$

where W is the point just defined.

(ii) *Suppose that* $u \parallel v$, *the case when* $\alpha + \beta = 2\pi$. (Compare Chapter 4, Section 7.) Let P be an arbitrary point (Figure 83), and write

$$P' = P\mathbf{u}, \quad P'' = P'\mathbf{v} = P\mathbf{uv} = P(\mathbf{ux})(\mathbf{xv}),$$

so that, exactly as before,

$$P'' = P\mathbf{U}_\alpha \mathbf{V}_\beta.$$

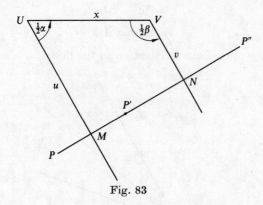

Fig. 83

Under the reflections $\mathbf{u}$, $\mathbf{v}$, the points P, P', P'' lie on the straight line through P perpendicular to u and v. Let this line meet u in M and v in N. Then

$$\vec{PM} = \vec{MP'}, \quad \vec{P'N} = \vec{NP''},$$

so that

$$\vec{PP''} = \vec{PM} + \vec{MP'} + \vec{P'N} + \vec{NP''}$$

$$= 2(\vec{MP'} + \vec{P'N})$$

$$= 2\vec{MN}.$$

Now $\vec{MN}$ is constant, being in the direction perpendicular to the lines u, v whose positions are determined by the given rotations, and of length equal to the distance (in the normal sense of the word) between those lines.

Hence in this case *the product* $\mathbf{U}_\alpha \mathbf{V}_\beta$ $(\alpha + \beta = 2\pi)$ *is equivalent to a translation* in the direction and of the magnitude indicated.

7. An identity for three concurrent lines

Let a, b, c be three given concurrent lines. To prove that $\mathbf{abc}$ *is a reflection*.

Let d be the line through the point of concurrence such that

$$(d, c) = (a, b) = \alpha, \quad \text{say (Figure 84).}$$

Then $$\mathbf{dc} = \mathbf{ab},$$

each being $\mathbf{U}_{2\alpha}$, where

$$U = a \cap b.$$

But $$\mathbf{dc} = \mathbf{ab}$$

$$\Rightarrow \mathbf{dc}^2 = \mathbf{abc}$$

$$\Rightarrow \mathbf{abc} = \mathbf{d},$$

where $\mathbf{d}$ is the operation of reflection in the line d.

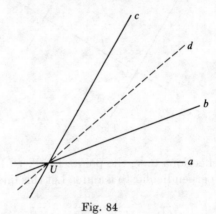

Fig. 84

Corollary 4. *To prove that, if a, b, c are concurrent, then*

$$(\mathbf{abc})^2 = \mathbf{I},$$

or, equivalently, $$\mathbf{abc} = \mathbf{cba}.$$

Since $$\mathbf{d}^2 = \mathbf{I},$$

it follows at once that

$$(\mathbf{abc})^2 = \mathbf{I}.$$

Thus, alternatively,

$$(\mathbf{abc}) = (\mathbf{abc})^{-1}$$

$$= \mathbf{c}^{-1}\mathbf{b}^{-1}\mathbf{a}^{-1}$$

$$= \mathbf{cba}.$$

Before considering the *converse* of this result, recall the result given in Chapter 4, Section 7, that, *if l, m, n are parallel lines, then* $(\mathbf{lmn})^2 = \mathbf{I}$. We therefore adapt the converse of the present result to the form:

If a, b, c are three lines, no two of which are parallel, such that $(\mathbf{abc})^2 = \mathbf{I}$, *then those lines are concurrent.*

Suppose that a, b, c are not concurrent but that, no two being parallel, they form the sides of a triangle ABC (Figure 85). Re-write the relation

$$\mathbf{abcabc} = \mathbf{I}$$

to give

$$\mathbf{abc} = \mathbf{cba},$$

and so

$$\mathbf{bc} = (\mathbf{ac})\,(\mathbf{ba}).$$

Reflect the triangle ABC in the line a to give the triangle XBC, where XB, XC are lines z, y respectively. Then, by equality of angles,

$$\mathbf{ac} = \mathbf{za}, \quad \mathbf{ba} = \mathbf{ay},$$

so that

$$\mathbf{bc} = (\mathbf{ac})\,(\mathbf{ba}) = (\mathbf{za})\,(\mathbf{ay}) = \mathbf{z}(\mathbf{a^2})\,\mathbf{y}$$

$$= \mathbf{zy}.$$

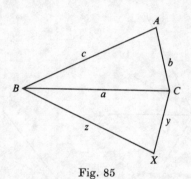

Fig. 85

There are now two possibilities:

(i) The rotation $\mathbf{bc}$ about A is the same as the rotation $\mathbf{zy}$ about X, neither being identity. This is impossible unless A and X coincide. But this they cannot do on the assumption that ABC is a genuine triangle. It follows that the triangle ABC cannot exist, and hence that a, b, c are concurrent.

(ii) The rotations $\mathbf{bc}$ and $\mathbf{zy}$ are both identity. This requires, in particular,

$$\mathbf{bc} = \mathbf{I},$$

so that

$$\mathbf{bc^2} = \mathbf{c},$$

or

$$\mathbf{b} = \mathbf{c}.$$

The two lines b, c are not distinct and the property $(\mathbf{abc})^2 = \mathbf{I}$, though true, loses significance.

The upshot, then, is that the lines a, b, c are concurrent.

8. The bisectors of an angle

Let a, b be two given intersecting lines, and let x, y be the bisectors of the angles between them (Figure 86), so that

$$\mathbf{ax = xb}, \quad \mathbf{ay = yb},$$

with $x \neq y$.

To prove that $x \perp y$.

From the identifying relations, just given,

$$\mathbf{axy = xby},$$

$$\mathbf{ayx = ybx}$$

$$= \mathbf{xby} \quad \text{(Section 7)}.$$

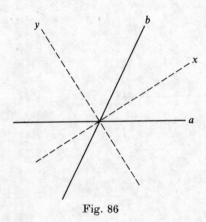

Fig. 86

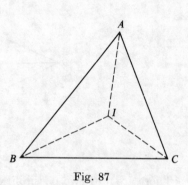

Fig. 87

Hence $\mathbf{axy = ayx}$,

so that $\mathbf{xy = yx}$,

and so $x \perp y$ (Section 4),

remembering that x and y are assumed distinct.

9. The bisectors of the angles of a triangle

To prove that *the bisectors of the (internal) angles of a triangle are concurrent.*

(i) Let the bisectors of the angles at B, C, obtained by folding BA on BC and CA on CB respectively, meet in I (Figure 87). Then I is equidistant from BA and BC in their folded positions and therefore equidistant from BA and BC in their original positions. Similarly I is equidistant from CA and CB. Hence I is equidistant from AB and AC, so that it lies on the bisector of the angle at A.

The point I, which is equidistant from the sides, is called the *in-centre* of the triangle. A circle can be drawn with its centre at A so as to touch all the three sides.

Exercise D

1. Prove that the bisectors of the external angles at B and C meet on the bisector of the internal angle at A. The point of intersection, I_1, is called the *e-centre* (escribed centre) opposite to A.

2. Prove that, if I_2, I_3 are similarly defined, then $II_1 \perp I_2 I_3$ (Figure 88).

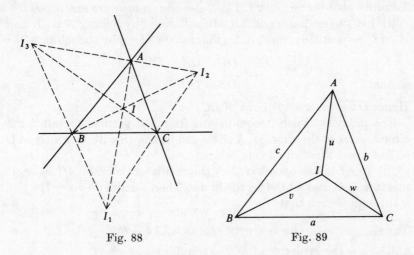

Fig. 88   Fig. 89

(ii) *Proof by the operators:* Let the internal bisectors of the angles at B and C be v and w, meeting at I (Figure 89). Then

$$\mathbf{av} = \mathbf{vc}, \qquad \mathbf{va} = \mathbf{cv},$$

$$\mathbf{aw} = \mathbf{wb}, \qquad \mathbf{wa} = \mathbf{bw},$$

so that

$$\mathbf{vw} = (\mathbf{va})(\mathbf{aw}) \quad (\mathbf{a}^2 = \mathbf{I}, \text{ the unit transformation})$$

$$= (\mathbf{cv})(\mathbf{wb})$$

$$= \mathbf{cvwb}.$$

Now let p be the line through I perpendicular to the side b, so that

$$\mathbf{pb} = \mathbf{bp}.$$

Then

$$\mathbf{vwp} = \mathbf{cvwbp} = \mathbf{cvwpb}.$$

But (Section 7) **vwp** is equivalent to a reflection **x** in a line x through **I**. Hence the relation is

$$\mathbf{x} = \mathbf{cxb} \quad \text{or} \quad \mathbf{cx} = \mathbf{xb},$$

so that (i) $A \in x$ since $c \cap x = x \cap b$, (ii) x bisects the angle at A.

But x passes through I; and so the three bisectors are concurrent in I.

Remark. It does not seem easy to distinguish between the two bisectors of an angle by these methods.

10. The mediators of the sides of a triangle

To prove that *the mediators of the sides of a triangle are concurrent*.

(i) Let the mediators of AB, AC, obtained by folding A on B and A on C respectively, meet in O (Figure 90). Then, by the foldings,

$$OA = OB, \quad OA = OC,$$

so that $$OB = OC.$$

Hence O lies on the mediator of BC.

The point O, which is equidistant from the vertices, is called the *circumcentre* of the triangle. A circle can be drawn with its centre at O so as to pass through all three sides.

(ii) *Proof by the operators.* Let the mediators of AB, AC be w, v, meeting in O, and let OA be the line x. Then there is (Section 7) a line u through O such that

$$\mathbf{u} = \mathbf{wxv}.$$

Thus $$\mathbf{B}\mathbf{u} = \mathbf{Bwxv} = \mathbf{A}\mathbf{xv} = \mathbf{A}\mathbf{v} = C,$$

and so u is the mediator of BC, as required.

11. The altitudes of a triangle

It is a standard result of elementary geometry that *the altitudes of a triangle are concurrent*, in the *orthocentre*, usually called H.

This theorem will now be proved in a way that illustrates the technique we are now using. [The method makes no pretence at simplicity.]

Let ABC be the triangle and AP, BQ, CR the altitudes, not yet proved concurrent. Let the mediators of BC, CA, AB be OL, OM, ON, meeting in O. For the lines, use the notation indicated in Figure 91:

$$BC = a, \quad CA = b, \quad AB = c;$$
$$AP = p, \quad BQ = q, \quad CR = r;$$
$$OA = x, \quad OB = y, \quad OC = z.$$

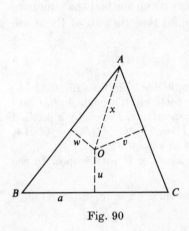

Fig. 90

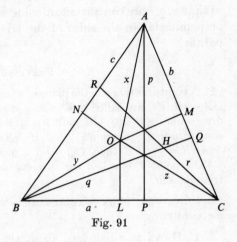

Fig. 91

Then $\qquad\qquad x,y,z$ are concurrent

$$\Rightarrow \mathbf{xyz = zyx}.$$

By folding B onto C, we have

$$\angle CBO = \angle BCO\,;$$

thus, by similar argument,

$$\angle OCB + \angle ACO + \angle BAO = \tfrac{1}{2}\text{ (sum of angles of triangle)}$$
$$= \text{right angle},$$

so that $\qquad\qquad \angle ACB + \angle BAO = \text{right angle},$

giving $\qquad\qquad \angle BAO = \text{right angle} - \angle ACB$
$$= \angle PAC.$$

Thus $\qquad\qquad \mathbf{bp = xc}$

$$\Rightarrow \mathbf{p = bxc}$$

and, similarly, $\qquad\qquad \mathbf{q = cya},$

$$\mathbf{r = azb}.$$

Hence $\qquad\qquad \mathbf{(pqr) = (bxc)\,(cya)\,(azb)}$
$$= \mathbf{bxyzb},$$

so that $\qquad\qquad \mathbf{(pqr)^2 = (bxyzb)\,(bxyzb)}$
$$= \mathbf{b(xyz)^2\,b}$$
$$= \mathbf{b^2},$$

since x, y, z are concurrent. Thus

$$\mathbf{(pqr)^2 = I},$$

so that p, q, r are concurrent, it being clear (from the fact that they are perpendicular to the sides of the triangle) that no two of them are parallel.

Exercise E

1. A point U is taken in the plane of a triangle ABC. The lines $BC, CA, AB,$ UA, UB, UC are called a, b, c, x, y, z respectively. Through A, B, C are drawn lines AP, BQ, CR, called p, q, r respectively. Prove, by a method similar to that of Section 11, that, if $\angle BAP = \angle UAC,$ $\angle CBQ = \angle UBA,$ $\angle ACR = \angle UCB$, then AP, BQ, CR meet in a point V.

[The point V is called the *isogonal conjugate* of U with respect to the triangle ABC.]

2. Prove that, if $\mathbf{bx} = \mathbf{xc}$ and $\mathbf{ax} = \mathbf{xa}$, then $\mathbf{ba} = \mathbf{ac}$. Interpret geometrically.

3. $\mathbf{C}_C \mathbf{B}_B \mathbf{A}_A$ is a half-turn about the foot of the perpendicular from B to CA.

4. $\mathbf{A}_{2A} \mathbf{C}_{2C} \mathbf{B}_{2B} = \mathbf{I}$, where the angles of $\triangle ABC$ have (counterclockwise) magnitudes A, B, C.

5. $\mathbf{P}_\pi \mathbf{l} = \mathbf{l} \mathbf{P}_\pi \Leftrightarrow P \in l$.

6. $\mathbf{P}_\pi \mathbf{l} = \mathbf{l} \mathbf{Q}_\pi \Leftrightarrow l$ is the mediator of PQ.

7. The sides BC, CA, AB of an isosceles triangle ABC $(AB = AC)$ are a, b, c. The middle point of BC is U and the line AU is named u. Prove that $\mathbf{c} = \mathbf{ubu}$, and deduce that

$$\mathbf{ac} = (\mathbf{au})(\mathbf{bu}).$$

Verify this result by submitting B and C in turn first to the operation $\mathbf{ac}$ and second to the product of $\mathbf{au}$ followed by $\mathbf{bu}$.

8. Repeat Question 7 with the modification that the triangle ABC is not isosceles, but that U is the point where the internal bisector of $\angle BAC$ meets BC.

9. The sides AB, BC, CD, DA of a rectangle $ABCD$, named in the counterclockwise sense, are a, b, c, d; the diagonals AC, BD are u, v, meeting in U. The angle $\angle BAU = \theta$. Prove that

$$\mathbf{B}_{2\theta} \mathbf{B}_\pi \mathbf{C}_\pi \mathbf{D}_\pi \mathbf{A}_{\pi+2\theta} = \mathbf{U}_{4\theta}.$$

Verify this result for the transformations of the points U and D, checking the positions by geometrical argument.

10. Prove that, if a, b, c, x are reflections, then

$$(\mathbf{cb}) = (\mathbf{cx})(\mathbf{xa})(\mathbf{ab}).$$

ABC is an equilateral triangle whose centre is U, and AX is a median (passing through U). BU is produced its own length to $U_1, U_1 X$ is produced

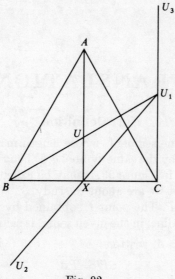

Fig. 92

its own length to U_2, and CU_1 is produced its own length to U_3 (Figure 92). Prove that $CU_3 = CU_2$ and that the angle $\measuredangle U_3 C U_2$ is $\frac{4}{3}\pi$.

Using the opening result, verify that these results follow from the relation

$$U \mathbf{A}_{\frac{1}{3}\pi} \mathbf{X}_\pi \mathbf{C}_{\frac{4}{3}\pi} = U \mathbf{A}_{\frac{2}{3}\pi}.$$

6

TRANSLATIONS

1. Definition

Let d be a given line segment, whose length may also, without confusion, be denoted by the same symbol d. When traversed in a definite sense, as indicated in Figure 93, it may be called the *base line* for the transformation that we are about to study.

Take any point P. The point P' obtained by moving a distance d parallel to the base line, in the given sense, is said to be obtained from P by the *translation* $\vec{\mathbf{d}}$, written

$$P' = P\vec{\mathbf{d}}.$$

The inverse operation $\vec{\mathbf{d}}^{-1}$, which might also be written $\overleftarrow{\mathbf{d}}$, returns P' back to P.

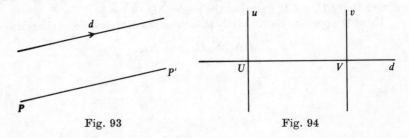

Fig. 93   Fig. 94

Since every point is moved by $\vec{\mathbf{d}}$, *there are no self-corresponding points*, but every straight line parallel to d is self-corresponding, though not point-for-point.

It is immediate that straight lines translate to straight lines, and also that *orientation is preserved*.

2. Translation by reflection in two parallel lines

Take any two points U, V on d (with $\vec{UV}$ in the sense of $\vec{\mathbf{d}}$) so that their distance apart is $\frac{1}{2}d$, and through them draw the lines u, v perpendicular to d (Figure 94). Then (Chapter 4, Section 7)

$$\vec{\mathbf{d}} = \mathbf{uv}.$$

[82]

Thus *the translation is equivalent to the product of reflections in two parallel lines distant $\frac{1}{2}d$ apart and each perpendicular to d.*

Note that *one of these two lines can be selected arbitrarily.* The other is then determined *uniquely* in order to give correct sense.

3. Translation as a product of half-turns

Take two points U, V on the base line distant $\frac{1}{2}d$ apart (with $\overrightarrow{UV}$ in the sense of $\overrightarrow{\mathbf{d}}$). Let P be any point of the plane, and subject it to two half-turns $\mathbf{U}_\pi$, $\mathbf{V}_\pi$ in succession (Figure 95), so that

$$Q = P\mathbf{U}_\pi,$$

$$P' = Q\mathbf{V}_\pi,$$

giving $\qquad\qquad P' = P\mathbf{U}_\pi\mathbf{V}_\pi.$

We prove that

$$\overrightarrow{\mathbf{d}} = \mathbf{U}_\pi\mathbf{V}_\pi.$$

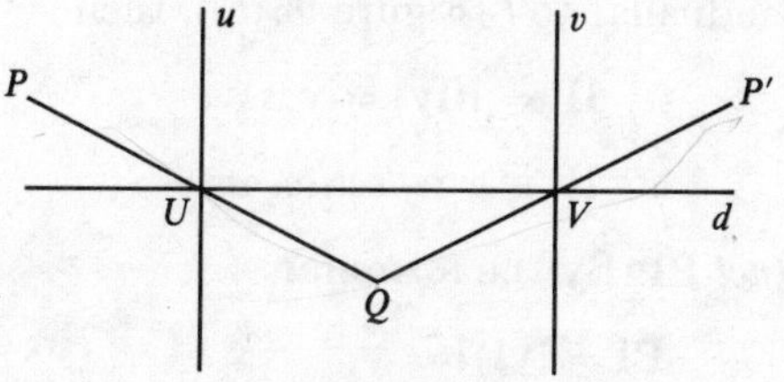

Fig. 95

If $\mathbf{d}$ (without arrow) denotes reflection in d, then

$$\mathbf{U}_\pi = \mathbf{ud} = \mathbf{du},$$

$$\mathbf{V}_\pi = \mathbf{vd} = \mathbf{dv},$$

where u, v are the lines through U, V perpendicular to d. Thus

$$\mathbf{U}_\pi\mathbf{V}_\pi = (\mathbf{ud})(\mathbf{dv})$$

$$= \mathbf{u}(\mathbf{d}^2)\mathbf{v}$$

$$= \mathbf{uv} \quad (\mathbf{d}^2 = \mathbf{I})$$

$$= \overrightarrow{\mathbf{d}},$$

by Section 2.

Exercise A

1. Use the result of Section 3 to verify that the straight line joining the middle points of two sides of a triangle is parallel to the third side and equal in length to half of it.

4. Further uses of operators

Let l, m be two parallel lines and x a line perpendicular to them Figure 96 (a), such that
$$l \cap x = A, \quad m \cap x = B.$$

Omitting the suffix π for the present, use notation such as **A** to denote a half-turn about the point A. Then
$$\mathbf{A} = \mathbf{xl} = \mathbf{lx}, \quad \mathbf{B} = \mathbf{xm} = \mathbf{mx}.$$

We start by identifying some products.

(i) *The product* **lm**: As we have seen, this is the *translation* $2\overrightarrow{AB}$.

(ii) *The product* **lP**, *where* $P \in l$: By the formula, if y is the line through P perpendicular to l (Figure 96 (b)), then
$$\mathbf{lP} = \mathbf{l(ly)} = \mathbf{y},$$
and   **lP** is a *reflection* in y.

(iii) *The product* **Pl**: By the formula,
$$\mathbf{Pl} = \mathbf{(yl)l} = \mathbf{y},$$
and   **Pl** is again a *reflection* in y.

(iv) *The product* **Pm**, *where* $P \in l$, *so that* $P \notin m$ (Figure 96 (c)): By the formula,
$$\mathbf{Pm} = \mathbf{(yl)\,m} = \mathbf{y(lm)},$$

and **Pm** is a reflection in **y**, followed by a translation $2\overrightarrow{PQ}$, where Q is the point $m \cap y$. This is the transformation called a *glide reflection*, to be studied shortly.

(v) *The product* **mP**: By the formula,
$$\mathbf{mP} = \mathbf{m(ly)} = \mathbf{(ml)\,y},$$

which is the 'glide' $2\overrightarrow{QP}$ followed by reflection in y.

(vi) *The product* **PQ**: By the formulae,
$$\mathbf{PQ} = \mathbf{(ly)\,(ym)} = \mathbf{lm},$$

and (as we have already seen)
$$\mathbf{PQ} = 2\overrightarrow{PQ}.$$

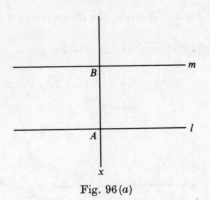

Fig. 96 (a)

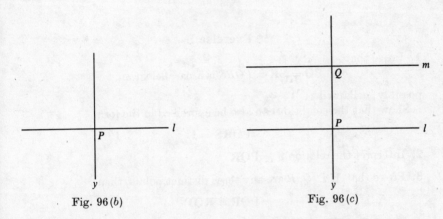

Fig. 96 (b)   Fig. 96 (c)

5. The product of two translations

Let $\vec{\mathbf{u}}$, $\vec{\mathbf{v}}$ be two given translations. We prove that *the product $\vec{\mathbf{u}}\vec{\mathbf{v}}$ is the translation defined* (in a way to be explained) *by the diagonal of a parallelogram of which* $\vec{\mathbf{u}}$, $\vec{\mathbf{v}}$ *are adjacent sides.*

Let P be an arbitrary point and submit it to the translation $\vec{\mathbf{u}}$, giving a point Q, where

$$Q = P\vec{\mathbf{u}}.$$

Similarly displace Q to R, where

$$R = Q\vec{\mathbf{v}}.$$

Then $$R = P\vec{\mathbf{u}}\vec{\mathbf{v}}.$$

Now PR is the diagonal of a parallelogram $PQRS$ (Figure 97) in which the sides PQ, SR are in the direction of $\vec{\mathbf{u}}$ and of magnitude

4

denoted by u; and QR, PS are in the direction of $\vec{v}$ and of magnitude denoted by v.

This is the result stated, P being arbitrary.

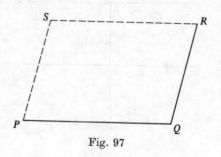

Fig. 97

Exercise B

1. Prove that
$$PQ = SR \Leftrightarrow PQRS \text{ is a parallelogram,}$$
possibly 'collapsed'.

Show that the condition can also be expressed in the form
$$PQRS = I.$$

2. Interpret the relation $S = PQR$.

3. Prove that, if P, Q, R are any three distinct points, then
$$PQR = RQP.$$

4. Prove that $PR = RQ \Leftrightarrow R$ is the middle point of PQ.

5. Prove from the results given in Section 4 that
   (i) $Pl = lP \Leftrightarrow P$ lies on l,
   (ii) $Pl = lQ \Leftrightarrow l$ is the mediator of PQ.

6. Points P, Q, R, S, U are so related that
$$PU = UR, \quad SU = UQ.$$

Prove that
$$SR = UQPU,$$

and hence, using Question 3, that $PQRS$ is a parallelogram.

7. Given two parallelograms $ABCD$, $ABQR$, prove that
$$D = ABC, \quad R = QBA,$$

and deduce that $CDRQ$ is a parallelogram.

Remark. The work of Section 5 is closely linked with the theory of *vectors*, for which a text-book should be consulted.

6. The product uvw when the three lines are parallel

We have proved, under rotations, that, when lines u, v, w are con-current, then there is a line λ such that $\boldsymbol{\lambda} = \mathbf{uvw}$, thus obtaining the concurrency condition $(\mathbf{uvw})^2 = \mathbf{I}$ or, more conveniently sometimes, $\mathbf{uvw} = \mathbf{wvu}$. We also proved the converse result that, if no two of u, v, w are parallel and if $\mathbf{uvw} = \mathbf{wvu}$, then the three lines are concurrent.

The problem now is to examine the analogous results when parallelism is allowed.

(i) Let u, v, w be three parallel lines and let p be a line perpendicular to them, meeting them in U, V, W respectively (Figure 98). Recall that, in terms of translations,

$$\mathbf{uv} = 2\overrightarrow{UV}, \quad \mathbf{wu} = 2\overrightarrow{WU}, \quad \mathbf{vw} = 2\overrightarrow{VW}.$$

Then the relation

$$\overrightarrow{UV} + \overrightarrow{VW} + \overrightarrow{WU} = \text{zero translation}$$

gives

$$\overrightarrow{UV} + \overrightarrow{WU} + \overrightarrow{VW} = \text{zero translation},$$

so that

$$(\mathbf{uv})(\mathbf{wu})(\mathbf{vw}) = \mathbf{I},$$

or

$$(\mathbf{uvw})^2 = \mathbf{I}.$$

Now let L be the *uniquely determined* point on p such that

$$\overrightarrow{LW} = \overrightarrow{UV},$$

and let l be the line through L and parallel to u, v, w (Figure 99). Then

$$\mathbf{lw} = \mathbf{uv}.$$

It follows that

$$\mathbf{uvw} = (\mathbf{lw})\,\mathbf{w} = \mathbf{lw}^2$$
$$= \mathbf{l},$$

so that *the product* $\mathbf{uvw}$ *of reflections in three parallel lines* u, v, w *is equivalent to a reflection in the single line l defined as above.*

This gives an alternative confirmation of the preceding result, since

$$(\mathbf{uvw})^2 = \mathbf{l}^2$$
$$= \mathbf{I}.$$

(ii) Consider next *the converse problem*. Let u, v, w be three distinct lines, with $u \parallel v$, where

$$\mathbf{uvw} = \mathbf{wvu}.$$

It is required *to prove that w is parallel to u and v.*

4-2

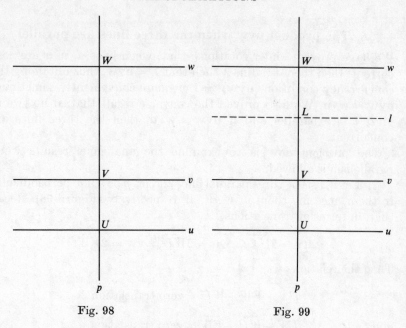

Fig. 98   Fig. 99

Suppose that, on the contrary, w meets v in a point P (Figure 100). Since $u \parallel v$, there is a line p through P perpendicular to both. Further, let the line through P perpendicular to w be a. Then

$$\mathbf{pu} = \mathbf{up},$$

$$\mathbf{pv} = \mathbf{vp} = \mathbf{wa} = \mathbf{aw} \quad \text{(half-turns about } P\text{)},$$

$$\mathbf{uvw} = \mathbf{wvu} \quad \text{(given)}.$$

Thus

$$\mathbf{wa} = \mathbf{vp} \Rightarrow \mathbf{w} = \mathbf{vpa},$$

$$\mathbf{aw} = \mathbf{pv} \Rightarrow \mathbf{w} = \mathbf{apv},$$

$$\mathbf{uvw} = \mathbf{wvu} \Rightarrow \mathbf{uv}(\mathbf{vpa}) = (\mathbf{apv})\,\mathbf{vu}$$

$$\Rightarrow \mathbf{upa} = \mathbf{apu}.$$

[Note that this last relation would have been automatic for u, p, a concurrent. Here it is more significant.]
Further,

$$\mathbf{upa} = \mathbf{apu}$$

$$\Rightarrow \mathbf{pa} = \mathbf{uapu} = \mathbf{uaup} \quad (\mathbf{pu} = \mathbf{up})$$

$$\Rightarrow \mathbf{papa} = \mathbf{uaua}.$$

Now $\mathbf{pa}$ is a rotation about P through twice the angle (p, a), so that $\mathbf{papa}$ is a rotation about P through four times $\angle(p, a)$. But $\mathbf{uaua}$ is either identity, or a translation, or a rotation about the point $u \cap a$ which, if it exists, is necessarily different from P. Hence *each of* **papa**, **uaua** *can only be identity*. We therefore need (p, a) to be some multiple of a right angle. Since $p \perp u$, it is therefore necessary that a is either perpendicular to u or parallel to u; and so w is either parallel to u or perpendicular to u.

But
$$w \parallel u \Rightarrow w \text{ coincides with } v,$$

a case which we have excluded.

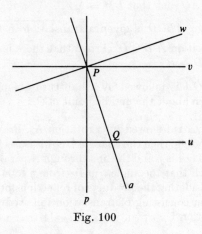

Fig. 100

Hence we need
$$w \perp u, \quad w \perp v$$

so that
$$\mathbf{uw} = \mathbf{wu}, \quad \mathbf{vw} = \mathbf{wv}.$$
The given relation
$$\mathbf{wvu} = \mathbf{uvw}$$

thus gives
$$\mathbf{wvu} = \mathbf{uwv} = \mathbf{wuv},$$

so that
$$\mathbf{vu} = \mathbf{uv}.$$

The lines u, v are therefore either coincident or perpendicular, each contradicting the hypothesis.

The existence of P is therefore impossible, and so w is parallel to v and u.

Note. What we have proved is that, under the conditions stated, three distinct parallel lines exist. This does not of itself prove that the case can happen, but that has been cleared under (i) where we obtained three distinct parallel lines that do have the property $\mathbf{uvw} = \mathbf{wvu}$.

Exercise C

1. Prove that, if p is perpendicular to the parallel lines u, v, then $\mathbf{puv} = \mathbf{uvp}$, and $\mathbf{pvu} = \mathbf{vup}$.

2. Prove that, if u and v are distinct, $p \perp u$, and $\mathbf{puv} = \mathbf{uvp}$, then u and v are either parallel or perpendicular.

3. Two lines AP, AQ are given in position and $\overrightarrow{XY}$ is a segment of given length and direction. By translating AP, AQ, show how to find points L on AP and M on AQ such that $\overrightarrow{LM} = \overrightarrow{XY}$.

4. A parallelogram $ABCD$ is given a translation in the direction of the line $\overrightarrow{AC}$ to the position $A'B'C'D'$. Prove that there is a half-turn $A \to C'$, $B \to D'$, $C \to A'$, $D \to B'$.

5. A translation $\overrightarrow{OA}$ is followed by a half-turn about A. Prove that the result is a half-turn about the middle point of OA.

6. A translation $\overrightarrow{OA}$ is followed by a rotation $\mathbf{A}_\theta$. Prove that, if the point U is self-corresponding, then the triangle UOA is isosceles and $\angle OUA = \theta$.

    The mediator of OA is p and the line through A parallel to p is q. The line r through A is such that the angle $\angle qAr$ (from q to r) is $\frac{1}{2}\theta$. The lines p, r meet in U. By considering the products of reflections $\mathbf{pq}$ and $\mathbf{qr}$, prove that the transformation consisting of translation followed by rotation is equivalent to the rotation $\mathbf{U}_\theta$.

7. The middle points of the sides AB, AC of a triangle ABC are Q, R. The triangle is given a translation $\overrightarrow{QR}$ to the position $A'B'C'$. Prove that AB' is a median of the triangle ABC.

    The triangle $A'B'C'$ is given a translation $\overrightarrow{BA}$ to the position $A''B''C''$. Prove that A' is the middle point of $A''B''$.

8. An arbitrary point B' is taken on the side AD of a parallelogram $ABCD$, and the parallelogram is given a translation $\overrightarrow{BB'}$ to the position $A'B'C'D'$. Prove that C' also lies on AD.

    Prove that the triangles $AA'B'$, $C'DC$ are congruent.

7

GLIDE REFLECTIONS

The transformation now to be studied is somewhat unfamiliar, and we slacken the pace accordingly.

1. A product of three reflections

Let u, v be distinct parallel lines and x a line perpendicular to each (Figure 101). Consider the product

$$\mathbf{uxv},$$

which received mention in Chapter 6, Section 4.

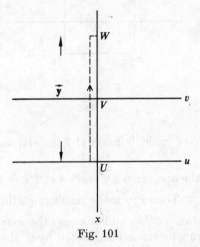

Fig. 101

Since $\mathbf{ux} = \mathbf{xu}$, $\mathbf{vx} = \mathbf{xv}$, the product can be written in the alternative forms
  (i) $(\mathbf{uv})\mathbf{x}$,
  (ii) $\mathbf{x}(\mathbf{uv})$.

Write $x \cap u = U$, $x \cap v = V$. Then $\mathbf{uv}$ is the translation which we might denote by $\{2\overrightarrow{UV}\}$; but, to agree with the notation given at the start of Chapter 6, we prefer to write $\{2\overrightarrow{UV}\} = \overrightarrow{\mathbf{y}}$, where y itself denotes a

segment UW of length $2UV$ on the line x, in the sense from U to V.
Then

$$\mathbf{uxv} = \vec{\mathbf{yx}} = \vec{\mathbf{xy}}.$$

Consider first the operation of $\vec{\mathbf{yx}}$ on a point P (Figure 102). Let
$P\vec{\mathbf{y}} = P_1$, where $\vec{PP_1} = 2\vec{UV}$. Then $P_1\mathbf{x} = P_2$, where P_2 is the reflection
of P_1 in x. Hence the point

$$P\vec{\mathbf{yx}}$$

*is found by 'gliding' P to P_1 by the translation $2\vec{UV}$, and then reflecting
P_1 in x.*

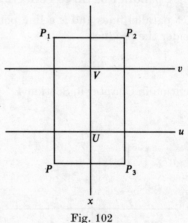

Fig. 102

This operation of glide followed by reflection is called a *glide
reflection*.

Consider next the operation $\vec{\mathbf{xy}}$ on P. Let $P\mathbf{x} = P_3$, where P_3 is the
reflection of P in $\mathbf{x}$. Then $P_3\vec{\mathbf{y}}$ is the result of gliding from P_3 parallel
to x through a distance $2\vec{UV}$; and *this gives the same point P_2 as before*.
Hence, if the transformation is denoted by $\mathfrak{g}$, then

$$\mathfrak{g} = \vec{\mathbf{yx}} = \vec{\mathbf{xy}}.$$

It is essential to note that *the glide takes place parallel to the axis of the
reflection*.
Note that
$$\mathfrak{g}^2 = (\vec{\mathbf{yx}})(\vec{\mathbf{xy}}) = (\vec{\mathbf{y}})^2,$$

where $(\vec{\mathbf{y}})^2$ is the translation $4\vec{UV}$.

Exercise A

1. Illustrate the result $\mathbf{g}^2 = 4\overrightarrow{UV}$ by means of a diagram.

Verify that $\mathbf{g}^3$ is a glide reflection.

2. Prove that the inverse of a glide reflection is also a glide reflection.

3. The triangle ABC has a right angle at A. The points of the plane are subjected to two glide reflections in succession: the first has axis AB and translation $\overrightarrow{AB}$; the second has axis AC and translation $\overrightarrow{AC}$. Draw in a diagram the position $A'B'C'$ to which the triangle ABC is transformed, and prove that AA', BB', CC' have a common middle point O.

Prove also that, if an arbitrary point P is transformed to P', then the middle point of PP' is also at O.

4. The middle points of the sides AB, AC of a triangle ABC are R, Q respectively. The figure is given a translation $\overrightarrow{RQ}$ to position A_1, B_1, C_1, R_1, Q_1 and the result is reflected in BC to give the position A', B', C', R', Q'. Prove that $QQ' \parallel RR'$.

Prove also that, if $U = AC \cap A'C'$, then the triangle UCC' is isosceles.

Is it possible for AC, $A'C'$ to be (i) parallel, (ii) coincident?

5. The middle points of the sides AB, AC of a triangle ABC are R, Q respectively. Through R, Q lines r, q are drawn perpendicular to the side BC, named a. Indicate in a diagram the position $A'B'C'$ to which the triangle is transformed by the operation $\mathbf{rqa}$.

Under what condition can the points A, C, A' be collinear?

2. The nature of glide reflection

Consider as a preliminary a summary of the self-corresponding elements of the isometries met in the preceding chapters.

(i) *A reflection* has a line of self-corresponding points and also an infinity of lines (perpendicular to the preceding line) that are self-corresponding, though not point-for-point.

(ii) *A rotation* has a single self-corresponding point and, in general, no self-corresponding lines; but the half-turn has an infinity of lines that are self-corresponding, though not point-for-point.

(iii) *A translation* has no self-corresponding points, but an infinity of lines that are self-corresponding, though not point-for-point.

As far as *self-corresponding points* are concerned, these isometries give none, one, or an infinity. For lines that are corresponding, though not point-for-point, they give none or infinity; the glide reflection fills a gap by giving the case of a single such line, and it is of interest to derive the transformation from that starting-point.

The aim, then, is to have an isometry with a single line l that is self-corresponding, though not point-for-point.

Let A, B be two *fixed* points on l. Their mates A', B' are to be on l, and, by the isometry property, *either*

$$\overrightarrow{A'B'} = \overrightarrow{BA}$$

or
$$\overrightarrow{A'B'} = \overrightarrow{AB}.$$

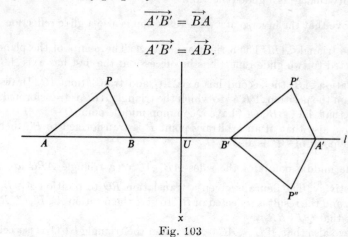

Fig. 103

(i) *Suppose that* $\overrightarrow{A'B'} = \overrightarrow{BA}$ (a case we are, in fact, to exclude). An *arbitrary* point P transforms to P' so that the triangles $A'B'P'$, ABP are congruent. Two positions are possible for P', according to orientation, and these are distinguished by the names P', P'' in the diagram (Figure 103), where P' is on the same side of l as P, and P'' is on the other.

Let U be the middle point of AA', and consequently of BB', and draw the line x through U perpendicular to l. By folding about x, the points A', B', P' fall exactly on A, B, P by virtue of the congruence of the triangles. Hence P, a point selected arbitrarily, gives rise to its reflection in x, so that the whole transformation in this case is a *reflection*. But this has an infinity of self-corresponding lines and must therefore be excluded.

It follows further that P'' is obtained from P by the *half-turn* $\mathbf{x}l$ and must also be excluded since the infinity of lines through U are self-corresponding.

Hence the case $\overrightarrow{A'B'} = \overrightarrow{BA}$ is excluded.

(ii) *Suppose that* $\overrightarrow{A'B'} = \overrightarrow{AB}$. With notation analogous to that just used, the transformation $P \rightarrow P'$ is obtained by the *translation* parallel to l through the distance $\overrightarrow{AA'} = \overrightarrow{BB'}$. This, once more, is ruled out, since there is an infinity of self-corresponding lines.

Consider, finally, the transformation $P \rightarrow P''$, by a translation from P to P' followed by a reflection in l to P'' (Figure 104). This is precisely the desired *glide reflection*, and the only self-corresponding line (not point-for-point) is l.

The same point P'' is obtained by first reflecting in l and then applying the translation $\overrightarrow{AA'}$.

The study of the self-corresponding elements of isometries thus leads inevitably to the existence of the glide reflection; this is indeed the unique isometry (see p. 50) $A \to A'$, $B \to B'$, $P \to P''$.

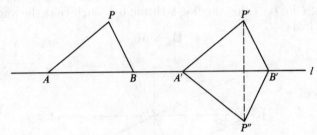

Fig. 104

Exercise B

1. The triangle ABC is subjected to the half-turn $\mathbf{A}$ so that

$$(ABC)\,\mathbf{A} = AQR,$$

and then the triangle AQR is subjected to the glide reflection of axis $\overrightarrow{AB}$ and distance AB. Show how the resulting triangle can be transformed to the triangle ABC by reflection.

2. $ABCD$ is a parallelogram; P is the point such that A is the middle point of PB, and Q is the point such that A is the middle point of QD. The triangle APQ is subjected to the glide reflection of axis $\overrightarrow{AB}$ and distance AB, and the transformed triangle is subjected to the further glide reflection of axis $\overrightarrow{AD}$ and distance AD. Prove that the resultant triangle $A'P'Q'$ can be obtained from the triangle APQ by a translation $\overrightarrow{AC}$ followed by a rotation about D.

3. Two glide reflections $\mathbf{G}$, $\mathbf{H}$ are defined as follows:

$OXZY$ is a given parallelogram; $\mathbf{G}$ is the transformation that has $\overrightarrow{OX}$ as axis and distance OX, while $\mathbf{H}$ is the transformation that has $\overrightarrow{OY}$ as axis and distance OY.

(i) By considering the transforms of the vertex O in the products $\mathbf{GH}$, $\mathbf{HG}$, prove that they are not commutative.

(ii) If $\overrightarrow{XO}$ is produced its own length to L, so that O is the middle point of LX, prove that $L\mathbf{GH} = Y$.

(iii) Prove that $OGH = Q$, where Q is the reflection of Z in OY.

(iv) Prove that $LOYQ$ has $OY \parallel LQ$ and $LY = OQ$.

(v) Prove that the product $\mathbf{GH}$ is a rotation.

3. The product $U_\alpha l$, where the point U is not on the line l

(This discussion involves some important points of technique.)

Let U and l be a given point and line, where $U \notin l$ (Figure 105). To describe the rotation $\mathbf{U}_\alpha$, let b be the line through U perpendicular to l, meeting l in L. Take the line a through U such that the angle (a, b) is $\frac{1}{2}\alpha$. Then

$$\mathbf{U}_\alpha = \mathbf{ab}.$$

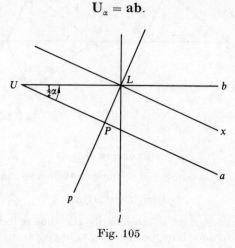

Fig. 105

The product $\mathbf{U}_\alpha l$ is then given by the formula

$$\mathbf{U}_\alpha l = (\mathbf{ab})\,l = \mathbf{a}(\mathbf{b}l)$$

$$= \mathbf{aL}_\pi.$$

The evaluation of $\mathbf{aL}_\pi$ is suggested by Section 1: let p be the line through L perpendicular to a and meeting a in P. Draw through L the line x parallel to a. Then

$$\mathbf{aL}_\pi = \mathbf{a}(\mathbf{xp})$$

$$= (\mathbf{ax})\,\mathbf{p}$$

$$= (2\overrightarrow{PL})\,\mathbf{p},$$

which is *a glide reflection with axis p and distance $2\overrightarrow{PL}$.*

4. The general product *bac*, where the lines *a*, *b*, *c* are arbitrary

Let ABC be a ('genuine') triangle, and let Q, R be the feet of the perpendiculars from B to CA and from C to AB (Figure 106). It is to be proved that **bac** *is a glide reflection with axis QR*.

The nature of the result implies that the argument will require some subtlety, but it is very instructive.

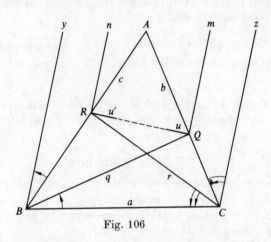

Fig. 106

Write BC, CA, AB as a, b, c and BQ, CR as q, r. Draw through B the line y such that $\mathbf{aq} = \mathbf{cy}$ and through C the line z such that $\mathbf{zb} = \mathbf{ra}$. Then

$$\mathbf{bac} = \mathbf{bqqac}$$
$$= (\mathbf{bq})(\mathbf{yc})\,\mathbf{c}$$
$$= \mathbf{bqy}.$$

Draw through Q the line m parallel to y and the line u perpendicular to m. Then $\mathbf{bq} = \mathbf{Q}_\pi = \mathbf{um}$, so that

$$\mathbf{bac} = (\mathbf{um})\,\mathbf{y} = \mathbf{u}(\mathbf{my}),$$

which, by Section 1, is *the glide reflection with u as axis and translation 2d, where d is the distance from Q to y.*

Exercise C

1. Taking n, u' as the lines through R parallel and perpendicular to z, prove that
$$\mathbf{bac} = (\mathbf{zn})\,\mathbf{u'}.$$

2. Deduce from Question 1 that

  (i) u and u' are along the line QR;

  (ii) the distance from m to y is equal to the distance from z to n;

  (iii) y and z are the lines through B and C perpendicular to QR.

3. Prove by elementary trigonometry that the distances named in Question 2 (ii) are equal to $2R \sin A \sin B \sin C$, where R is the radius of the circumcircle of the triangle ABC.

4. Prove that $(\mathbf{bac})^2$ is a translation in the direction $\overrightarrow{QR}$, of magnitude four times the distance from m to y.

5. Prove that, if ABC is an isosceles triangle right-angled at A, then $\mathbf{bac}$ is the glide reflection through a distance $\overrightarrow{CB}$ with axis the line through A parallel to BC.

6. Prove that if a triangle ABC is carried to a triangle $A'B'C'$ by glide reflection, then those two triangles are oppositely orientated.

5. The 'glide box'

This device helps to make some of the diagrams clearer when dealing with problems involving glide reflections.

Let AB, $A'B'$ be two equal line segments. The problem is *to exhibit a glide reflection in which* $A \to A'$, $B \to B'$.

Let U, V be the middle points of AA', BB'. Reflect the figure in UV so that

$$A \to A_1, \quad B \to B_1, \quad A' \to A'_1, \quad B' \to B'_1.$$

Through A, B, A', B' draw the lines parallel to UV, and perpendicular to UV, as shown in Figure 107.

Now

$$A'B' = AB \qquad \text{(given)}$$

$$= A_1 B_1 \quad \text{(reflection in } UV),$$

so that the two rectangles $A_1 X_1 B_1 Y_1$, $A'MB'N$, having $A_1 B_1$ and $A'B'$ as diagonals and corresponding sides parallel, are equal. Hence

$$\overrightarrow{BB'_1} = \overrightarrow{X_1 M} = \overrightarrow{A_1 A'}.$$

Thus $A'B'$ is obtained from AB by (i) reflecting AB in UV to give $A_1 B_1$, (ii) translating $A_1 B_1$ parallel to UV to give $A'B'$. This is the glide reflection.

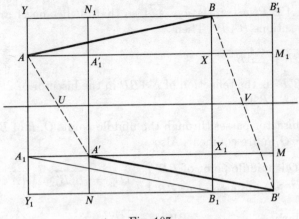

Fig. 107

6. The glide reflection connecting two oppositely-orientated congruent triangles

Let ABP, $A'B'P'$ be two oppositely-orientated congruent triangles (Figure 108), so that

$$\triangle \overrightarrow{ABP} \equiv \triangle \overleftarrow{A'B'P'},$$

and let U, V, W be the middle points of AA', BB', PP'. We now prove that:

Theorem 1. *The points U, V, W are collinear when distinct.* (See Question 1 below.)

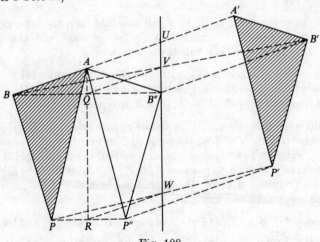

Fig. 108

Give $\triangle A'B'P'$ a translation $\overrightarrow{A'A}$ so that A' lies on A and B', P' assume positions B'', P''. Then

$$\triangle \overrightarrow{ABP} \equiv \triangle \overleftarrow{AB''P''}$$

$\Rightarrow \triangle AB''P''$ is the reflection of $\triangle ABP$ in the bisector of $\angle BAB''$ (or PAP'').

But this bisector passes through the middle points Q, R of BB'', PP'', so that A, Q, R are collinear. Also

$$\left.\begin{array}{l} Q \text{ is middle point of } BB'' \\ V \text{ is middle point of } BB' \end{array}\right\} \Rightarrow \overrightarrow{QV} = \tfrac{1}{2}\overrightarrow{B''B'} = \tfrac{1}{2}\overrightarrow{AA'},$$

and, similarly, $$\overrightarrow{RW} = \tfrac{1}{2}\overrightarrow{AA'}.$$

Hence U, V, W, being the translations $\tfrac{1}{2}\overrightarrow{AA'}$ of the collinear points, are themselves collinear.

It follows *that $A \to A'$, $B \to B'$, $P \to P'$ under the glide reflection whose axis is the line UV and whose magnitude is the projection of $\overrightarrow{AA'}$ upon UV.* Note that this transformation is determined *by the two pairs A, A' and B, B'.* The mate of an arbitrary point P is found by following the geometrical formula just outlined. [Hence the notation P, P' for the third vertex of the triangle.]

Exercise D

1. In the work of Section 6, the points U, V, W must lie on a line if two of them coincide.

Prove, however, that, if U, V, W all coincide then the triangles ABP, $A'B'P'$ are necessarily orientated in the same sense and the isometry $A \to A'$, $B \to B'$, $P \to P'$ is a half-turn.

2. An isosceles triangle ABC, with $AB = AC$, is subjected to a glide reflection whose axis is the line joining the middle points of AB, AC. Prove that the isometry $A \to A'$, $B \to C'$, $C \to B'$ is equivalent to a half-turn.

3. A right-angled triangle ABC, with the right angle at A, is subjected to two glide reflections. The first, taking it to position $A_1B_1C_1$, has as its axis (including magnitude and sense) the line joining the middle points of CA, CB; the second, taking it to position $A_2B_2C_2$, has as its axis the line joining the middle points of BA, BC. Prove that the isometry $A_1 \to A_2$, $B_1 \to B_2$, $C_1 \to C_2$ is equivalent to a half-turn.

4. The sides AB, BC, CD, DA of a rectangle $ABCD$ are denoted by a, b, c, d respectively. Prove that **dba** defines the glide reflection of axis $2\overrightarrow{AB}$.

Prove that the transformation given by the successive applications of glide reflections with axes $2\overrightarrow{AB}$, $2\overrightarrow{BC}$, $2\overrightarrow{CD}$, $2\overrightarrow{DA}$ is equivalent to the translation $2\overrightarrow{DB}$.

5. In the figure described in Question 4, $AC \cap BD = O$, and u, v are the lines through O parallel to AD, AB respectively. Prove that **uba** defines the glide reflection of axis $\overrightarrow{AB}$.

Prove that the transformation given by the successive applications of glide reflections with axes $\overrightarrow{AB}$, $\overrightarrow{BC}$, $\overrightarrow{CD}$, $\overrightarrow{DA}$ is identity.

Give a geometrical proof by taking an arbitrary point P and its successive transforms P_1, P_2, P_3, P_4 and proving that P_4 is P.

6. Given a triangle ABC and a circle whose centre is at B, prove that, if that circle is transformed successively by a glide reflection with axis $\overrightarrow{BC}$, a glide reflection with axis $\overrightarrow{CA}$ and a glide reflection with axis $\overrightarrow{AB}$, the circle is transformed into itself, though not point for point. [No properties of a circle are needed except the definition. See p. 119 if necessary.]

8

THE ANALYSIS OF
ISOMETRIES; GROUPS

1. First steps

We have obtained four types of isometry. These, with their orientations, are:

    (i) rotation, direct;
    (ii) translation, direct;
    (iii) reflection, indirect;
    (iv) glide reflection, indirect.

We have also proved that a rotation may be obtained as a product of two reflections in non-parallel lines; a translation as a product of two reflections in parallel lines; and a glide reflection as a product of three reflections, in lines in general position.

All *these* isometries can therefore be expressed as products of reflections; and, conversely, products of reflections yield one or other of these isometries, or identity. The problem arises whether the list is complete, or whether there are other isometries hitherto unsuspected and not obtainable in this way.

2. The direct isometries

Let $\mathbf{T}$ be any given direct isometry. Any pair of reflections gives a rotation or a translation (each of which is a direct isometry), so it is natural to consider whether $\mathbf{T}$ itself can be expressed as a product $\mathbf{uv}$ of two reflections. For this, we should require the relation

$$\mathbf{T} = \mathbf{uv} \quad \text{or} \quad \mathbf{Tvu} = \mathbf{I}.$$

To make progress, we require two lemmas

Lemma 1. *A direct isometry with two fixed points is the identity.*

Suppose, in fact, that $\mathbf{S}$ is an isometry such that $A\mathbf{S} = A$, $B\mathbf{S} = B$, and let R be any point of the line AB (Figure 109). The transforms of A, B, R are A, B, R', where, by isometry,

$$AR' + R'B = AR + RB = AB.$$

[102]

Hence R' lies on AB, with $AR' = AR$, so that $R' \equiv R$ and *AB is a line of self-corresponding points*, which we call x for reference.

Now let P be any point of the plane, and let PM be drawn perpendicular to AB; let P' be the mate of P in **S**. Then $PM \to P'M$, and, because of the isometry, the fact that $PM \perp x$ gives $P'M \perp x$ also.

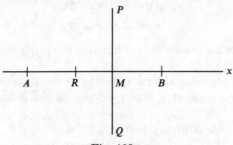

Fig. 109

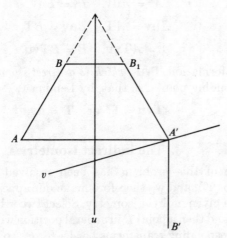

Fig. 110

Hence P' lies on the line PM and, since $P'M = PM$, that point is either at P itself or at the point $Q = P\mathbf{x}$. But the orientations of $\triangle APB$ and $\triangle AQB$ are opposite, so that P is not at Q. It follows that P' is at P, so that **S** is the identity.

Lemma 2. *If AB and $A'B'$ are two equal segments, there exist two lines u, v such that $(A, B)\mathbf{uv} = (A', B')$. If u, v are parallel, then $\mathbf{uv}$ is a translation; otherwise it is a rotation.*

Let u be the mediator of AA' (Figure 110), so that

$$A\mathbf{u} = A'.$$

Let $B\mathbf{u} = B_1$.

If $B_1 \equiv B'$, then $A'B_1$ can be obtained from AB by rotation about the point of intersection $A'B_1 \cap AB$; and this rotation can be expressed as a product of two reflections.

Otherwise, let v be the mediator of B_1B'. Since $A'B' = AB = A'B_1$, the point A' lies on v. Hence

$$Auv = A'v = A',$$
$$Buv = B_1v = B',$$

and so u, v form a suitable pair of lines for the product uv to send A, B to A', B'.

We can now establish the main result: *the given direct isometry* T *can be expressed as a product of two reflections, to give either a rotation or a translation.*

Let A, B be two arbitrary points, and let $A' = AT$, $B' = BT$. Then $A'B' = AB$, so that, by Lemma 2, there are reflections u, v such that

$$A' = Auv, \quad B' = Buv.$$

Hence $\qquad\qquad Auv = AT, \quad Buv = BT,$

or $\qquad\qquad A = ATvu, \quad B = BTvu.$

The transformation Tvu, *which is a direct isometry*, has thus two self-corresponding points, so that, by Lemma 1,

$$Tvu = I \quad \text{or} \quad T = uv,$$

as required.

3. The indirect isometries

The essence of this problem has been resolved in Theorem 1 of Chapter 7 (p. 99), and we therefore make our appeal to it.

Let T be a given indirect isometry. Select two arbitrary points A, B of the plane and then a point P in general position with respect to them. Let the corresponding transforms be A', B', P', so that

$$\triangle \overrightarrow{A'B'P'} \equiv \triangle \overleftarrow{ABP}.$$

The conditions of the theorem are then satisfied.

Let U, V be the middle points of AA', BB'. These two points must be distinct for arbitrary choice of A and B, otherwise T would be a half-turn about the common middle point – a *direct* isometry. Denote by $\overrightarrow{d}$ the projection of the segment $\overrightarrow{AA'}$ on the line UV. Then the result of Chapter 7, Section 6, shows that P' is that point obtained from P by reflection in UV followed by the glide $\overrightarrow{d}$.

Hence *every indirect isometry is equivalent to a glide reflection, or, as a special case (when* $\overrightarrow{d}$ *is the zero displacement) a reflection.*

4. Groups; short introduction

It is unlikely that anyone having reached the present stage in mathematics will not have had at least an introduction to the theory of groups. If necessary, an appropriate text-book should be consulted.

Briefly, a group $(G, *)$ consists of a set G of elements (of any kind – points, lines, operations, numbers, ...) and a rule, denoted here by the symbol $*$, for combining them in pairs subject to the following conditions:

(i) *If a, $b \in G$, then the 'product' $a * b$ obtained from the rule of combination is also in G.* This property is known as *closure*.

For example, if G denotes the set of rotations about a given point O, and if $*$ denotes the product operation discussed in Chapter 5, Section 5, then
$$\mathbf{O}_\alpha * \mathbf{O}_\beta$$
is the rotation $\mathbf{O}_{\alpha+\beta}$, which is also a member of G.

(ii) *Any three elements a, b, c of G combine according to the associative law.*
$$a * (b * c) = (a * b) * c.$$
In the example quoted,
$$\mathbf{O}_\alpha * (\mathbf{O}_\beta * \mathbf{O}_\gamma) = (\mathbf{O}_\alpha * \mathbf{O}_\beta) * \mathbf{O}_\gamma,$$
each being
$$\mathbf{O}_{\alpha+\beta+\gamma}.$$

(iii) *There is a unit element e* with the property that
$$a * e = e * a = a$$
for all elements a of G.

In the example quoted, the identity transformation $\mathbf{I}$ is the unit.

(iv) *Each element a of G has an inverse*, often denoted by a^{-1}, with the property that
$$a^{-1} * a = a * a^{-1} = e.$$

In the example quoted,
$$\mathbf{O}_{-\alpha} * \mathbf{O}_\alpha = \mathbf{O}_\alpha * \mathbf{O}_{-\alpha} = \mathbf{I},$$
so that $\mathbf{O}_{-\alpha}$ is the inverse of $\mathbf{O}_\alpha$.

Notation. The symbol of operation $*$ is often omitted and a product written in the more familiar form ab.

Exercise A

These examples are standard results that should be noted

1. Prove that $(a^{-1})^{-1} = a$.

2. Prove that $(ab)^{-1} = b^{-1}a^{-1}$.

3. Prove that, if $a^2 = e$, then $a^{-1} = a$, where a^2 denotes the product aa or $a*a$.

4. Prove that, if $ab = ac$, then $b = c$.

Definition. It is not necessarily true that the products $a*b$ and $b*a$ are the same. A group $(G, *)$ with the property

$$a*b = b*a$$

for all pairs a, b is said to be *commutative* or *Abelian*.

It is perfectly possible for a group to have *some* elements that commute even though not all of them do. The group then is *not* Abelian.

5. The order of a group

When the number of elements in a group is *finite*, the group itself is called a *finite group*. Otherwise it is *infinite*.

The number of elements in a finite group is called the *order* of the group.

Exercise B

1. Prove that the set consisting of the numbers $+1$ and -1 under the rule of ordinary multiplication is a group of order 2.

2. Prove that the set consisting of the group of all integers under the rule of addition is an infinite group.

6. Sub-groups

Let H be a subset of the elements of a group $(G, *)$, and subject the elements of H to the rule of combination operating within $(G, *)$. If the elements of $(H, *)$ retain all the four properties of combination listed in Section 4, then H is called a *sub-group* of G.

The set consisting of the single unit element, and the set consisting of the whole of G, are both sub-groups, but are given the name *improper* sub-groups. Other sub-groups are *proper*.

7. The group of all isometries

Let G denote the set of all isometries in a given plane. Define a 'product' $*$ in G by the rule that

$$\mathbf{P} * \mathbf{Q}$$

means the result of applying to the points of the plane, first the isometry **P** and then the isometry **Q**. It is to be proved that $(G, *)$ *as so defined is a group.*

We follow in order the four properties of Section 4:

(i) **P** $*$ **Q** is certainly an isometry, consisting as it does of the isometry **P** followed by the isometry **Q**.

(ii) **P** $*$ (**Q** $*$ **R**) = (**P** $*$ **Q**) $*$ **R**, each being the result of applying first **P**, then **Q**, then **R**.

(iii) The identity **I** is the unit isometry.

(iv) Any isometry **P** has an inverse $\mathbf{P}^{-1}$ whose operation restores all points of the plane to the position from which they started.

Following Jeger, we denote the group of all isometries by the symbol **K**.

Exercise C

1. Prove that **P** $*$ **Q** transforms straight lines to straight lines.

2. Prove that **P** $*$ **Q** transforms parallel lines to parallel lines; and middle points of segments to middle points of segments.

8. Some sub-groups of K

The isometries we have met are unwilling to form subgroups on their own. For example, the product of two reflections is not a reflection at all, but either a rotation or a translation; the law of closure is not obeyed. Some genuine sub-groups do, however, emerge:

(*a*) *The sub-group B of direct isometries.* By inspection of the four individual properties, the set of *direct* isometries can be proved to form a sub-group of **K**. Associativity and the possession of an inverse are immediate, and the identity transformation itself is also an element since it certainly preserves orientation. Closure is verified, since the product of two transformations, neither of which changes orientation, is also orientation-preserving. The conditions for a sub-group are therefore satisfied.

Exercise D

1. Prove that the set of indirect isometries does not form a sub-group.

2. Prove that the set of rotations (with various centres) does not by itself form a sub-group.

3. Prove that the set of translations forms a sub-group.

(*b*) *The sub-group of rotations and translations.* Once again, associativity, unit and inverse are clear, but attention must be given to closure:

It was proved (Chapter 5, Section 6) that the product of two rotations about different points is, *in general*, another rotation. Exception occurs, however, when, in the notation used there, $\alpha + \beta = 2\pi$, in which case the resulting product is a *translation*.

If, then, we are to have a sub-group containing all rotations, it must contain translations as well. This forces us to consider for closure three further sets of products:

    (i) translation followed by translation;
    (ii) rotation followed by translation;
    (iii) translation followed by rotation.

Case (i) presents no difficulties; the product of two translations is a translation.

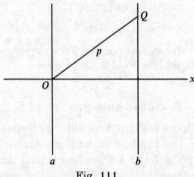

Fig. 111

For *case* (ii), let O be the centre of a rotation, and x the line through O in the direction of a translation (Figure 111). Then the translation can be exhibited by taking two lines, a (through O) and b, at a distance apart equal to ($\frac{1}{2}$ magnitude of translation), each perpendicular to the line x. Let p be the line through O such that

$$\mathbf{pa} = \mathbf{O}_\alpha,$$

where α is the angle of the rotation.

Since the translation $\mathbf{t}$ is given by the relation

$$\mathbf{t} = \mathbf{ab},$$

it follows that

$$\mathbf{O}_\alpha \mathbf{t} = (\mathbf{pa})(\mathbf{ab})$$
$$= \mathbf{pb}.$$

In the nature of the case, p does not coincide with a, so that it meets b; and so $\mathbf{pb} = \mathbf{Q}_\alpha$, a *rotation* through an angle α about the point of intersection $Q = p \cap b$.

Exercise E

1. Investigate *case* (iii) similarly.

The property of closure is therefore established, and so the set of all rotations and translations is indeed a sub-group of **K**.

9. Some finite sub-groups of K.

All isometries can be expressed as products of reflections. Consider then a group G consisting of the identity **I** together with a certain number of reflections **l, m, n,** ... under the rule of combination that has been adopted throughout.

Observe that the associative law $(\mathbf{ab})\,\mathbf{c} = \mathbf{a}(\mathbf{bc})$ is always satisfied, and that G has a unit element in **I**. Further any element of the group G, such as **abcd**, has an inverse **dcba**, since, for reflections,

$$(\mathbf{abcd})\,(\mathbf{dcba}) = (\mathbf{abc})\,(\mathbf{cba}) \quad (\mathbf{d}^2 = \mathbf{I})$$

$$= (\mathbf{ab})\,(\mathbf{ba}) \qquad (\mathbf{c}^2 = \mathbf{I})$$

$$= \mathbf{a}^2 \qquad\qquad (\mathbf{b}^2 = \mathbf{I})$$

$$= \mathbf{I}.$$

We may therefore restrict attention to problems of *closure*, illustrated in Exercise F, which involve groups with a finite number of elements.

Exercise F

1. Prove that the set consisting of **I** and one reflection **l** forms a group.

2. Prove that the set consisting of **I** and the two rotations **ab, ba** forms a group when the angle between the lines a and b is $\frac{1}{3}\pi$.

3. Prove that the set consisting of **I** and the half-turn about a given point forms a group.

4. Prove that, if n is a positive integer, the set consisting of **I** and the rotations $\mathbf{O}_{2\pi/n}, \mathbf{O}_{4\pi/n}, \mathbf{O}_{6\pi/n}, \ldots, \mathbf{O}_{(2n-2)\pi/n}$ forms a group of order n. Identify two sub-groups when $n = 6$.

10. Group tables

Elementary calculations of group products are often exhibited conveniently in tabular form. This may be explained by reference to the next example of a finite group.

Let u, v be two given lines meeting in a point U (Figure 112), and consider a set containing $\mathbf{I}$ and the reflections $\mathbf{u}$, $\mathbf{v}$, with the normal law of combination. For this to define a group, the set will have to be extended to include both $\mathbf{uv}$ and $\mathbf{vu}$.

Note that $\mathbf{uv}$, $\mathbf{vu}$ are indeed new isometries, since

$$\mathbf{uv} = \mathbf{I} \Rightarrow \mathbf{u} = \mathbf{v},$$
$$\mathbf{uv} = \mathbf{v} \Rightarrow \mathbf{u} = \mathbf{I},$$
$$\mathbf{uv} = \mathbf{u} \Rightarrow \mathbf{v} = \mathbf{I},$$

and these possibilities must be excluded if $\mathbf{I}$, $\mathbf{u}$, $\mathbf{v}$ are distinct.

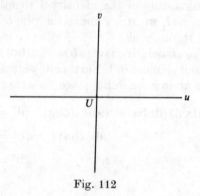

Fig. 112

The extension can however be made to consist of just a *single* element, by selecting u, v so that $\mathbf{uv} = \mathbf{vu}$: that is, so that $u \perp v$, in which case $\mathbf{uv}$ or $\mathbf{vu}$ gives the half-turn U.

Exercise G

1. Prove that *the system is now closed*, in that

$$\mathbf{Uu} = \mathbf{uU} = \mathbf{v},$$
$$\mathbf{Uv} = \mathbf{vU} = \mathbf{u},$$
$$\mathbf{U}^2 (= \mathbf{UU}) = \mathbf{I}.$$

2. Prove that the isometries $\mathbf{I}$, $\mathbf{u}$, $\mathbf{v}$, $\mathbf{uv}$ then form a finite group of order 4.

As indicated at the start, the products establishing the group property can be exhibited in tabular form

	I	u	v	U
I	I	u	v	U
u	u	I	U	v
v	v	U	I	u
U	U	v	u	I

where, for example, the element in the row indicated by **u** and the column indicated by **v** is precisely the product **uv**, or **U**. In the same way, the element in the row indicated by **v** and the column indicated by **u** is the product **vu**; that this is again **U** is *not* necessarily the case for a general group.

The property that each of the elements **I**, **u**, **v**, **U** occurs once in each row and once in each column is, by standard theory, necessary if the set under the given rule of combination is to form a group. The converse may not be true – the feature does not of itself ensure a group; associativity may need an independent check.

11. Symmetry

We have, up to now, regarded an isometry as operating on all points of the plane. There is further interest in considering the effects on a finite number of points only, disregarding what is happening in the plane as a whole.

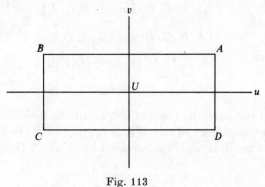

Fig. 113

Suppose, for example, that u, v are two perpendicular lines meeting in U, and take an arbitrary point A (Figure 113). Reflect A in u, v successively to give points

$$A, A\mathbf{u}, A\mathbf{uv}, A\mathbf{uvu}, A\mathbf{uvuv}, \ldots,$$

say, for convenience,

$$A, B, C, D, \ldots.$$

By the work of Part I, the points A, B, C, D are at the vertices of a rectangle, and, *after that, the points repeat according to the pattern* $A, B, C, D, A, B, \ldots$.

Starting with A, the successive reflections give the four points A, B, C, D and those four only.

This can be re-worded:

The rectangle, regarded as consisting of four vertices and four sides, is left unchanged as a whole when reflected in u, and when reflected in v.

Definition. A figure which remains unchanged as a whole after reflection in a line is said to be *symmetrical* about that line.

Thus the rectangle is symmetrical about u and symmetrical about v. The rectangle, further, is left unchanged as a whole when subjected to the half-turn about the point U.

Definition. A figure which remains unchanged as a whole, after a half-turn about a point, is said to be *symmetrical* about that point.

The reflections **u**, **v** and the half-turn **U**, though leaving the rectangle unchanged *as a whole*, have very differing effects on the individual vertices. Adding the identity **I** to these operations, the effects may be summarised in the form:

$$(A, B, C, D)\,\mathbf{I} = (A, B, C, D),$$

$$(A, B, C, D)\,\mathbf{v} = (B, A, D, C),$$

$$(A, B, C, D)\,\mathbf{U} = (C, D, A, B),$$

$$(A, B, C, D)\,\mathbf{u} = (D, C, B, A).$$

Note that the pattern of sets of four points on the right-hand side is the same as the pattern of sets of four operations in the group table in Section 10 when **I**, **u**, **v**, **U** are replaced by A, B, C, D respectively.

Exercise H

State what symmetry, if any, is possessed by each of the following figures:

1. Isosceles triangle.

2. Equilateral triangle.

3. Square.

4. Regular pentagon.

5. Regular hexagon.

6. Right-angled triangle.

7. Parallelogram.

8. Rhombus.

9. Kite.

12. Groups associated with symmetrical figures

Consider, in illustration, an equilateral triangle ABC. Let u, v, w be the bisectors of the angles at A, B, C respectively (Figure 114).

Reflection in u gives the transformation **u** for which

$$A \to A, \quad B \to C, \quad C \to B,$$

so that *the position of the triangle as a whole is unaffected, though individual vertices are in different places.*

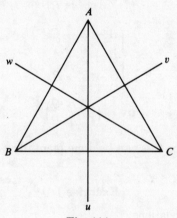

Fig. 114

Similarly **v** gives

$$A \to C, \quad B \to B, \quad C \to A,$$

and **w** gives

$$A \to B, \quad B \to A, \quad C \to C.$$

Each transformation is said to effect a *permutation* of the vertices, and we may write

$$\mathbf{u} = \begin{pmatrix} A & B & C \\ A & C & B \end{pmatrix}, \quad \mathbf{v} = \begin{pmatrix} A & B & C \\ C & B & A \end{pmatrix}, \quad \mathbf{w} = \begin{pmatrix} A & B & C \\ B & A & C \end{pmatrix},$$

where each letter is permuted to that which lies below it. Order is not important, and we may equally write

$$\mathbf{u} = \begin{pmatrix} B & C & A \\ C & B & A \end{pmatrix}$$

so long as the 'columns' are correct. Similar notation will be used later for other permutations.

We are thinking of groups, and therefore of the effects of *successive* operations. The notation of the permutations is very convenient here. For example, to find the product **uv**, start with

$$\mathbf{u} = \begin{pmatrix} A & B & C \\ A & C & B \end{pmatrix}$$

and then rearrange the 'columns' of **v** so that they take the order of the transforms:

$$\mathbf{v} = \begin{pmatrix} A & C & B \\ C & A & B \end{pmatrix}$$

Then **uv** transforms $\quad \begin{cases} A \to A \to C, \\ B \to C \to A, \\ C \to B \to B, \end{cases}$

so that $\qquad \mathbf{uv} = \begin{pmatrix} A & B & C \\ C & A & B \end{pmatrix}.$

With a little practice this can be done mentally.

Exercise I

Prove the following relations:

1. $\mathbf{vu} = \begin{pmatrix} A & B & C \\ B & C & A \end{pmatrix}.$

2. $\mathbf{uw} = \begin{pmatrix} A & B & C \\ B & C & A \end{pmatrix}, \quad \mathbf{wu} = \begin{pmatrix} A & B & C \\ C & A & B \end{pmatrix}.$

3. $\mathbf{u}^2 = \begin{pmatrix} A & B & C \\ A & B & C \end{pmatrix}.$

Note that $\mathbf{uv} \neq \mathbf{vu}$. The order of operation makes a decisive difference.

The point now reached shows that the reflections **u**, **v**, **w**, together with the identity **I**, do *not* form a group when acting on the vertices of the equilateral triangle ABC. The law of closure is violated.

To salvage a group, we need two other operators,

$$\alpha = \begin{pmatrix} A & B & C \\ C & A & B \end{pmatrix}, \quad \beta = \begin{pmatrix} A & B & C \\ B & C & A \end{pmatrix}.$$

Exercise J

1. Prove the relations:

(i) $\alpha^2 = \beta$, $\beta^2 = \alpha$;

(ii) $\alpha^3 = I$, $\beta^3 = I$;

(iii) $\alpha u = w$: [That is, prove that

$$\begin{pmatrix} A & B & C \\ C & A & B \end{pmatrix} \text{ followed by } \begin{pmatrix} A & B & C \\ A & C & B \end{pmatrix} \equiv \begin{pmatrix} C & A & B \\ B & A & C \end{pmatrix} \text{ is } \begin{pmatrix} A & B & C \\ B & A & C \end{pmatrix}.]$$

(iv) $u\alpha = v$: [That is, prove that

$$\begin{pmatrix} A & B & C \\ A & C & B \end{pmatrix} \text{ followed by } \begin{pmatrix} A & B & C \\ C & A & B \end{pmatrix} \equiv \begin{pmatrix} A & C & B \\ C & B & A \end{pmatrix} \text{ is } \begin{pmatrix} A & B & C \\ C & B & A \end{pmatrix}.]$$

(v) $v\beta = u$, $\beta w = u$.

2. Confirm the following table:

	I	α	β	u	v	w
I	I	α	β	u	v	w
α	α	β	I	w	u	v
β	β	I	α	v	w	u
u	u	v	w	I	α	β
v	v	w	u	β	I	α
w	w	u	v	α	β	I

where, for example, αu is the element in the row headed α and the column headed u, so that $\alpha u = w$.

3. Confirm that the six elements $I, \alpha, \beta, u, v, w$ have inverses $I, \beta, \alpha, u, v, w$ respectively.

4. Check that the six permutations, subject to this table for 'products', form a group.

5. Check that the following sets form proper sub-groups:

$$(I, u), \ (I, v), \ (I, w), \ (I, \alpha, \beta).$$

6. Prove that the group is not Abelian (commutative) as defined in 3, and list the pairs of elements that do not commute. For example, $uv \neq vu$.

To complete the discussion, we have to identify the two operations α, β. This can be done in two ways:

(i) From the table,

$$\alpha = uv, \quad \alpha = vw, \quad \alpha = wu.$$

Thus α is a *rotation* about the common point of intersection of u, v, w, through an angle $2(u, v)$, or $\frac{4}{3}\pi$, in the counterclockwise sense.

Similarly β is a rotation through $2(u, w)$, or $\frac{2}{3}\pi$, in the counterclockwise sense.

(ii) The 'missing' operations to map the triangle ABC onto itself are the rotations about its centre through angles of $\frac{2}{3}\pi$ and $\frac{4}{3}\pi$. Spinning the triangle about its centre establishes visually the relations

$$\alpha^2 = \beta, \quad \beta^2 = \alpha, \quad \alpha^3 = I, \quad \beta^3 = I.$$

Remark. If these operations are carried out upon a triangular piece of cardboard, reflection about a line such as u is effected by rotating the triangle *in space* about the line u. The six operations are identity, 'flips' about u or v or w, rotations about the centre through $\frac{2}{3}\pi$ or $\frac{4}{3}\pi$.

Extension. Other symmetrical figures may be treated similarly.

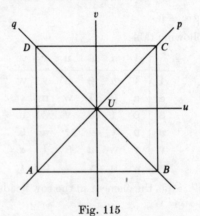

Fig. 115

The square. (Compare the discussion of the rectangle in Section 11.)
The square $ABCD$ has *four* axes of symmetry (Figure 115):
   (i) the line u through the centre U parallel to AB, DC;
   (ii) the line v through U parallel to AD, BC;
   (iii) the diagonal AC, named p;
   (iv) the diagonal BD, named q.

For convenience, we now omit the upper line in naming a permutation, so that

$$\begin{pmatrix} A & B & C & D \\ B & D & C & A \end{pmatrix} \text{ is written } (B \quad D \quad C \quad A)$$

and $\quad \begin{pmatrix} A & B & C & D \\ D & C & A & B \end{pmatrix} \text{ is written } (D \quad C \quad A \quad B).$

It is implicit that the (omitted) upper line consists of A, B, C, D *in that order*.

The four symmetries just named give the permutations

$$\mathbf{u} = (D \quad C \quad B \quad A),$$

$$\mathbf{v} = (B \quad A \quad D \quad C),$$

$$\mathbf{p} = (A \quad D \quad C \quad B),$$

$$\mathbf{q} = (C \quad B \quad A \quad D).$$

The products of these reflections taken in pairs are all rotations about U. Thus,

$$\mathbf{uv} = \mathbf{vu} = \mathbf{pq} = \mathbf{qp} = \mathbf{U}_\pi,$$

the half-turn about U.

Again,

$$\mathbf{up} = \mathbf{pv} = \mathbf{vq} = \mathbf{qu} = \mathbf{U}_{\frac{1}{2}\pi}$$

and

$$\mathbf{pu} = \mathbf{vp} = \mathbf{qv} = \mathbf{uq} = \mathbf{U}_{\frac{3}{2}\pi}.$$

As in the case of the equilateral triangle, the four reflections defined by the symmetries are not enough to give a group, and they have to be supplemented by the four rotations about the centre given by

$$\mathbf{I} = (A \quad B \quad C \quad D),$$

$$\boldsymbol{\alpha} = \mathbf{U}_{\frac{1}{2}\pi} = (B \quad C \quad D \quad A),$$

$$\boldsymbol{\alpha}^2 = \mathbf{U}_\pi = (C \quad D \quad A \quad B),$$

$$\boldsymbol{\alpha}^3 = \mathbf{U}_{\frac{3}{2}\pi} = (D \quad A \quad B \quad C).$$

Exercise K

1. Establish the table given below and verify that it defines a group:

	I	α	α^2	α^3	u	v	p	q
I	I	α	α^2	α^3	u	v	p	q
α	α	α^2	α^3	I	q	p	u	v
α^2	α^2	α^3	I	α	v	u	q	p
α^3	α^3	I	α	α^2	p	q	v	u
u	u	p	v	q	I	α^2	α	α^3
v	v	q	u	q	α^2	I	α^3	α
p	p	v	q	u	α^3	α	I	α^2
q	q	u	p	v	α	α^3	α^2	I

MGB

2. A *regular hexagon* has six equal sides, and adjacent sides contain an angle of $\frac{2}{3}\pi$. Prove that there are six axes of symmetry, of which three, u, v, w, are shown in Figure 116.

If the three other axes are p, q, r, show that all products of pairs of reflections such as **uv**, **up**, **pq** are rotations about the centre U of the form $\mathbf{U}_{\frac{1}{3}k\pi}$, where $k = 0, 1, 2, 3, 4, 5$.

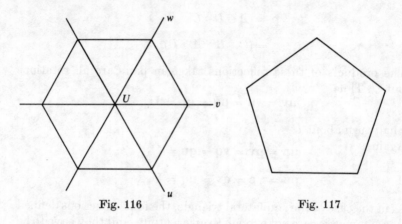

Fig. 116   Fig. 117

Denoting the rotations by the notation $\mathbf{I}$, α, α^2, α^3, α^4, α^5, examine the group of symmetries of the hexagon by methods analogous to those just used for the square.

3. Examine similarly the regular pentagon (Figure 117).

9

CIRCLES

1. Symmetry properties

A *circle* is a plane figure whose points are at a constant distance (the *radius* of the circle) from a fixed point O (its *centre*).

As a matter of common usage, the word *circle* is taken to mean either the 'outer rim' or the area enclosed. The outer rim itself is called the *circumference*. There is seldom, if ever, ambiguity in practice.

When the plane of the circle is folded by a crease through O, the two parts of the circle lie in complete contact. The crease, AOB in Figure 118, is called a *diameter* of the circle. The circle is *symmetrical* about all its diameters.

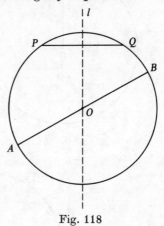

The two arcs into which a circle is divided by a diameter are called *semicircles*.

The straight line joining two points P, Q of a circle is called the *chord PQ*. The mediator of PQ is a straight line l which, since $OP = OQ$, is a diameter passing through the centre O.

Fig. 118

Exercise A

The properties in Questions 1–6 are standard, quotable, results that are almost automatic consequences of the complete symmetry of the circle. Check that you are quite clear of their correctness.

1. The straight line from the centre perpendicular to a chord bisects that chord (Figure 119).

2. The straight line from the centre to the middle point of a chord is perpendicular to that chord.

3. Equal chords are equidistant from the centre.
   [Given that $AB = CD$, rotate AB 'round the circle' till A falls on C and B on D (Figure 120). The foot of the perpendicular from O to the new position of AB coincides with the foot of the perpendicular from O to CD.]

[119]

4. Chords that are equidistant from the centre are equal.

5. If $AB = CD$, then $BC \parallel AD$.
[Fold B onto C; then A is folded onto D.]

6. If two circles have a point A in common, then they meet in a second point B, and the common chord AB is perpendicular to the line UV joining the two centres (Figure 121). Indeed, UV is the mediator of AB.

[In a limiting case, B may coincide with A. This is the phenomenon of *tangency*, and will be discussed later.]

Any of the properties in Questions 1–6 may be quoted in support of an argument.

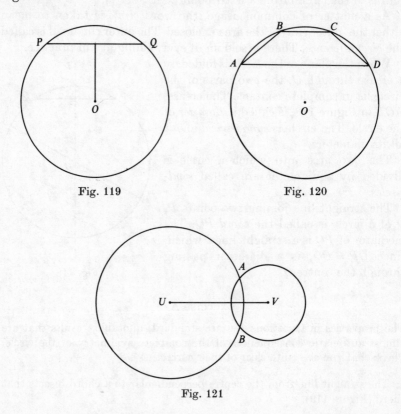

Fig. 119   Fig. 120

Fig. 121

7. Two equal circles meet in A, B, and M is the middle point of AB (Figure 122). A point P is taken on the first circle, and R is the point of the second circle obtained from P by a half-turn about M. Prove that $PARB$ is a parallelogram.

PA meets the second circle in Q and QM meets the first circle in S as shown. Prove that $PQRS$ is a parallelogram and that RS passes through B.

8. A square and a circle, having a common centre U, meet in points A_1, A_2, B_1, B_2, C_1, C_2, D_1, D_2, as in Figure 123. Prove that $A_1 U C_1$ is a straight line and name three other such lines.

Regarding the square as given, show how to select the radius of the circle so that the line segments $A_1 A_2$, $A_2 B_1$, $B_1 B_2$, $B_2 C_1$, $C_1 C_2$, $C_2 D_1$, $D_1 D_2$, $D_2 A_1$ are all equal in length.

9. Two circles, with centres U and V, meet in A and B. A line through A cuts the first circle in P and the second in Q. The middle points of AP, AQ are L, M. Prove that $LU \parallel MV$.

10. Two equal circles intersect in A, B. The point C on the first circle is such that $AC = AB$; the point D on the second circle is such that $BD = BA$. Prove that the points A, B, C, D are at the vertices of a parallelogram.

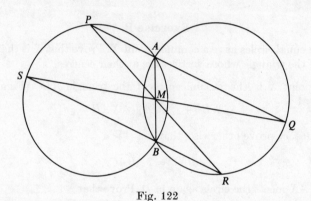

Fig. 122

2. The circumcircle of a triangle

Let ABC be a given triangle. It is to be proved that *a circle can be drawn to pass through the three vertices* A, B, C.

The circle is called the *circumcircle* of the triangle ABC and its centre is the *circumcentre*.

Let the mediator u of AB meet the mediator v of AC in X (Figure 124). [These mediators do meet, since they cannot be parallel unless the points A, B, C are collinear.] Then

$$\left. \begin{array}{l} X \in u \Rightarrow XB = XA \\ X \in v \Rightarrow XC = XA \end{array} \right\} \Rightarrow XA = XB = XC.$$

Hence, by definition, a circle with centre X passes through A, B, C.

Corollary 1. *The centre X is unique, and so the circumcircle is also unique. It follows, too, that two circles with three points in common must be identical.*

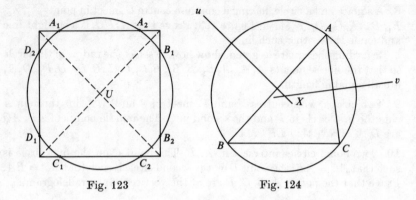

Fig. 123   Fig. 124

Exercise B

1. Three equal circles have a common point X. Prove that X is the circum-centre of the triangle whose vertices are at their centres.

2. The point X is the circumcentre of the triangle ABC (Figure 125). Prove that

$$\angle XBC + \angle XCA + \angle XAB = \tfrac{1}{2}\pi$$

and deduce, or prove otherwise, that

$$\angle BXC = 2\angle BAC.$$

The line AX meets the circle again in D. Prove that

$$\angle ABD = \angle ACD = \tfrac{1}{2}\pi.$$

3. Properties of arcs

Definition. Two points A, B on the circumference of a circle divide that circumference into two curved parts called *arcs*. Each of the arcs is said to be *subtended* by the chord AB.

If AB, CD are two equal arcs (Figure 126), rotation of A to C round the circle carries B to D. Hence, if O is the centre,

$$\text{chord } AB = \text{chord } CD,$$

$$\angle AOB = \angle COD.$$

If, then, we are given a pair of (i) equal arcs, *or* (ii) equal chords, *or* (iii) equal angles subtended at the centre, the above or analogous argument shows that arcs *and* chords *and* angles subtended at the centre are equal.

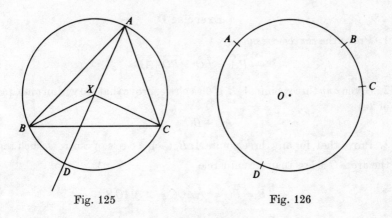

Fig. 125   Fig. 126

Exercise C

1. Prove that a circle can be drawn through the vertices of a square, and that these vertices divide the circumference into four equal parts.

2. Four points A, B, C, D on a circle of centre O are such that

$$\operatorname{arc} AB = 2 \operatorname{arc} CD.$$

Prove that $\angle AOB = 2\angle COD$.
    But check, by careful drawing or otherwise, that chord $AB \neq 2$ chord CD.

Suppose next that PQ, AB are parallel chords of a circle whose centre is O (Figure 127). The line through the centre perpendicular to them bisects each, and so P, A can be folded onto Q, B. Hence

$$\operatorname{chord} AP = \operatorname{chord} BQ,$$

$$\operatorname{arc} AP = \operatorname{arc} BQ.$$

For precision, define (analogously to the counterclockwise sense for an angle) a sense of *description* round a circle; in the diagram, P, A, B, Q follow in the *counterclockwise* sense.
    An arc measured subject to sense will be denoted by a symbol such as

$$\overset{\frown}{PA}.$$

What we have proved is that

$$\overrightarrow{PQ} \parallel \overrightarrow{AB} \Rightarrow \overset{\frown}{PA} = \overset{\frown}{BQ}.$$

Exercise D

1. Prove the *converse result*:

$$\overset{\frown}{PA} = \overset{\frown}{BQ} \Rightarrow \overrightarrow{PQ} \,\|\, \overrightarrow{AB}.$$

2. Given *any* three points A, B, C on a circle, prove that (to within multiples of 2π)

$$\overset{\frown}{AB} + \overset{\frown}{BC} = \overset{\frown}{AC}.$$

3. Prove that, for any three points A, B, C on a circle of centre O, such that the arc $\overset{\frown}{AC}$ is less than a semi-circle,

$$\overset{\frown}{AB} = \overset{\frown}{BC} \Rightarrow \triangle AOC = 2 \triangle AOB.$$

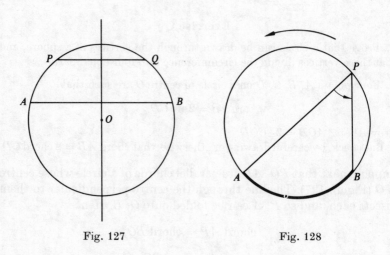

Fig. 127   Fig. 128

4. Angle theorems for a circle

Definitions. The arcs $\overset{\frown}{AB}$, $\overset{\frown}{BA}$ are called *complementary*.

If P is any point on the arc $\overset{\frown}{BA}$, then the angle $\triangle APB$ is said to be *subtended at P by the arc $\overset{\frown}{AB}$*.

[The need for $\overset{\frown}{BA}$ and $\overset{\frown}{AB}$ is an unfortunate consequence of the conventions. It is the arc $\overset{\frown}{AB}$, darkened in Figure 128, that subtends the angle.]

Theorem 1. *The angle $\triangle AOB$ subtended at the centre O by an arc $\overset{\frown}{AB}$ is double the angle $\triangle APB$ subtended by $\overset{\frown}{AB}$ at any point P on $\overset{\frown}{BA}$.*

Let $\overrightarrow{XOU}$, $\overrightarrow{YOV}$ be the diameters parallel to $\overrightarrow{AP}$, $\overrightarrow{BP}$ (Figure 129). Then

(i) $\triangle APB = \triangle XOY$,

(ii) $\overset{\frown}{UV} = \overset{\frown}{XY}$.

Further,
$$\overrightarrow{AP} \parallel \overrightarrow{XU} \Rightarrow \overset{\frown}{AX} = \overset{\frown}{UP},$$
$$\overrightarrow{BP} \parallel \overrightarrow{YV} \Rightarrow \overset{\frown}{YB} = \overset{\frown}{PV}.$$

Hence
$$\overset{\frown}{AB} = \overset{\frown}{AX} + \overset{\frown}{XY} + \overset{\frown}{YB}$$
$$= \overset{\frown}{UP} + \overset{\frown}{XY} + \overset{\frown}{PV}$$
$$= \overset{\frown}{XY} + (\overset{\frown}{UP} + \overset{\frown}{PV})$$
$$= \overset{\frown}{XY} + \overset{\frown}{UV}$$
$$= 2\overset{\frown}{XY}.$$

Hence
$$\triangle AOB = 2\triangle XOY$$
$$= 2\triangle APB.$$

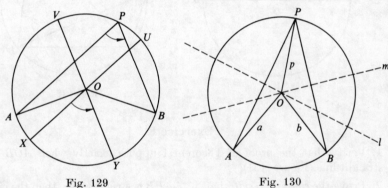

Fig. 129   Fig. 130

Corollary 2. *The angle subtended by a semicircle at a point of the circumference is equal to a right angle.*

Alternative proof of Theorem 1. With the same notation as before for points on the circle, denote the lines OA, OB, OP by the symbols a, b, p and let l, m be the bisectors of the angles $\triangle POA$, $\triangle BOP$ (Figure 130). Then
$$\mathbf{al = lp,} \quad \mathbf{la = pl,}$$

and
$$\mathbf{bm = mp,} \quad \mathbf{mb = pm,}$$

so that
$$\mathbf{almb = lppm = lm.}$$

But the lines l, m, b are concurrent, so that

$$\mathbf{lmb = bml.}$$

Hence $\qquad\qquad\qquad\qquad \mathbf{abml = lm,}$

so that $\qquad\qquad\qquad\qquad \mathbf{abm = lml}$

and $\qquad\qquad\qquad\qquad \mathbf{ab = lmlm = (lm)^2.}$

The angle $\triangle AOB$ is therefore double the angle $\triangle(l,m)$ (the rotation from OA to OB being the rotation *from* the line l *to* the line m, repeated).

But, by the symmetry of the circle,

$$l \perp AP, \quad m \perp BP.$$

Hence the angle from l to m is equal to the angle from PA to PB. That is, $\qquad\qquad\qquad \triangle AOB = 2\,\triangle APB.$

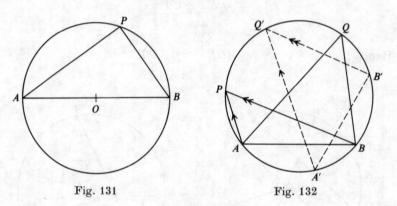

Fig. 131   Fig. 132

Exercise E

1. Verify that the proof of Theorem 1 applies exactly when AOB is a straight line (Figure 131).

2. Prove the *converse result*, that, if $\triangle APB$ is a right angle, then the circle on AB as diameter passes through P.

Theorem 2.

Definition. The two arcs into which a chord AB divides the circumference of a circle are sometimes called *segments* of the circle.

Theorem 2 is usually enunciated in the form:

Angles in the same segment of a circle are equal.

More precisely: *let A, B be two given points of a circle and P, Q two points of the arc $\overset{\frown}{BA}$ (Figure 132). Then*

$$\triangle APB = \triangle AQB.$$

(i) The result is an immediate corollary of Theorem 1.

(ii) *Aliter*. Rotate the triangle AQB round the circle to the position $A'Q'B'$ such that

$$\vec{A'Q'} \parallel \vec{AP}.$$

Then $$\overset{\frown}{Q'P} = \overset{\frown}{AA'}$$

$$= \overset{\frown}{BB'} \quad \text{(by the rotation)}$$

so that $$\vec{B'Q'} \parallel \vec{BP}.$$

Hence $$\angle APB = \angle A'Q'B'$$

$$= \angle AQB \quad \text{(by the rotation)}.$$

Exercise F

1. Prove that Q' is the middle point of $\overset{\frown}{QP}$.

Theorem 3. Essentially, this theorem is wanted in order to take the place of Theorem 2 when P and Q are on opposite arcs AB (Figure 133).

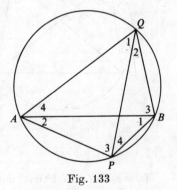

Fig. 133

Informally stated, Theorem 2 gives, in the notation of the diagram, the equality of angles marked 1, 2, 3, 4. Since the sum of all the angles of the quadrilateral is four right angles, it follows that

'$1+2+3+4$' = two right angles,

so that (using unsigned angles)

$$\angle APB + \angle AQB = \text{two right angles},$$

$$\angle PAQ + \angle PBQ = \text{two right angles}.$$

More formally:

Definition. If four points A, P, B, Q are taken in order on a circle, the quadrilateral $APBQ$, with sides AP, PB, BQ, QA is said to be *cyclic*. The four points are said to be *concyclic*.

Theorem 3 asserts that *the opposite angles of a cyclic quadrilateral are supplementary*.

From Theorem 2, with unsigned angles,

$$\angle APQ = \angle ABQ,$$

$$\angle BPQ = \angle BAQ,$$

$$\angle AQP = \angle ABP,$$

$$\angle BQP = \angle BAP.$$

Adding corresponding sides and re-arranging:

$$(\angle APQ + \angle BPQ) + (\angle AQP + \angle BQP)$$

$$= (\angle ABQ + \angle ABP) + (\angle BAQ + \angle BAP),$$

or $\angle APB + \angle AQB = \angle PBQ + \angle PAQ.$

Since the total sum of the four angles just named is four right angles, the sum on each side is two right angles, as was to be proved.

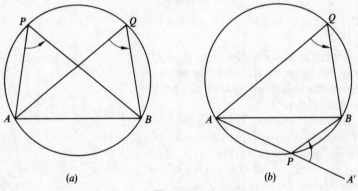

Fig. 134

It is to be noted that, *with signed angles, Theorems 2 and 3 are the same:*

For Theorem 2, with P and Q on the same arc AB, we have

$$\triangle APB = \triangle AQB.$$

For Theorem 3, with P and Q on opposite arcs AB, let AP be produced beyond AP to A' (Figure 134(b)). Then

$$\angle A'PB = \text{supplement of } \angle APB$$

$$= \angle AQB$$

but $\triangle APB = \triangle A'PB,$

being the same rotation, so that

$$\triangle APB = \triangle AQB.$$

Thus *the sensed angles subtended by two given points A, B on the circumference of a circle at varying points on the circumference are all equal, independently of the arc AB on which those points are taken.*

The *converse* of Theorems 2 and 3 is also true:

If four points A, B, P, Q are so related that

$$\triangle APB = \triangle AQB,$$

then the four points A, B, P, Q lie on a circle (Figure 135).

Suppose that, instead, the circle through A, B, P cuts AQ in Q_1, not shown in the diagram. Then

$$\triangle AQ_1B = \triangle APB \quad \text{(by Theorems 2 and 3)}$$

$$= \triangle AQB \quad \text{(given)},$$

so that $$BQ_1 \parallel BQ.$$

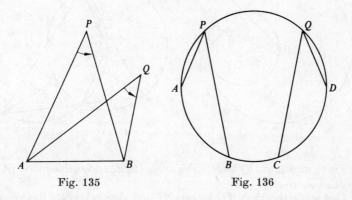

Fig. 135   Fig. 136

But this is impossible for two lines with the point B in common unless BQ_1 and BQ are the same line. Hence Q must coincide with Q_1 and so be on the circle ABP.

Generalisation. It is an immediate extension of the preceding work that *equal arcs, or equal chords, subtend equal sensed angles at the circumference.*

If, for example, $\overset{\frown}{AB} = \overset{\frown}{CD}$ in Figure 136, the rotation $A \to C, B \to D$ moves P to P' where

$$\triangle APB = \triangle CP'D \quad \text{(by the rotation)}$$

$$= \triangle CQD \quad \text{(by Theorem 2)}.$$

Exercise G

1. A point A is taken on a circle of centre O, and the circle is drawn whose diameter is OA (Figure 137). A line through O cuts the second circle in P and the line AP meets the first circle again in B. Prove that $PO \perp AB$ and that $PA = PB$.

2. Two circles, named V and W for reference, are so related that W passes through the centre O of V (Figure 138). The circles meet in A and B. A point P is taken on V, and PB meets W again in Q. Give reasons for the statements

    (i) $\angle APB = \frac{1}{2}\angle AOB$,

    (ii) $\angle AQB =$ supplement of $\angle AOB$ $(= \pi - \angle AOB)$,

and deduce that $QA = QP$.

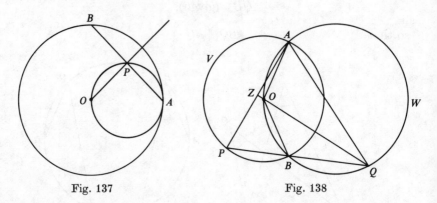

Fig. 137   Fig. 138

Prove also that OQ bisects the angle AQP, and deduce that OQ is perpendicular to AP.

Deduce further that, if OQ meets AP in Z, then, wherever P is taken on the circle V, the point Z lies on the circle whose diameter is OA.

3. A circle has diameters AB and PQ, and X is a point on the circle (Figure 139). Prove that the arcs AP, BQ are equal and show that the line bisecting $\angle AXQ$ also bisects $\angle PXB$.

4. Two circles meet in A and B. A straight line through A meets one circle in P and the other in Q (Figure 140). Prove that the magnitude of $\angle PBQ$ does not depend on the particular line selected.

5. Six points A, B, C, D, E, F are taken equally spaced round a circle, so that the arcs

$$AB, BC, CD, DE, EF, FA$$

are all equal (Figure 141). Prove that each of these arcs subtends an angle of $\frac{1}{3}\pi$ $(= 60°)$ at the centre O, and deduce that the six triangles AOB, BOC, ..., FOA are equilateral.

Verify that the diagram can be constructed by drawing arcs of circles with radius equal to that of the given circle and with centres A, B, C, D, E, F.

Prove that the triangles such as BOF have angles $\frac{2}{3}\pi, \frac{1}{6}\pi, \frac{1}{6}\pi$.

6. The mediator of a chord AB meets a circle in points X, Y of which X is on the major arc AB and Y on the minor. A point P is taken on the arc AXB. Prove that, in Figure 142, PY is the internal bisector of $\angle APB$ and PX the external bisector.

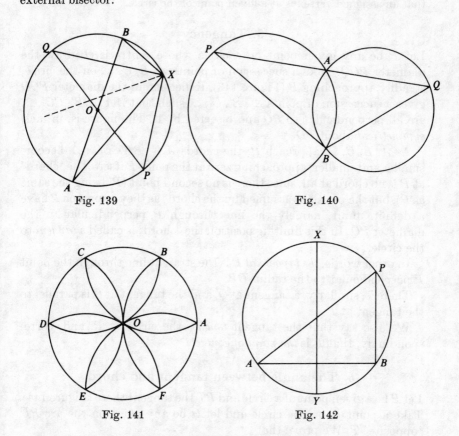

Fig. 139   Fig. 140

Fig. 141   Fig. 142

7. The points D, E, on AC, AB respectively, are the feet of the perpendiculars from the vertices B, C of a triangle ABC to the opposite sides. The circumcentre of the triangle is O. Prove that $\angle OAE = \frac{1}{2}\pi - \angle ACB$.

By proving that the quadrilateral $BCDE$ is cyclic, or otherwise, deduce that $AO \perp DE$.

8. The diagonals $ABCD$ of a quadrilateral meet in O, and P, Q, R, S are the feet of the perpendiculars from O to AB, BC, CD, DA respectively. Prove that
$$\angle SPQ = \angle SAO + \angle QBO$$
and obtain a similar expression for $\angle SRQ$.

It is now given that the quadrilateral $PQRS$ is cyclic. By considering the sum of the angles of the triangles OAD, OBC, or otherwise, prove that $AC \perp BD$.

9. Give a construction to draw a triangle of given shape with its vertices on a given circle.

Give a construction to draw a triangle of given shape in a given circle so that an assigned vertex is at a given point of the circle.

5. Tangency

Let P be any given point on a circle whose centre is O; draw the diameter POQ. Take a succession of points A, B, C, ... on the circle, steadily approaching P (Figure 143). Reflection in the diameter POQ gives a succession of points A', B', C', ... such that AA', BB', CC', ... are all perpendicular to PQ and bisected by it. The figure is, in fact, *symmetrical* about PQ.

As A, B, C, ... approach P; the chords AA', BB', CC', ... become smaller and smaller, approaching zero at the point P itself. The 'chord' at P is no chord at all, since there is no second point (P' being the same as P), but the positions assumed by the chords as they approach P have a definite limit, namely the line through P perpendicular to the diameter PQ. In this limiting position the 'chord' is called a *tangent* to the circle.

In other words, *the tangent at P is the straight line through the point P perpendicular to the radius OP.*

There is, similarly, a tangent at Q, and the tangent at Q is parallel to the tangent at P.

We also say that the tangent *touches* the circle at P, and, correspondingly, that P is *the point of contact*.

6. The angle between tangent and chord

Let P be a given point of a circle and PT the tangent there (Figure 144). Take a point U on the circle and let Q be any point on the arc PU 'opposite' T. We prove that

$$\triangle TPU = \triangle PQU,$$

so that *the angle between the tangent PT and the chord PU is equal to the angle $\angle PQU$ in the opposite segment.*

To show what is involved, imagine PT replaced by a chord $AA'T$ parallel to it and close to it (Figure 145). Then we have proved that

$$\triangle TA'U = \triangle AQU,$$

and the required result appears when, as AA' moves towards P, the points A' and A are each replaced by P.

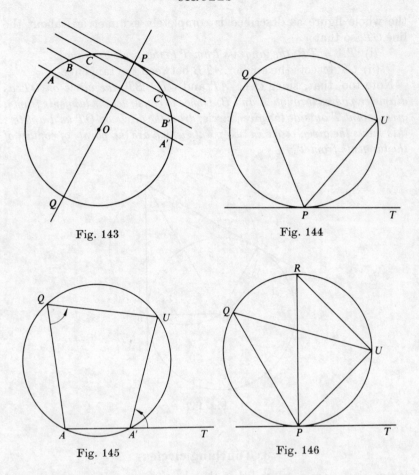

Fig. 143   Fig. 144

Fig. 145   Fig. 146

Aliter. A firmer proof can be obtained by drawing the diameter PR (Figure 146). Then

$$PR \text{ diameter}$$

$$\Rightarrow \angle PUR = \text{right angle}$$

$$\Rightarrow \angle PQU = \angle PRU \text{ (same segment)}$$

$$= \text{right angle} - \angle RPU$$

$$= \angle TPU.$$

7. Symmetry results for tangents

Let A, B be two points on a given circle, and let the tangents at A and B (assumed not to be parallel) meet at T (Figure 147). If O is the centre, the whole figure as described is completely symmetrical about the line OT, so that

(i) $TA = TB$; *the tangents from T to the circle are equal;*

(ii) OT bisects the angle $\angle ATB$ between the tangents.

Note too, that, since $OA \perp AT$ and $OB \perp BT$, *the circle on OT as diameter passes through A and B. Hence to construct the tangents from a given point T outside the given circle, draw the circle on OT as diameter; this meets the given circle in two points which are the points of contact of the tangents from T.*

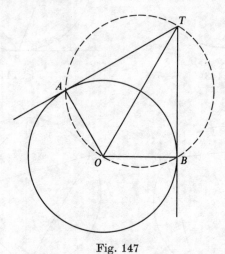

Fig. 147

8. Touching circles

If two circles are so placed that they have a point P in common and the same tangent there, they are said to *touch* or to have *contact* at P. When they lie outside each other the contact is *external*; when one is inside the other, the contact is *internal* (Figure 148).

If U, V are the centres and P the point of contact, then PU, PV are each perpendicular to the common tangent, so that U, V, P are collinear; that is, *the centres and the point of contact are collinear.*

Exercise H

1. Prove that, if two circles of radii a and b touch, then the distance apart of their centres is either $a+b$ or (assuming a to be greater than b) $a-b$.

2. Two circles touch at P; a line through P meets one circle in X and the other in Y. Prove that the tangents at X and Y are parallel.

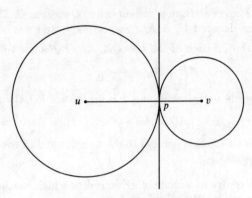

External contact

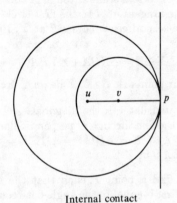

Internal contact

Fig. 148

3. A point T is taken on the tangent at P to a given circle, and a line through T cuts the circle at A and B. Prove that the triangles TAP, TPB are equiangular.

4. The triangle ABC has a right angle at A, and D is the foot of the perpendicular from A to BC. Prove that AB, AC are the tangents at A to the circles ADC, ADB respectively.

5. Two circles are so placed that they have a common point P where the tangents are perpendicular. Prove that the centre of either circle lies on the tangent at P to the other.

6. Points P, Q, R, S are taken in order round a circle. The tangents at P, Q meet at A; the tangents at Q, R meet at B; the tangents at R, S meet at C; the tangents at S, P meet at D. Prove that $BC + AD = AB + CD$.

7. Points P, Q, R are taken on a circle. The tangents at Q, R meet at A;

the tangents at R, P meet at B; the tangents at P, Q meet at C. The lengths of BC, CA, AB are denoted by a, b, c respectively, and s is written for $\frac{1}{2}(a+b+c)$. Prove that, if each of the arcs $\overarc{QR}$, $\overarc{RP}$, $\overarc{PQ}$ is less than a semi-circle, then

$$AR = AQ = s-a,$$

but that, if $\overarc{QR}$ exceeds a semi-circle and P is on the arc $\overarc{RQ}$, then

$$AQ = AR = s.$$

8. The chord QR of a circle is parallel to the tangent at P. Prove that the triangle PQR is isosceles.

9. Prove that the centre of a circle of given radius which touches a given circle lies on one or other of two fixed circles.

10. Two circles meet at A, B and a line through A cuts the first circle at P and the second at Q. The tangent at A to the first circle cuts BQ at X, and the tangent at A to the second circle cuts BP at Y. Prove that, if A lies between P and Q,

$$\angle XAY = \angle XQA + \angle YPA,$$

and deduce that the four points A, B, X, Y lie on a circle.

11. $ABCD$ is a cyclic quadrilateral; the diagonals AC, BD meet at right angles at U. Prove that the line through U perpendicular to AD bisects BC. [Consider the argument $\angle BUX = \angle DUY = \angle YAU = \angle UBX$, where the line meets BC in X and AD in Y.]

12. Given two circles, find a point P such that the angle between the tangents from P to the first is equal to the angle between the tangents from P to the second, these angles being given in magnitude. It is assumed that the configuration is such that a point such as P exists.

Prove that, if the given angle is a right angle, no such point P exists if the distance between the centres of the circles exceeds the diagonal of a square of sides equal to the sum of the radii.

9. A rotation isometry for a circle

Let U be a given circle and rotate it about a point O of its circumference to a position U' (Figure 149). Then U, U' are two equal circles which, having one common point O, must have another, say A. We assume that A is not at O: that is, that the rotation is not through an angle π.

The diameter OP of U is rotated to the diameter OP' of U'. Hence

$$\angle OAP = \angle OAP' = \text{right angle},$$

so that P, A, P' are collinear.

Now let X be any other point of U, rotated to the position X' on U'.

[It is, at the moment, without prejudice that XX' is drawn to pass through A.] Then

$$OX = OX' \quad \text{(by the rotation)}$$

$$\Rightarrow \angle OX'X = \angle OXX'.$$

Similarly $\qquad\qquad \angle OP'P = \angle OPP'.$

Further, by the rotation

$$\angle XOX' = \angle POP',$$

so that, the sum of the angles of a triangle being 2 right angles,

$$\angle OX'X = \angle OXX' = \angle OP'P = \angle OPP'.$$

(But we do not know that XX' passes through A.)

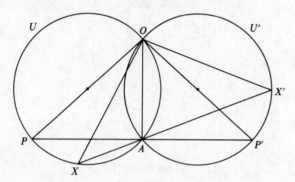

Fig. 149

Now let $XX' \cap PP' = B$. Then

$$\angle P'PO = \angle X'XO$$

$$\Rightarrow \angle BPO = \angle BXO$$

$$\Rightarrow \quad B, P, X, O \text{ are concyclic.}$$

Hence B lies on U and, similarly, on U'. That is, B is at A and the diagram, as drawn, is correct.

The *fundamental theorem* is thus:

If a circle U is rotated about one of its points O to a circle U' meeting U again in A, then any point X of U is rotated to that point X' of U' such that XAX' is a straight line.

Illustration 1. Three equal circles U, V, W pass through a point O. The further intersections are A for V, W; B for W, U; C for U, V

(Figure 150). An arbitrary point P is taken on U; PC meets V again in Q, and QA meets W again in R. It is to be proved that *the points P, B, R are collinear.*

Rotate U about O to V; thus P rotates to Q. Then rotate V about O to W; thus Q rotates to R.

The net result is to rotate U to W, so that P rotates to a point on PB. But this point is to be R and so P, B, R are collinear.

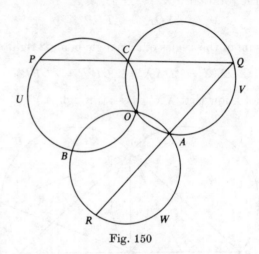

Fig. 150

Exercise I

1. Given a point O on a circle U, prove that a half-turn about O transforms U to a circle U' touching U at O.

Two unequal circles have a common point O. Give a construction for a straight line XOY, meeting one circle in X and the other in Y, so that O is the middle point of XY. (The two circles are assumed not to touch at O.)

2. Two equal circles U, V meet in points O, A, and $\mathbf{O}_\theta$ is the rotation about O that transforms U to V. A point P is taken not lying on either circle. By drawing two chords of U through P, or otherwise, devise a construction for the point $P\mathbf{O}_\theta$.

3. Two equal circles U, V meet in points O, A, and a square $PQRS$ is drawn with its vertices on the circumference of U. The lines PA, QA, RA, SA meet V again in points P', Q', R', S'. Prove that $P'Q'R'S'$ is a square.

4. Two equal circles U, V meet in points O, A. The tangent at A to U meets V in A', and a line PAP' meets U in P and V in P'. Prove that $P'A' = PA$.

5. A point P inside a parallelogram $ABCD$ is such that

$$\angle APB + \angle CPD = \pi.$$

Prove that the circles ABP, CPD are equal, and that the circles APD, BPC are equal.

The triangle CPD is subjected to the translation $\overrightarrow{DA}$ to the position BQA. Prove that $PAQB$ is a cyclic quadrilateral and deduce that

$$\angle DCP = \angle DAP.$$

Deduce finally that the four circles named in the first paragraph are all equal.

10

RATIO PROPERTIES: ENLARGEMENTS

1. Preamble

The links between length and angle are very hard to establish by reasonably intelligible argument; but we must try. Basically, we all 'know' (a word that itself will hardly stand scrutiny) that if two triangles have the same angles, then their sides are in the same proportion; this, indeed, is an assumption many readers may well wish to make straight away and to leave it at that.

The only comparison of lengths at our disposal so far comes from the process of folding, and that will be our starting-point. Let XYZ be a triangle with a right angle at Y (Figure 151). Fold X on Y and let the crease meet XY, XZ in M, U respectively. Then M is the middle point of XY and MU is the mediator of XY, so that $MU \perp XY$ and $XU = UY$. Since $YZ \perp XY$ also, we have $MU \parallel YZ$. Thus the crease is, in fact, the line parallel to YZ through the middle point of XY.

Further

$$\angle UYZ = \text{right angle} - \angle UYX$$

$$= \text{right angle} - \angle YXU \quad \text{(folding)}$$

$$= \angle UZY \quad \text{(triangle } XYZ\text{)}$$

so that

$$UZ = UY$$

$$= UX.$$

Thus, *for the right-angled triangle, the straight line through the middle point of XY and parallel to YZ passes also through the middle point of XZ.*

Exercise A

1. Prove (the converse of the result just proved) that, for the right-angled triangle, the straight line through the middle point of XZ parallel to YZ bisects XY (Figure 152).

2. Prove that, for the right-angled triangle, the straight line joining the middle points of XY, XZ is parallel to YZ.

3. Prove that the length of MU is half that of YZ.

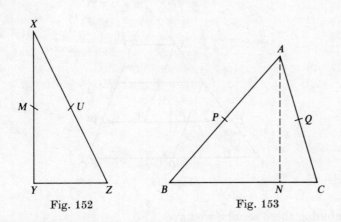

Fig. 152   Fig. 153

4. *The mid-point theorems:* Points P, Q are taken on the sides AB, AC respectively of a triangle ABC (Figure 153). By drawing AN perpendicular to BC, or otherwise, prove that:

  (i) if P is the middle point of AB and $PQ \parallel BC$, then Q is the middle point of AC;

  (ii) if P and Q are the middle points of AB and AC, then $PQ \parallel BC$;

  (iii) if either (i) or (ii) holds, then the length of PQ is half that of BC.

  Alternative enunciation: The straight line joining the middle points of two sides of a triangle is parallel to the third side and equal in length to half of it.

  Give a similar statement for a converse of this result.

2. The next step

Suppose now that the side AB of a triangle ABC is divided into four equal parts by points X, L, U and that lines through these points parallel to BC cut AC in Y, M, V.

Draw the lines XNW, LPQ, as shown in Figure 154, parallel to AC. From the parallelograms thus formed, we have the equalities

$$XN = YM; \quad LP = NW = MV; \quad PQ = VC.$$

Now

$$\left. \begin{array}{l} AX = XL \\ XY \parallel LM \end{array} \right\} \Rightarrow AY = YM,$$

$$\left. \begin{array}{l} XL = LU \\ LN \parallel UW \end{array} \right\} \Rightarrow XN = NW$$

and

$$\left. \begin{array}{l} LU = UB \\ UP \parallel BQ \end{array} \right\} \Rightarrow LP = PQ.$$

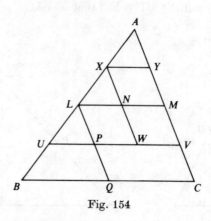

Fig. 154

Combining these results, we have

$$AY = YM = MV = VC,$$

so that AC is divided into four equal parts, at Y, M, V.

The method is perfectly general and it follows, by natural extension, that, *if n is any positive integer, then*

$$AX = \frac{1}{n}AB, \quad AY = \frac{1}{n}AC.$$

The trend, we hope, is now clear. If n is any rational number, say

$$n = p/q,$$

where p, q are positive integers, then identical argument applied to sub-units of length $\frac{1}{q}AX$ leads to the result

$$AX = \frac{1}{n}AB, \quad AY = \frac{1}{n}AC.$$

When n is irrational, we meet the same difficulties that we had for length itself and overcome them (or, to be more truthful, circumvent them) in a similar way.

Be all this as it may, we now feel justified in making the *basic assumption* (Figure 155):

$$XY \parallel BC \Leftrightarrow \frac{AX}{AB} = \frac{AY}{AC}.$$

3. Alternative statements

Some variants of the ratio statement are found useful. Let ABC be a given triangle, and $X \in AB$, $Y \in AC$ such that

$$XY \parallel BC.$$

Then, as we have seen

$$\frac{AX}{AB} = \frac{AY}{AC},$$

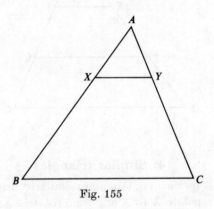

Fig. 155

or, equivalently, there exists a number n such that

$$AX = \frac{1}{n}AB, \quad AY = \frac{1}{n}AC.$$

Thus
$$XB = AB - AX = \left(\frac{n-1}{n}\right)AB,$$

$$YC = AC - AY = \left(\frac{n-1}{n}\right)AC,$$

so that
$$\frac{AX}{XB} = \frac{AY}{YC}, \quad \frac{AB}{XB} = \frac{AC}{YC}.$$

Exercise B

1. Given a triangle ABC, with two lines XY, PQ, each parallel to BC and meeting AB in X, P and AC in Y, Q (Figure 156), prove the following results:

$$\frac{XP}{PB} = \frac{YQ}{QC}, \quad \frac{XB}{XP} = \frac{YC}{YQ},$$

$$\frac{AX}{PB} = \frac{AY}{QC}, \quad \frac{PB}{PX} = \frac{QC}{QY}.$$

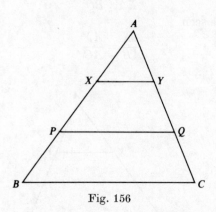

Fig. 156

4. Similar triangles

Let ABC, XYZ be two equiangular, similarly orientated, triangles (Figure 157). Translate X to A and then rotate $\triangle XYZ$ about A until Y is at V on AB. Then, necessarily, Z is at a point W of AC.

But

$$\angle AVW = \angle XYZ = \angle ABC$$

$$\Rightarrow VW \parallel BC$$

$$\Rightarrow \frac{AV}{AB} = \frac{AW}{AC}$$

$$\Rightarrow \frac{XY}{AB} = \frac{XZ}{AC}.$$

Repetition of the argument with reference to other corresponding vertices gives the *fundamental result for equiangular triangles*:

$$\frac{YZ}{BC} = \frac{ZX}{CA} = \frac{XY}{AB}.$$

In other words, *equiangular triangles have corresponding sides proportional*.

Two such triangles are said to be *similar*, written

$$\triangle ABC \simeq XYZ.$$

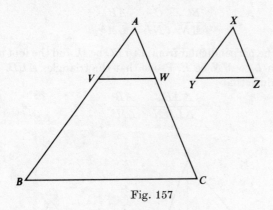

Fig. 157

Exercise C

1. Prove that similarity is an equivalence relation.

2. Prove that
$$\left.\begin{array}{l} \triangle ABC \simeq \triangle XYZ \\ \triangle ABC \simeq \triangle UVW \\ YZ = VW \end{array}\right\} \Rightarrow \triangle XYZ \equiv \triangle UVW,$$

the two triangles being congruent.

3. Given $\triangle ABC$ and a segment YZ, prove that $\exists \triangle XYZ$ such that

$$\triangle ABC \simeq \triangle XYZ.$$

4. Prove that, if $\triangle ABC$ and $\triangle XYZ$ have corresponding sides proportional, then they are equiangular. [This is a standard theorem.]

5. The middle points of the sides AD, BC of a parallelogram $ABCD$ are P, X respectively. Prove that the lines AX, PC meet the diagonal BD at its points of trisection.

Prove also that $BD \cap PC$ is a point of trisection of PC and that $BD \cap AX$ is a point of trisection of AX.

6. A quadrilateral $ABCD$ has the properties $AB \parallel DC$ and $BU = UD$, where $U = AC \cap BD$. Prove that $ABCD$ is a parallelogram.

7. A line parallel to the side BC of a triangle ABC meets AB in Q and AC in P. The line through Q parallel to BP meets AC in R. Prove that

$$AP^2 = AR.AC.$$

8. *The area-ratio theorem for similar triangles.* It is an important result that *the areas of similar triangles are proportional to the squares of corresponding sides.* Let the triangles ABC, LMN be similar (Figure 158), so that

$$\hat{A} = \hat{L}, \quad \hat{B} = \hat{M}, \quad \hat{C} = \hat{N},$$

$$\frac{BC}{MN} = \frac{CA}{NL} = \frac{AB}{LM}.$$

Let the foot of the perpendicular from A to BC be D, and the foot of the perpendicular from L to MN be P. Prove that the triangles ABD, LMP are similar, and deduce that

$$\frac{\triangle ABC}{\triangle LMN} = \frac{AB^2}{LM^2}.$$

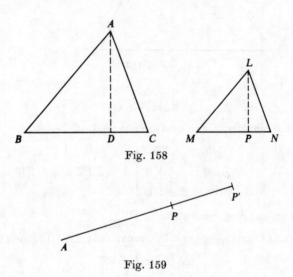

Fig. 158

Fig. 159

5. Enlargements

Let A be a given point and k a given number. The transformation (Figure 159) which sends a point P to the point P' on AP such that

$$\overrightarrow{AP'} = k\overrightarrow{AP}$$

is called an *enlargement* with centre A and ratio k, written

$$P' = P\mathbf{A(k)},$$

or, when no ambiguity is possible, simply

$$P' = P\mathbf{A}.$$

When all the points of a given configuration are subjected to this transformation, the result is an *enlargement* of the given configuration (Figure 160).

If $k > 1$, then P' lies on AP produced beyond P;

if $k = 1$, then P' coincides with P;

if $0 < k < 1$, then P' lies between A and P;

if $k = 0$ (a poor enlargement), then P is at A;

if $k < 0$, then conditions exactly analogous to those just given hold on the *opposite* side of A; and, in particular, when $k = -1$, A is the middle point of PP', the transformation being a *half-turn* about A.

It is now assumed that $k \neq 0$.

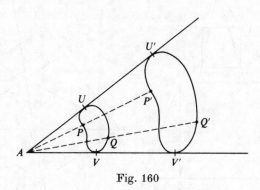

Fig. 160

The *inverse* of the enlargement is the enlargement $\mathbf{A(k^{-1})}$, since

$$\overrightarrow{AP'} = k\overrightarrow{AP} \Leftrightarrow AP = k^{-1}\overrightarrow{AP'}.$$

If a segment PQ transforms to $P'Q'$, so that $P \to P'$, $Q \to Q'$, then, by similar triangles,

$$\left.\begin{array}{l} AP' = kAP \\ AQ' = kAQ \end{array}\right\} \Rightarrow \left\{\begin{array}{l} P'Q' \parallel PQ \\ P'Q' = kPQ. \end{array}\right.$$

Thus *corresponding lines are parallel* and *the length of a transformed segment is k times the length of the original segment*.

Exercise D

1. Prove that $\triangle XYZ\mathbf{A(k)} \simeq \triangle XYZ$.

2. Prove that P, Q, R collinear

$$\Rightarrow P', Q', R' \text{ collinear and } \overrightarrow{P'Q'}/\overrightarrow{Q'R'} = \overrightarrow{PQ}/\overrightarrow{QR}.$$

3. Prove that enlargement preserves orientation, whether k is positive or negative.

4. Prove the following construction for 'inscribing' a square $PQRS$ in a triangle ABC, as shown in Figure 161.

Let UV be any line parallel to BC, meeting AB in U and AC in V. Complete the square $UVWX$ with the line WX on the side of UV remote from A. Then AX, AW meet BC in the required points P, Q.

Illustration 1. *The centroid of a triangle.* Let ABC be a given triangle, with E, F the middle points of AC, AB (Figure 162). Let $G = BE \cap CF$.

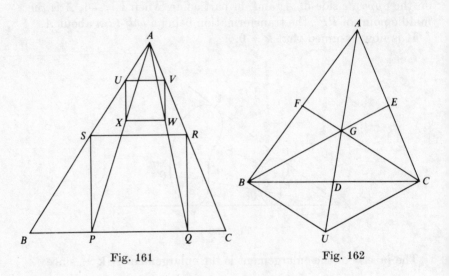

Fig. 161   Fig. 162

Consider the enlargement $\mathbf{A(2)}$ under which

$$F \to B, \quad E \to C.$$

Suppose that $G \to U$, so that G is the middle point of AU.
Then

$$\left. \begin{array}{l} F \to B \\ G \to U \end{array} \right\} \Rightarrow FG \parallel BU,$$

$$\left. \begin{array}{l} E \to C \\ G \to U \end{array} \right\} \Rightarrow EG \parallel CU.$$

Hence $BGCU$ is a parallelogram, so that D *is the middle point of the diagonal BC*.

The lines AD, BE, CF joining the vertices to the middle points of the opposite sides, are called the *medians* of the triangle. We have just proved that *the medians of a triangle are concurrent*.

Exercise E

1. Using the enlargement $\mathbf{G}(-\frac{1}{2})$, prove that each median is trisected at G.

2. A circle has diameter AB, and centre O; C is that point of the diameter for which B is the middle point of OC (Figure 163). A variable point P is taken on the circle, and Q is the middle point of CP. Use the enlargement $\mathbf{C}(\frac{1}{2})$ to prove that Q lies on a circle of centre B.

3. Given a circle and a point U outside it, use the enlargement $\mathbf{U}(\frac{1}{3})$ to find a chord UAB such that $UA = \frac{1}{3}UB$ (Figure 164).

Harder: Prove that the construction is not possible if the distance of U from the centre of the circle exceeds a diameter.

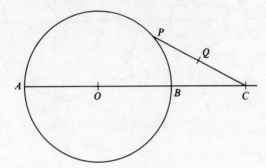

Fig. 163

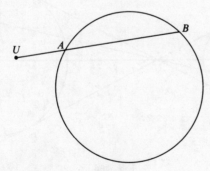

Fig. 164

Illustration 2. *Circles under enlargement.* Let U be a given point outside a given circle α (Figure 165). Let r be a given ratio, and denote by α' the circle given by

$$\alpha' = \alpha\mathbf{U}(\mathbf{r}).$$

The centre O of α transforms to the centre O' of α', and the points of contact P, Q of tangents from U to α transform to the points of

6

contact P', Q' of tangents from U to α'. If X is any point of α, its transform is a point X' of α', where

$$O'X' \parallel OX, \quad O'X' = rOX.$$

We have, by implication, taken r to be positive. Figure 166 shows the analogous configuration when r is negative.

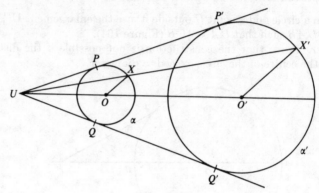

Fig. 165

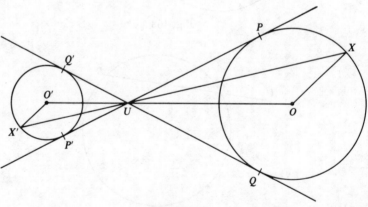

Fig. 166

It will be noticed that, when r is positive, $\overrightarrow{OX}$, $\overrightarrow{OX'}$ have like senses, but that, when r is negative, $\overrightarrow{OX}$, $\overrightarrow{OX'}$ have opposite senses. In the first case U is 'beyond both circles'; in the second case it is 'between them'.

The converse configuration may be mentioned briefly.

Let α, α' be two unequal circles, which we take to be non-intersecting, with centres at O, O' and with radii a, a'. Then there are four common tangents, denoted in Figure 167 by TT', SS' meeting in U, and PP', QQ' meeting in V. Those meeting in U are said to be *direct* and those meeting in V are said to be *transverse*.

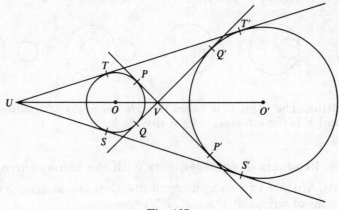

Fig. 167

Let the length of OO' be d. From the similar triangles UTO, $UT'O'$,

$$\frac{UO}{a} = \frac{UO'}{a'}$$

and each of these ratios, by elementary algebra, is

$$\frac{UO' - UO}{a' - a} = \frac{d}{a' - a},$$

so that

$$UO = \frac{ad}{a' - a}, \quad UO' = \frac{a'd}{a' - a}.$$

Exercise F

1. Prove that

$$VO = \frac{ad}{a + a'}, \quad VO' = \frac{a'd}{a + a'}.$$

2. Prove that the following construction gives U geometrically, and give a similar construction for V:

Let OX, $O'X'$ be parallel radii in the same sense. Then XX' meets the line of centres in U.

3. Prove that, when U is determined, the following construction gives S, T, and give a similar construction for P, Q:

The circle on OU as diameter meets the circle α in S, T.

4. A line through U cuts α in L, M and α' in L', M'. Prove that the triangles OLM, $O'L'M'$ are similar.

5. Prove that the pairs of circles in the following diagrams have in common $0, 1, 2, 3, 4$ tangents respectively:

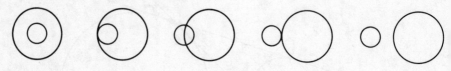

Definition. The point U is called the *external centre of similitude* for α, α' and V is the *internal centre of similitude*.

6. Products of enlargements with the same centre

If $\mathbf{A(m)}$, $\mathbf{A(n)}$ are two such enlargements, then the successive transformations of any point P are P', P'', where

$$P' = P\mathbf{A(m)},$$

$$P'' = P'\mathbf{A(n)}$$

$$= P\{\mathbf{A(m)}\,\mathbf{A(n)}\}.$$

Further, $\qquad\qquad \overrightarrow{AP'} = m\overrightarrow{AP},$

$$\overrightarrow{AP''} = n\overrightarrow{AP'} = mn\overrightarrow{AP},$$

so that the product is the enlargement $\mathbf{A(mn)}$. Hence

$$\mathbf{A(m)\,A(n) = A(mn)}.$$

Exercise G

1. Prove that $\mathbf{A(m)\,A(m^{-1})}$ is the identity transformation.

2. Prove that $\mathbf{A(m)\,A(-m^{-1})}$ is a half-turn.

7. Products of enlargements with different centres

Let $\mathbf{A(m)}$, $\mathbf{B(n)}$ be two given enlargements. Write

$$P_1 = P\mathbf{A(m)}, \quad P' = P_1\mathbf{B(n)},$$

so that the 'product' transformation is given by

$$P' = P\{\mathbf{A(m)\,B(n)}\}.$$

If Q is a second point (not shown in Figure 168), with Q_1, Q' defined similarly, then

$$P_1Q_1 = mPQ, \quad P_1Q_1 \parallel PQ;$$
$$P'Q' = nP_1Q_1, \quad P'Q' \parallel P_1Q_1,$$

so that $\qquad\qquad P'Q' = mnPQ, \quad P'Q' \parallel PQ.$

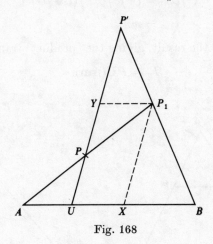

Fig. 168

Suppose now that $P'P$ meets AB in U. We are *to prove that*

$$P' = PU(\mathbf{mn}),$$

the point U being fixed. (The case $P'P \parallel AB$ will be considered later.)

Draw P_1X parallel to $P'P$ to meet AB in X. Then, by properties of parallel lines,

$$\overrightarrow{AX}/\overrightarrow{AU} = \overrightarrow{AP_1}/\overrightarrow{AP} = m,$$

so that $\qquad\qquad \overrightarrow{AX} = m\overrightarrow{AU};$

and $\qquad\qquad \overrightarrow{XB}/\overrightarrow{UB} = \overrightarrow{P_1B}/\overrightarrow{P'B} = n^{-1},$

so that $\qquad\qquad \overrightarrow{XB} = n^{-1}\overrightarrow{UB}.$

Thus $\qquad m\overrightarrow{AU} + n^{-1}\overrightarrow{UB} = \overrightarrow{AX} + \overrightarrow{XB} = \overrightarrow{AB},$

so that U *is a fixed point for all positions of P.* In fact,

$$m\overrightarrow{AU} + n^{-1}(\overrightarrow{UA} + \overrightarrow{AB}) = \overrightarrow{AB},$$

or $\qquad\qquad \overrightarrow{AU} = \left(\dfrac{n-1}{mn-1}\right)\overrightarrow{AB},$

assuming that $mn \neq 1$.

Next draw P_1Y parallel to AB to meet PP' in Y. Then

$$\overrightarrow{UY}/\overrightarrow{UP} = \overrightarrow{AP_1}/\overrightarrow{AP} = m,$$

$$\overrightarrow{UP'}/\overrightarrow{UY} = \overrightarrow{BP'}/\overrightarrow{BP_1} = n,$$

so that $\overrightarrow{UP'}/\overrightarrow{UP} = (\overrightarrow{UP'}/\overrightarrow{UY})(\overrightarrow{UY}/\overrightarrow{UP})$

$$= mn.$$

This establishes the result, giving the 'product' transformation:

$$P' = P\mathbf{U(mn)}.$$

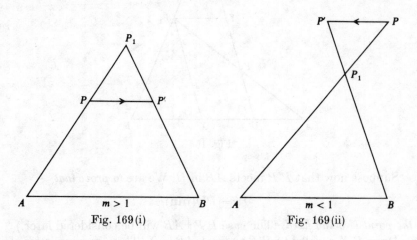

Fig. 169(i)   Fig. 169(ii)

The case $mn = 1$. When $mn = 1$, then, since

$$m = \overrightarrow{AP_1}/\overrightarrow{AP} \quad \text{and} \quad n^{-1} = \overrightarrow{BP_1}/\overrightarrow{BP'},$$

it follows that

$$\overrightarrow{AP_1}/\overrightarrow{AP} = \overrightarrow{BP_1}/\overrightarrow{BP'}$$

so that $PP' \parallel AB.$

Further, $\dfrac{PP'}{AB} = \dfrac{PP_1}{AP_1} = \dfrac{AP_1 - AP}{AP_1} = 1 - m^{-1};$

hence $PP' = (1 - m^{-1})AB = \text{constant},$

and so *the product* $\mathbf{A(m)B(m^{-1})}$ *is a translation* parallel to AB, of magnitude $(1 - m^{-1})\overrightarrow{AB}$.

Note that, if $m < 1$ (Figure 169(ii)), *then the translation is in the sense* $\overrightarrow{BA}$. The positive value of the distance of translation is $(m^{-1} - 1)AB$.

Exercise H

1. Prove that $\mathbf{B(n)\,A(m)} = \mathbf{U^*(mn)}$, where $U^* \in BA$ such that

$$\overrightarrow{BU^*} = \frac{m-1}{mn-1}\,\overrightarrow{BA} \quad (mn \neq 1).$$

2. Deduce from Question 1 that $\mathbf{B(n)A(m)}$ cannot be the same as $\mathbf{A(m)B(n)}$ unless *either* one of $\mathbf{A(m)}$, $\mathbf{B(n)}$ is the identity transformation *or* A and B coincide.

Illustration 3. *Properties of a triangle.*

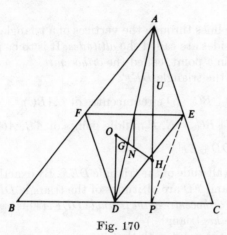

Fig. 170

Definitions (cf. Section 5, Illustration 1, and Exercise E, Question 1). The *medians* of a triangle are the lines joining the vertices to the middle points of the opposite sides. The *centroid* is the point where (Section 5) the medians meet, and it is a point of trisection for each of them.

Thus, if D, E, F are the middle points of the sides BC, CA, AB of a triangle ABC (Figure 170), then AD, BE, CF meet in G, and

$$\overrightarrow{AG}/\overrightarrow{GD} = \overrightarrow{BG}/\overrightarrow{GE} = \overrightarrow{CG}/\overrightarrow{GF}.$$

Further, since $FE \parallel BC$ and $AF = FB$, $AE = EC$, it follows that AD, joining A to the middle point of BC, also bisects EF. Thus G is *also the centroid of the triangle DEF*.

We are to make use of the enlargement $\mathbf{G}(-\tfrac{1}{2})$, under which $A\mathbf{G}(-\tfrac{1}{2}) = D$, $B\mathbf{G}(-\tfrac{1}{2}) = E$, $C\mathbf{G}(-\tfrac{1}{2}) = F$. For better appeal to the eye, though, we shall, *for this section*, use notation such as

$$A \to D, \quad B \to E, \quad C \to F$$

for that enlargement.

Then   circle $ABC \rightarrow$ circle DEF,

so that, if the centre of circle DEF is denoted by N, and the centre of circle ABC by O (the *circumcentre* of triangle ABC), we have

$$O \rightarrow N.$$

Hence N is the point on the line OG such that

$$\overrightarrow{GN} = \tfrac{1}{2}\overrightarrow{OG}.$$

Also *the radius of circle DEF is one half of the radius of the circumcircle of the triangle ABC.*

Definition. The lines through the vertices of a triangle perpendicular to the opposite sides are called the *altitudes*. It is to be proved shortly that they meet in a point, called the *orthocentre*.

Consider first the triangle DEF:

$$OD \perp BC \quad (O \text{ circumcentre of } \triangle ABC)$$

$$EF \parallel BC \quad (E, F \text{ middle points of } AB, AC)$$

$$\Rightarrow OD \perp EF.$$

That is, DO is an altitude of the triangle DEF. By exactly symmetrical arguments, EO and FO are altitudes of the triangle DEF.

Hence *O is the orthocentre of the triangle DEF.* (This argument proves its existence for *this* triangle.)

Now let H be the point such that

$$H \rightarrow O.$$

Then $A, B, C, G, O, H \rightarrow D, E, F, G, N, O,$

and so G, N, O stand in relation to the triangle DEF as G, O, H stand to the triangle ABC.

Since O, as we have proved, is the point of intersection of the altitudes of the triangle DEF, so H *is the point of intersection of the altitudes of the triangle ABC.* That is, the *orthocentre* exists, and it is at H.

We have proved incidentally that *the four points O, G, N, H lie on a straight line*, called the *Euler line* of the triangle ABC.

Let AH meet BC in the point P. Then, since H is the orthocentre, $AP \perp BC$.

For reference shortly, let U be the middle point of AH.

Consider next the enlargement $\mathbf{H}(\tfrac{1}{2})$ centred on the orthocentre H. For brevity, call the enlargement $\mathbf{H}$. Then

$$O\mathbf{H} = N, \quad A\mathbf{H} = U.$$

Further, the circle ABC, of centre O, transforms to a circle of centre N, whose radius is half that of the circle ABC; and this, as we have proved, is precisely the circle DEF. Thus

$$(\text{circle } ABC)\,\mathbf{H} = \text{circle } DEF.$$

But $A\mathbf{H} = U$, and points V, W may be defined similarly as the middle points of BH, CH, so that

$$BH = V, \quad CH = W.$$

Hence the points U, V, W lie on the circle DEF. Note, incidentally, that the relations

$$OH = N, \quad AH = U,$$

give the result that $NU = \tfrac{1}{2}OA$, confirming that U is on the circle of centre N and radius $\tfrac{1}{2}OA$.

Finally, since E is the middle point of AC and $\angle APC$ is a right angle, E is the centre of the circle APC, so that $EP = EC$, and therefore

$$\angle EPC = \angle ECP.$$

But $EFDC$ is a parallelogram, so that

$$\angle ECP = \angle DFE.$$

Hence $\qquad\qquad \angle EPC = \angle DFE,$

and so the quadrilateral $DFEP$ is cyclic.

The circle DEF thus contains P and, similarly, the points Q, R which are the feet of the perpendiculars from B to CA and C to AB.

Hence *the points D, E, F, P, Q, R, U, V, W all lie on a circle, called the nine-point circle of the triangle ABC.*

Exercise I

Let HD meet the circle ABC at L and let AP meet the circle ABC at X.

1. Prove that D is the middle point of HL and P the middle point of HX.

2. Prove that $LX \parallel BC$.

3. Prove that AOL is a straight line and that $OD = \tfrac{1}{2}AH$.

4. By applying the 'product' transformation $\mathbf{B}(\tfrac{1}{2})\mathbf{C}(\tfrac{2}{3})$ to the vertex A of a triangle ABC, verify that the medians through A and C meet at a point at which each is trisected.

Illustration 4. *The theorem of Apollonius.* (a) *The 'equal ratio'* *property.* Let AB be a given line segment (Figure 171). Produce $\overrightarrow{AB}$ to V, and (for future reference) let

$$\overrightarrow{AV}/\overrightarrow{BV} = r/s.$$

Suppose that any line l is drawn through V, and reflect the segment AB in l so that

$$Al = A', \quad Bl = B'$$

and, of course, $Vl = V$.

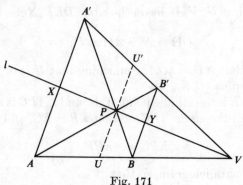

Fig. 171

Let $AB' \cap A'B = P$. Then $P \in l$ since $(A'B)l = AB'$. Draw through P the line UPU' meeting AB in U and $A'B'$ in U', where $U' = Ul$, so that $UPU' \perp l$.

We are to prove that (numerically) *the segments* AU, UB, AV, VB *satisfy the relation*

$$\frac{AU}{UB} = \frac{AV}{VB}.$$

By the reflection, $AA' \parallel BB'$

$$\Rightarrow \frac{AV}{VB} = \frac{AA'}{BB'} = \frac{AX}{B'Y} \quad \text{(halves)}$$

$$= \frac{XP}{PY},$$

since the triangles AXP, $B'YP$ are equiangular.

But $XA \parallel PU \parallel YB$

$$\Rightarrow \frac{XP}{PY} = \frac{AU}{UB}$$

$$\Rightarrow \frac{AV}{VB} = \frac{AU}{UB},$$

which is what was to be proved.

Note certain equalities:
(i) by the reflection,

$$PA' = PA, \quad PB' = PB;$$

(ii) $\qquad \angle XPA = \angle XPA' = \angle YPB = \angle YPB'$

and $\qquad \angle APU = \angle A'PU' = \angle BPU = \angle B'PU'.$

Hence l is the external bisector of $\angle APB$ and PU is the internal bisector.

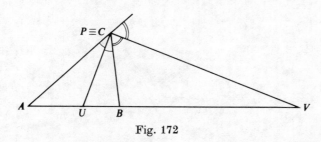

Fig. 172

(b) *The angle bisector theorem.* In the diagram of Figure 171, read P as C, a vertex of a given triangle ABC (Figure 172). Let CU be the bisector of the internal angle ACB and CV the external bisector. The configuration of Figure 171 is then determined in all its details, the line l being equated with VC. Then (compare the earlier diagram, Figure 171),

$$\frac{AC}{CB} = \frac{AC}{CB'} \quad (CB = CB')$$

$$= \frac{AU}{UB} \quad (CU \parallel B'B)$$

$$= \frac{AV}{VB} \quad \text{(as above).}$$

That is: *the bisectors of the angle C of a triangle ABC divide the side AB internally (at U) and externally (at V) in the ratio of the sides (AC/CB).*

(c) *The circle of Apollonius.* Let two points A, B be given, and a ratio r/s. It is required *to find the locus of a point P given that $AP/PB = r/s$.*

Let U, V be the internal and external points on AB such that $AU/UB = AV/VB = r/s$. Draw an arbitrary line l through V and, by reflection in l, obtain the diagram of Figure 171, where the point P is named without prejudice. Then

$$\frac{AP}{PB} = \frac{AP}{PB'} = \frac{AU}{UB} = \frac{r}{s},$$

so P is a point such as is required. Further it is the only point on l (other than V itself) with the property $XP/PY = XV/VY = r/s$. Hence the locus required is that of the point P uniquely defined in this way on the line l.

But U, V are fixed points, determined by A, B and the ratio r/s. Also $\angle UPV$ is a right angle. Hence *P lies on the circle having UV as a diameter*.

11

SIMILARITY TRANS-
FORMATIONS; SPIRAL
SIMILARITIES AND STRETCH
REFLECTIONS

1. Spiral similarities

Let A be a given point, r a given non-zero ratio (positive or negative) and α a given angle measured in the counterclockwise sense.

An arbitrary point P is transformed as follows (Figure 173):

 (i) rotate AP through the angle α to AP_1;

 (ii) enlarge $\overrightarrow{AP_1}$ to $\overrightarrow{AP'}$ so that $\overrightarrow{AP'} = r\overrightarrow{AP_1}$.

The transformation $P \to P'$ is called a *spiral similarity* with centre A, ratio r and angle α, and is denoted by the notation $\mathbf{A(r, \alpha)}$.

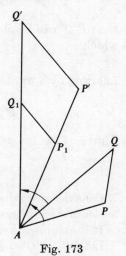

Fig. 173

The same point P' is obtained if the operations (i), (ii) are performed in the reverse order. (This is sometimes more convenient, and will, in fact, be used in Section 2.)

Let P, Q be two given points, transforming to P', Q'. By similarity considerations,

$$\frac{P'Q'}{PQ} = \frac{P'Q'}{P_1Q_1} = \frac{OP'}{OP_1} = r,$$

so that
$$P'Q' = rPQ.$$

Thus *all magnitudes are transformed in the ratio r*.

Exercise A

1. Prove that, if $P \to P'$ and $Q \to Q'$ by the spiral similarity $\mathbf{A(r, \alpha)}$, then there is an *induced spiral similarity* $Q \to P, Q' \to P'$ given by $\mathbf{A(t, \beta)}$, where $t = AQ/AP, \beta = \angle PAQ$.

2. Prove that, if $P \to P'$ and $Q \to Q'$ by the spiral similarity $\mathbf{A(r, \alpha)}$, then the counterclockwise angle between PQ and $P'Q'$ (from PQ to $P'Q'$) is α.

[161]

Deduce that, if $U = PQ \cap P'Q'$, then each of the circles APP', AQQ' passes through U.

3. Use the preceding two questions to prove that *each of the circles APQ, $AP'Q'$ passes through the point $PP' \cap QQ'$.*

4. Prove that, for two spiral similarities with the same centre,

$$\mathbf{A}(\mathbf{r}, \alpha)\,\mathbf{A}(\mathbf{t}, \beta) = \mathbf{A}(\mathbf{rt}, \alpha + \beta).$$

Verify that $$\mathbf{A}(\mathbf{1}, 0) = \mathbf{I},$$

the unit transformation, and find the inverse of $\mathbf{A}(\mathbf{r}, \alpha)$.

2. The transform of a segment

If a segment PQ is transformed to $P'Q'$ (Figure 174) by the relations

$$P' = P\mathbf{A}(\mathbf{r}, \alpha), \quad Q' = Q\mathbf{A}(\mathbf{r}, \alpha),$$

then $P'Q'$ can be obtained from PQ by an extension $\mathbf{A}(\mathbf{r})$ to P_2Q_2 for which

$$P_2Q_2 = rPQ, \quad P_2Q_2 \parallel PQ,$$

followed by a rotation $\mathbf{A}(\alpha)$ from P_2Q_2 to $P'Q'$ for which

$$P'Q' = P_2Q_2, \quad \triangle(\overrightarrow{P_2Q_2} \text{ to } \overrightarrow{P'Q'}) = \alpha.$$

Thus $$P'Q' = rPQ,$$

$$\triangle(\overrightarrow{PQ} \text{ to } \overrightarrow{P'Q'}) = \alpha.$$

Consider now the converse process: *given two segments PQ, $P'Q'$, to obtain a spiral similarity $P \to P'$, $Q \to Q'$.*

It is assumed that PQ, $P'Q'$ are not parallel. (See Exercise B.)

Let $PQ \cap P'Q' = U$. Then the angle of the similarity must be α, where $\alpha = \triangle(PQ \text{ to } P'Q')$.

Draw the circles UPP', UQQ' (Figure 175). Since they have one point U in common, they also have another, say A. We are to prove that A *is the centre of the spiral similarity*:

(i) $\qquad \triangle PAP' = \triangle PUP'$ (circle UPP')

$\qquad\qquad\quad \equiv \triangle QUQ'$ (same angle)

$\qquad\qquad\quad = \triangle QAQ'$ (circle UQQ').

Hence line $AP \to$ line AP' and line $AQ \to$ line AQ' by rotation through the angle $\triangle PUP' \equiv \triangle QUQ'$.

(ii) The triangles APQ, $AP'Q'$ are equiangular, since

$$\triangle PAQ = \triangle PAP' + \triangle P'AQ$$
$$= \triangle QAQ' + \triangle P'AQ$$
$$= \triangle P'AQ';$$

and $\quad\quad \triangle AQP \equiv \triangle AQU$
$$= \triangle AQ'U \quad \text{(circle } AUQQ')$$
$$\equiv \triangle AQ'P'.$$

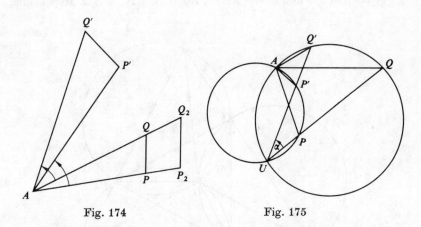

Fig. 174   Fig. 175

Corresponding lengths are therefore proportional, so that

$$\frac{AP'}{AP} = \frac{AQ'}{AQ}$$
$$= r, \quad \text{say.}$$

Thus $\mathbf{A}(\overrightarrow{\mathbf{AP'}}/\overrightarrow{\mathbf{AP}}, \triangle \mathbf{PAP'})$ is a spiral similarity $P \to P'$, $Q \to Q'$. It is completely determined when the two non-parallel corresponding segments are given.

Exercise B

1. Prove that, if the two segments PQ, $P'Q'$ are parallel, then there is an *enlargement* $P \to P'$, $Q \to Q'$ if PQ, $P'Q'$ are not equal and a *translation* or *half-turn* $P \to P'$, $Q \to Q'$ if PQ, $P'Q'$ are equal.

Corollary 1. *Two directly similar triangles ABC, PQR can be transformed into each other* ($\triangle ABC \to \triangle PQR$) *by a spiral similarity.*

When the triangles are oppositely orientated, this is not possible, since spiral similarities preserve orientation. (See Section 5.)

Exercise C

A sequence

To determine whether *a triangle A′ B′ C′ can be constructed similar to ABC, but with A′, B′, C′ on BC, CA, AB respectively.*

1. Assuming such a figure drawn (Figure 176) prove that each of the circles $AB'C'$, $BC'A'$, $CA'B'$ is equal to the circle $A'B'C'$, and that those three circles have a common point V.

2. Prove that the four circles $AB'C'$, $BC'A'$, $CA'B'$, $A'B'C'$ are all equal.

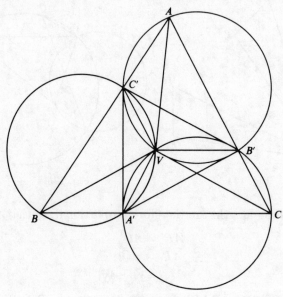

Fig. 176

3. Prove that $\angle VBA' = \angle VCA'$ and deduce that V is the circumcentre of the triangle ABC.

4. Prove that, if A' is *any* point selected arbitrarily on BC, then the circle $VA'C$ (where V is the circumcentre) meets AC in a point B' and the circle $VA'B$ meets AB in a point C' such that the triangle $A'B'C'$ is similar to the given triangle ABC.

5. Prove that, if V is also the centre of a spiral similarity $A \to A'$, $B \to B'$, $C \to C'$, then the triangle ABC must be equilateral.

3. The product of two spiral similarities
with different centres

Let $\qquad\qquad\qquad$ $\mathbf{A}(\mathbf{r}, \alpha), \quad \mathbf{B}(\mathbf{t}, \beta)$

be two given spiral similarities. It is immediate that the product

$$\{\mathbf{A}(\mathbf{r}, \alpha)\mathbf{B}(\mathbf{t}, \beta)\}$$

applied to any one segment enlarges it by a factor rt and turns it through an angle $\alpha + \beta$. We show that *there is a spiral similarity, the product of the given similarities, that does just this.*

We start by studying the fate of one segment, and naturally choose it to be as simple as possible (Figure 177). For ease of language, call the two similarities $\mathbf{A}$, $\mathbf{B}$. Let AB be of length a.

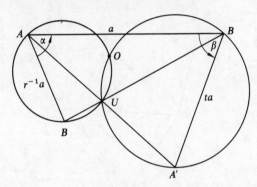

Fig. 177

(i) The point A is unaltered by $\mathbf{A}$, so that

$$A\mathbf{A} = A \quad \text{and} \quad A\mathbf{A}\mathbf{B} = A\mathbf{B} = A',$$

say, where $\qquad\qquad$ $BA' = ta, \quad \angle ABA' = \beta.$

(ii) Let $\bar{B}$ be the point that transforms to B by $\mathbf{A}$, so that

$$A\bar{B} = r^{-1}a, \quad \angle \bar{B}AB = \alpha.$$

Then $\qquad\qquad\qquad$ $\bar{B}\mathbf{A} = B, \quad \bar{B}\mathbf{A}\mathbf{B} = B.$

Combining (i) and (ii), $\bar{B}\mathbf{A}(\mathbf{A}\mathbf{B}) = \bar{B}A'$.

We restrict attention to the case when $\bar{B}A$ is not parallel to BA'.

The routine of Section 2 may now be applied. Let AA' meet $\bar{B}B$ in U, and then let O be the second point of intersection of the circles $UA\bar{B}$, $UA'B$. The product similarity is then

$$\mathbf{O}(\mathbf{rt}, \alpha + \beta)$$

and any segment PQ is transformed under it to a segment $P'Q'$ found by enlarging PQ by a factor rt and turning it through an angle $\alpha + \beta$.

Illustration. Let ABC be a given triangle (named in counter-clockwise sense) whose sides are a, b, c and angles $\hat{A}$, $\hat{B}$, $\hat{C}$. Draw equilateral triangles BPC, CQA, ARB outwards (Figure 178) and consider three spiral similarities

$$\mathbf{B} \equiv \mathbf{B}(c/a, \tfrac{1}{3}\pi + \hat{\mathbf{B}}),$$
$$\mathbf{A} \equiv \mathbf{A}(b/c, \tfrac{1}{3}\pi + \hat{\mathbf{A}}),$$
$$\mathbf{C} \equiv \mathbf{C}(a/b, \tfrac{1}{3}\pi + \hat{\mathbf{C}}),$$

taken in *clockwise* order round the triangle.

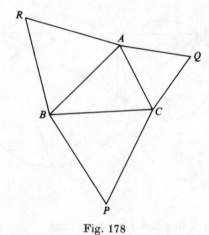

Fig. 178

We are to prove that $\mathbf{BAC}$ *is the identity transformation* $\mathbf{I}$ *which leaves the plane unaltered, where the order* $\mathbf{B}$, $\mathbf{A}$, $\mathbf{C}$ *is essential.*

From the similarities, we have the relations

$$C\mathbf{B} = R, \quad P\mathbf{B} = A,$$
$$B\mathbf{A} = Q, \quad R\mathbf{A} = C,$$
$$A\mathbf{C} = P, \quad Q\mathbf{C} = B.$$

Then
$$(\triangle BCP)\,\mathbf{BAC} = (\triangle BCP\,.\,\mathbf{B})\,\mathbf{AC}$$
$$= (\triangle BRA)\,\mathbf{AC}$$
$$= (\triangle BRA\,.\,\mathbf{A})\,\mathbf{C}$$
$$= (\triangle QCA)\,\mathbf{C}$$
$$= \triangle BCP.$$

Thus **BAC** carries $\triangle BCP$ to itself, thereby 'fixing' the whole plane. (Compare p. 50.) Hence
$$\mathbf{BAC = I}.$$

Corollary 2. *To prove that* **BA** *is the spiral similarity* **D** *given by*
$$\mathbf{D} = \mathbf{C}(b/a, \tfrac{2}{3}\pi + \hat{\mathbf{A}} + \hat{\mathbf{B}}):$$

Since **C**, **D** have the same centre C,
$$\mathbf{CD} = \mathbf{C}\left(\frac{a}{b} \cdot \frac{b}{a}, \; \tfrac{1}{3}\pi + \hat{\mathbf{C}} + \tfrac{2}{3}\pi + \hat{\mathbf{A}} + \hat{\mathbf{B}}\right)$$
$$= \mathbf{C}(1, 0)$$
$$= \mathbf{I},$$
the identity.

Then
$$\mathbf{BAC = I}$$
$$\Rightarrow \mathbf{BACD = D}$$
$$\Rightarrow (\mathbf{BA})(\mathbf{CD}) = \mathbf{D}$$
$$\Rightarrow \mathbf{BAI = D}$$
$$\Rightarrow \mathbf{BA = D}.$$

We have therefore succeeded in *expressing the product* **BA** *as a spiral similarity*. The relation
$$\mathbf{CD = I}$$
can be reversed by almost identical argument to give
$$\mathbf{DC = I}.$$
These two relations establish **D** as the *inverse* of **C**, and we may write
$$\mathbf{D = C^{-1}}.$$

Exercise D

1. P is a variable point on a given circle and A is a fixed point inside it. Prove that the spiral symmetry $P' = P\mathbf{A}(\mathbf{r}, \alpha)$ gives P' as a variable point of another fixed circle.

Three concentric circles have radii a, b, c where $a < b \leqslant c$. Show how to construct a triangle ABC of given shape ($\hat{A} = \alpha$, $\hat{B} = \beta$, $\hat{C} = \gamma$) with A, B, C on the circles of radii a, b, c respectively. (The point A can be given a fixed arbitrary position on the inner circle.)

4. The transform of a circle with respect to a point on it

Let A be a given point on a given circle Ω (Figure 179). Subject Ω to the spiral similarity

$$\mathbf{A(r, \alpha)}.$$

The effect is to rotate the circle about A through an angle α and then to enlarge it with ratio r, giving another circle Ω'. Since each of these circles contains A, there is a second point of intersection B, which we assume to be distinct from A (i.e. we assume that $\alpha \neq \pi$).

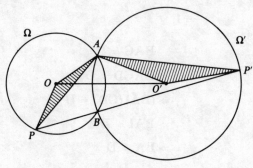

Fig. 179

The centre O of Ω transforms to the centre O' of Ω', so that

$$\angle OAO' = \alpha, \quad AO' = rAO.$$

Now let P be any point of Ω and P' the point of Ω' given by $P' = P\mathbf{A(r, \alpha)}$. Then

$$\left.\begin{array}{l} O \to O' \\ P \to P' \end{array}\right\} \Rightarrow \text{triangle } APP' \text{ similar to triangle } AOO'$$

$$\Rightarrow \angle APP' = \angle AOO'$$

$$= \tfrac{1}{2}\angle AOB \text{ (symmetry about } OO')$$

$$= \text{angle subtended at circumference by arc } AB.$$

Hence *PP' passes through B*, so that *corresponding points of Ω, Ω' are collinear with B.*

Exercise E

1. Prove that, conversely, if PB meets Ω' again in X, then X is the point corresponding to P.

Alternative treatment

Definition. The *shape* of a spiral similarity: Let

$$P' = P\mathbf{A}(\mathbf{r}, \boldsymbol{\alpha}).$$

Then the triangle APP' is fixed in shape, since

$$\triangle PAP' = \alpha, \quad AP'/AP = r,$$

where r, α are constant. This shape may conveniently be called *the shape of the spiral similarity*.

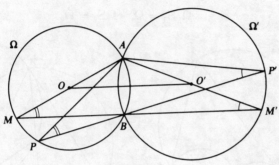

Fig. 180

Let Ω, Ω' be two given circles intersecting in A, B (Figure 180). It is required *to determine the spiral similarity* $\mathbf{A}(\mathbf{r}, \boldsymbol{\alpha})$ *sending* Ω *to* Ω' *and to prove that, under it, the straight lines joining corresponding points all pass through B.*

Since centres must transform to centres, it is necessary that $O \to O'$ and so AOA' *is a triangle giving the shape of the spiral similarity*. Let M, M' be the other ends of the diameters through A. Then

$$\angle ABM = \tfrac{1}{2}\pi, \quad \angle ABM' = \tfrac{1}{2}\pi \quad \text{(in semi-circles)}$$

$$\Rightarrow MBM' \text{ is a straight line.}$$

Draw any line through B cutting the circles in P, P'. Then, whether P lies on the major or minor arc AB,

$$\angle APP' = \angle AMB$$
$$= \angle AOO' \quad (OO' \parallel MM'),$$

and, similarly, $\quad \angle AP'P = \angle AO'O.$

Hence the triangle APP' is similar to the 'shape' triangle AOO', so that P *transforms to* P' *under the spiral similarity of centre* A, *ratio* AO'/AO *and angle* $\triangle OAO'$.

Illustration 2. *The Simson line. Let ABC be a given triangle and P any point on the circle ABC (Figure* 181*). Let PL, PM, PN be drawn perpendicular to BC, CA, AB. To prove that L, M, N are collinear.*

Denote the circle ABC by Ω. Then

$$\angle BNP = \angle BLP = \text{right angle}$$

$$\Rightarrow P, B, N, L \text{ on circle, } \Omega_1;$$

$$\angle CMP = \angle CLP = \text{right angle}$$

$$\Rightarrow P, M, C, L \text{ on circle, } \Omega_2.$$

Let S_1, S_2 be the spiral similarities with centres at P, such that

$$\Omega_1 S_1 = \Omega, \quad \Omega S_2 = \Omega_2$$

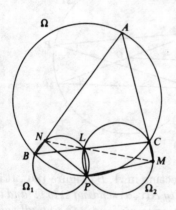
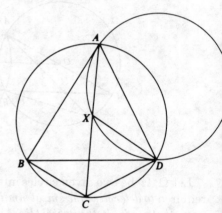

Fig. 181   Fig. 182

Then $NS_1 = A$ (Ω_1 meets Ω in P and B),

$AS_2 = M$ (Ω meets Ω_2 in P and C),

so that $NS_1 S_2 = M.$

But $S_1 S_2$ is the spiral similarity sending Ω_1 via Ω to Ω_2; that is

$$\Omega_1 S_1 S_2 = \Omega_2.$$

Hence the join of the corresponding points N, M passes through L, so that LMN is a straight line.

The line LMN is called the *Simson line* of P with respect to the triangle ABC.

Illustration 3. *The theorem of Ptolemy. Given a quadrangle ABCD with its vertices on a circle (Figure* 182*), to prove that*

$$AD.BC + CD.AB = BD.AC.$$

Consider the spiral similarity with centre D sending B to A – that is, with ratio DA/DB and angle $\angle BDA$. Under this, the given circle becomes another circle, through A and D. Let this circle meet AC again in X. Then, as we have seen,

$$C \to X,$$

so that
$$\triangle BCD \to \triangle AXD.$$

These triangles are thus similar, and so

$$\frac{BC}{AX} = \frac{BD}{AD},$$

or
$$AD.BC = AX.BD.$$

The similarity just established induces another (cf. Exercise A, Question 1), namely, that with centre D sending C to B. Under it, by equalities of ratios and angles, X is sent to A. Thus

$$\triangle CXD \to \triangle BAD,$$

and so
$$\frac{XC}{AB} = \frac{CD}{BD},$$

or
$$CD.AB = XC.BD.$$

Hence
$$AD.BC + CD.AB = (AX + XC)BD$$
$$= AC.BD.$$

Illustration 4. *Angles in the same segment*. Let U, A be two given points on a circle and P a variable point on the arc $\overarc{AU}$. To prove that *the angle $\angle UPA$ is constant as P varies* (Figure 183).

Let UP' be the diameter through U and apply the spiral similarity $\mathbf{U}(\mathbf{r}, \boldsymbol{\alpha})$, where $r = UP'/UP$, $\alpha = \angle PUP'$. Denote by A' the transform $A\mathbf{U}(\mathbf{r}, \boldsymbol{\alpha})$. Then the triangles UAP, $UA'P'$ are similar and, in particular, $\angle UPA = \angle UP'A'$. Further, in the 'induced' spiral similarity $\mathbf{U}(\mathbf{s}, \boldsymbol{\beta})$, where $s = UP/UA$, $\beta = \angle AUP$, we have $A \to P$, $A' \to P'$ so that the triangles UAA', UPP' are similar and, in particular,

$$\angle UAA' = \angle UPP',$$

which is a right angle since UP' is a diameter.

But $\angle UAP'$ is also a right angle, by the same diameter, so that we have
$$AA' \perp UA, \quad AP' \perp UA.$$

Hence $AA'P$ is a straight line, Thus

$$\triangle UPA = \triangle UP'A' \quad \text{(proved above)}$$

$$= \triangle UP'A,$$

which is constant since U and A are given.

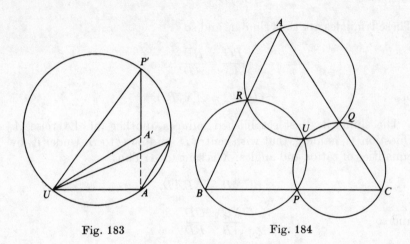

Fig. 183   Fig. 184

Exercise F

1. A point U is taken in the plane of a triangle ABC. A circle through U and A meets AB in R and AC in Q; a circle through U and B meets BC in P and BA in R (Figure 184). Prove, using an argument like the one just given for the Simson line, that U, C, Q, P lie on a circle.

2. Two circles Ω, Ω' meet in points A, B. A square $PQRS$ has its vertices on Ω. The straight lines PB, QB, RB, SB meet Ω' again in P', Q', R', S'. Prove that $P'Q'R'S'$ is a square.

3. Two circles Ω, Ω', of radii a, a' respectively, meet in points A, B. The tangent to Ω' at A meets Ω again in T and TB meets Ω' again in T''. Prove that

$$\frac{AT}{AT'} = \frac{a}{a'}.$$

4. To prove that *the altitudes of a triangle are concurrent*. Let ABC be a given triangle whose altitudes BQ, CR meet in H (Figure 185). Prove first that A, Q, H, R lie on a circle Ω. Let the circle Ω_1 through C, H, Q meet BC in P_1 and let the circle Ω_2 through B, H, R meet BC in P_2. By using the spiral similarities of centre H which (i) send $\Omega_1 \to \Omega$; (ii) send $\Omega \to \Omega_2$; (iii) send

$\Omega_1 \to \Omega_2$, prove that P_1, P_2 coincide in the point P which is the foot of the perpendicular from H to BC. By giving reasons for the statements

$$\triangle AHQ = \triangle ARQ = \triangle QCP,$$

or otherwise, prove that the line AP passes through H.

5. Equilateral triangles BCP, CAQ, ABR are drawn outwards from the sides of a triangle ABC. Prove that the three circles BCP, CAQ, ABR have a common point U at which, for an acute-angled triangle, each of the sides subtends an angle of $\frac{2}{3}\pi$.

Points P', Q', R' are taken on the arcs BC, CA, AB of these circles remote from U, and $P'CQ'$, $P'BR'$ are straight lines. Prove that $Q'AR'$ is a straight line and that $P'Q'R'$ is an equilateral triangle.

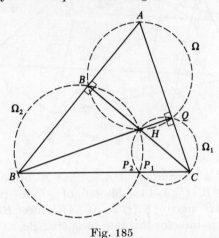

Fig. 185

5. Stretch-reflections

We have seen that a *segment PQ* can be transformed to a (non-parallel) segment $P'Q'$ by a spiral similarity. This similarity, if applied to the whole plane, *preserves the orientation for similar figures*, but it cannot deal with a case when the similarities are *opposite*.

In order to deal with an oppositely orientated transformation we must therefore look for a different technique.

The clue lies in the phrase 'opposite orientation', which implies that, somewhere, we ought to be using a reflection. We turn, in fact, to the discussion on glide reflections for isometries, and see how far we can progress while making obvious modifications. For ease of exposition, we follow closely the language of Chapter 7, Section 6.

Let ABC, $A'B'C'$ be two similar triangles (Figure 186), oppositely orientated, so that $$\overrightarrow{\triangle ABC} \simeq \overleftarrow{\triangle A'B'C'},$$

where $\qquad B'C' = kBC, \quad C'A' = kCA, \quad A'B' = kAB.$

Let U, V, W be the points on AA', BB', CC' such that

$$\overrightarrow{UA'} = k\overrightarrow{AU}, \quad \overrightarrow{VB'} = k\overrightarrow{BV}, \quad \overrightarrow{WC'} = k\overrightarrow{CW}.$$

We prove that U, V, W *are collinear.*

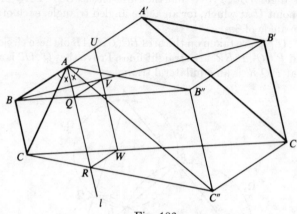

Fig. 186

Give $\triangle A'B'C'$ a translation $\overrightarrow{A'A}$ so that A' lies on A and B', C' assume positions B'', C''. Let the bisector of $\angle CAC''$ (which is also the bisector of $\angle BAB''$ since $\angle BAC = \angle C''AB''$) meet BB'' in Q and CC'' in R. By the angle-bisector theorem for a triangle,

$$\frac{BQ}{QB''} = \frac{BA}{AB''}$$

$$= \frac{BA}{A'B'} \quad \text{(translation)}$$

$$= \frac{1}{k},$$

so that $\qquad\qquad \overrightarrow{QB''} = k\overrightarrow{BQ}$

and, similarly, $\qquad\qquad \overrightarrow{RC''} = k\overrightarrow{CR}.$

Now, by the properties of similar triangles,

$$\frac{BQ}{BB''} = \frac{BV}{BB'} = \frac{1}{k+1}$$

$$\Rightarrow \frac{QV}{B''B'} = \frac{1}{k+1},$$

so that
$$\overrightarrow{QV} = (k+1)^{-1}\,\overrightarrow{B''B'}$$
$$= (k+1)^{-1}\,\overrightarrow{AA'}$$
$$= \overrightarrow{AU}$$

and, similarly,
$$\overrightarrow{RW} = \overrightarrow{AU}.$$

The points U, V, W therefore arise from A, Q, R under a translation $(k+1)^{-1}\,\overrightarrow{AU}$, and so U, V, W are collinear. Consider now the configuration drawn by analogy with the earlier 'glide box'.

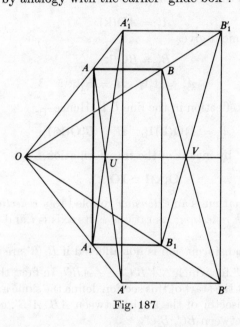

Fig. 187

We have two given line-segments AB, $A'B'$ (Figure 187), to be put into correspondence by an 'opposite' similarity. Take points $U \in AA'$, $V \in BB'$ so that
$$\overrightarrow{A'U}/\overrightarrow{UA} = \overrightarrow{B'V}/\overrightarrow{VB}$$
$$= \frac{A'B'}{AB}$$
$$= k, \quad \text{say.}$$

Then we have seen that UV makes equal angles with AB, $A'B'$.

Reflect the whole figure in UV, so that
$$A \to A_1, \quad B \to B_1, \quad A' \to A'_1, \quad B \to B'_1.$$

Then $$U = AA' \cap A_1A_1', \quad V = BB' \cap B_1B_1'.$$

Also AA_1', A_1A' meet at a point O on UV. Now

$$\frac{OA_1'}{OA} = \frac{A'A_1'}{A_1A} \quad (A'A_1' \parallel A_1A)$$

$$= \frac{A'U}{UA} \quad \text{(same parallels)}$$

$$= k \quad \text{(definition of } U\text{)}.$$

Hence, if $O(k)$ is the extension of vertex O and ratio k,

$$A_1' = AO(k).$$

Identical argument gives

$$B_1' = BO(k).$$

But $$A' = A_1'1, \quad B' = B_1'1,$$

where 1 denotes reflection in the line UV. Hence

$$A' = A\{O(k)1\}, \quad B' = B\{O(k)1\}.$$

Thus $AB \to A'B'$ by means of the transformation.

$$O(k)1 \equiv 1O(k).$$

This transformation is an *extension* coupled to a *reflection* and may be called a *stretch reflection*; its ratio is k, its axis is l and its centre is the point O on l.

Finally, the transformation is not affected if B, B' are replaced by other points C, C' for which $\triangle \overrightarrow{A'B'C'} \simeq \triangle \overleftarrow{ABC}$. In fact, the points U, V, W obtained at the start of this section define the same axis, which is parallel to the bisector of the angle between AB, $A'B'$, *and* between AC, $A'C'$, *and* between BC, $B'C'$.

Hence *an 'opposite' similarity is equivalent to a stretch reflection*, or to a glide reflection in the case of congruence.

Exercise G

1. Prove that a stretch reflection has one self-corresponding point and two lines that are self-corresponding, though not point-for-point.

2. Prove that, if a triangle ABC is subjected to a stretch reflection whose centre is A and whose axis is the bisector of the angle $\angle BAC$, so that $B \to B'$, $C \to C'$, then B, C, B', C' are concyclic.

3. Two circles Ω_1, Ω_2 meet in O and U. Prove that there is a stretch reflection of centre O sending Ω_1 to Ω_2.

Prove also that, if the stretch reflection has its axis meeting Ω_2 in L and if it sends U to U', then L is the middle point of the arc UU'.

4. The lines AB, CD have a common mediator. Find a point U that is the centre of (i) an enlargement $A \to C$, $B \to D$, (ii) a stretch reflection $A \to D$, $B \to C$.

Illustration 5. *To find points A', B', C' on the sides BC, AB, CA respectively of a triangle ABC so that the triangles $A'B'C'$, ABC are similar.*

Note that the orientations are reversed, so the result will be a *stretch reflection*.

The argument is hard, and may perhaps be followed best if the reader will work through a series of examples each of which is comparatively simple.

Exercise H

1. Lemma. *A line l is given and a point A' not on it; the shape (including orientation) of a varying triangle $A'XY$ is given. It is required to find the locus of Y as X moves along the line l (Figure 188).*

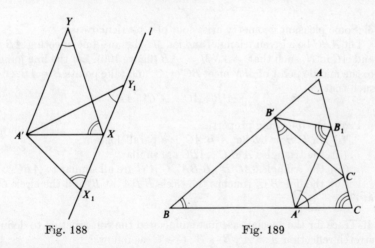

Fig. 188   Fig. 189

Let $A'X_1Y_1$ be the position when X_1 and Y_1 are *both* on l, determined since the angles $\angle Y_1X_1A'$ and $\angle A'Y_1X_1$ are known. Also let AXY be a general position of the varying triangle. Prove that the quadrilateral $A'XY_1Y$ is cyclic and hence that the angle $\angle YY_1X_1$ is constant. Hence Y moves on the line through Y_1 so defined.

2. Given a triangle ABC and an arbitrary point A' on BC, to find a triangle as defined in the statement of the problem:

Take the point B_1 on AC such that $\angle CA'B_1 = \angle A$ (Figure 189). Then the triangle $A'B_1C$ has the required shape ABC, and its orientation is *clockwise*. Through B_1 draw the line B_1B' (taking B' on AB) so that $\angle B'B_1A' = \angle C$. Take C' on AC so that $\angle A'B'C' = \angle B$. Prove (by a method similar to that used in the lemma of Question 1) that $A'C'B_1B'$ is cyclic and hence that the triangle $A'B'C'$ has the required shape and orientation.

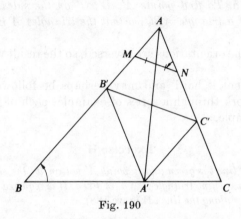

Fig. 190

3. Some pleasant geometry arises out of a particular case:

Let ABC be a given triangle, and let MN be any line, meeting AB in M and AC in N, such that $\angle ANM = \angle B$ (figure 190). Let the line joining A to the middle point of MN meet BC in A', and take points $B' \in AB$, $C' \in AC$ such that
$$A'B' \,\|\, AC, \quad A'C' \,\|\, AB.$$

Prove the following properties:
 (i) $BCC'B'$ is cyclic; $A'B'AC'$ is a parallelogram;
 (ii) the triangles $A'B'C'$, ABC are similar;
 (iii) the triangles $AC'B'$, $B'BA'$, $C'A'C$ are all similar to ABC.
 (iv) the line $B'C'$ touches the circle $B'BA'$ at B' and the circle $C'A'C$ at C'.

4. Trace for the special case just enunciated the construction to define the stretch reflection $A \to A'$, $B \to B'$, $C \to C'$ as follows:

Give the parallelogram $A'B'AC'$ a translation $\overrightarrow{A'A}$ to the position $AB''A''C''$ (Figure 191).
 (i) Prove that A is the middle point of $B'C''$ and of $C'B''$.

Let the bisector of the angle CAC'' meet BB'' in Q and CC'' in R. Let the lines through Q and R in the direction $\overrightarrow{AA'}$ meet BB' in V and CC' in W.

Prove that
$$\frac{B'V}{VB} = \frac{B''Q}{QB} = \frac{B'C'}{BC}$$

and that
$$\frac{C'W}{WC} = \frac{B'C'}{BC}.$$

Hence, as in the text, *VW is the axis of the stretch reflection.*

(ii) As in the text, prove that $A'U/UA = B'C'/BC$, and identify the centre of the stretch reflection.

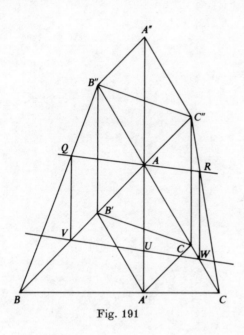

Fig. 191

PART III
THE USE OF MATRICES

12

MATRICES FOR GEOMETRY

There are many accounts of the elementary theory of matrices. The author thinks naturally of his own *Algebraic structure and matrices* (Cambridge University Press) but any text already familiar to the reader should be perfectly satisfactory.

The present summary is directed strongly towards those features that fit into the present work on transformations. Some acquaintance with the elements of coordinate geometry is assumed.

1. Notation and elementary operations

We start with a slight modification of the notation used in Part II. There we talked about transformations 1, U_α, $A(k)$, ..., and that language was convenient for our purposes. We now wish to use single-letter **bold** type (such as 1) in a different, though related, setting, and so from now on *transformations will be denoted exactly as before, but within square brackets*: $[1]$, $[U_\alpha]$, $[A(k)]$.

This will leave us free to use standard notation for matrices.

A *matrix* **a** is (when organised for processes of addition, multiplication, ...) a set of elements a_{ij} written as a rectangular array

$$\begin{pmatrix} a_{11} & a_{12} & a_{13} & \ldots & a_{1n} \\ a_{21} & a_{22} & a_{23} & \ldots & a_{2n} \\ \hdotsfor{5} \\ a_{m1} & a_{m2} & a_{m3} & \ldots & a_{mn} \end{pmatrix}$$

in which the first suffix denotes *row* and the second *column*. Thus the typical element a_{ij} lies in row i and column j. The matrix may also be denoted by the notation (a_{ij}), so that

$$\mathbf{a} \equiv (a_{ij}).$$

A matrix with m rows and n columns is said to be of *type* $m \times n$. When $n = 1$, the matrix of one column is called a *column vector*; when $m = 1$, the matrix of one row is called a *row vector*. The notation $\underset{(m \times n)}{\mathbf{a}}$ is sometimes used to emphasise that $\mathbf{a}$ is of type $m \times n$.

When the elements of rows and columns of a matrix $\mathbf{a}$ are interchanged, the result is a new matrix called the *transpose* of $\mathbf{a}$ and written $\mathbf{a}^T$. The notation $\mathbf{a}'$ is also used (but we shall keep to $\mathbf{a}^T$ here). Thus

$$a_{ij}^T = a_{ji};$$

that is, the element in row i and column j of $\mathbf{a}^T$ is the same as the element in row j and column i of $\mathbf{a}$. For example,

$$\begin{pmatrix} p & q & r \\ 1 & 2 & 3 \end{pmatrix}$$

transposes to

$$\begin{pmatrix} p & 1 \\ q & 2 \\ r & 3 \end{pmatrix}.$$

It follows immediately that
  (i) if $\mathbf{a}$ is of type $m \times n$, then $\mathbf{a}^T$ is of type $n \times m$;
  (ii) the transpose of $\mathbf{a}^T$ is $\mathbf{a}$ itself: $(\mathbf{a}^T)^T = \mathbf{a}$.

In general, $a_{ij} \neq a_{ji}$. When $a_{ij} = a_{ji}$ for all i, j, the matrix $\mathbf{a}$ is said to be *symmetric*. When $a_{ij} = -a_{ji}$, the matrix $\mathbf{a}$ is said to be *skew-symmetric*. For example,

$$\begin{pmatrix} 1 & 2 & 3 \\ 2 & 5 & 8 \\ 3 & 8 & 14 \end{pmatrix}$$

is a symmetric matrix

and

$$\begin{pmatrix} 0 & 3 & -2 \\ -3 & 0 & 1 \\ 2 & -1 & 0 \end{pmatrix}$$

is a skew-symmetric matrix.

The definitions are equivalent to $\mathbf{a}^T = \mathbf{a}$ and $\mathbf{a}^T = -\mathbf{a}$ respectively. Note that:
  (i) if $\mathbf{a}$ is symmetric or skew-symmetric, then $m = n$;
  (ii) if $\mathbf{a}$ is skew-symmetric, then $a_{ii} = 0$ for all i.

A matrix with the same number of rows and columns is said to be *square*. All symmetric and skew-symmetric matrices are square.

In the present context, the elements a_{ij} are taken to be *complex numbers* (usually *real*). A number by itself is often called a *scalar*, a name also given to a matrix of type 1×1.

When a matrix **a** is *multiplied by a scalar k*, the result is defined to be the matrix **b** such that

$$b_{ij} = ka_{ij}.$$

For example,

$$-3 \begin{pmatrix} 1 & 2 & 3 \\ 4 & 5 & 6 \end{pmatrix} = \begin{pmatrix} -3 & -6 & -9 \\ -12 & -15 & -18 \end{pmatrix}.$$

The *sum* $\mathbf{a} + \mathbf{b}$ of two matrices is defined to be the matrix **c** such that

$$c_{ij} = a_{ij} + b_{ij}.$$

For example,

$$\begin{pmatrix} 1 & 2 & 3 \\ 3 & 2 & 1 \end{pmatrix} + \begin{pmatrix} 1 & -2 & 3 \\ -3 & 2 & 1 \end{pmatrix} = \begin{pmatrix} 2 & 0 & 6 \\ 0 & 4 & 2 \end{pmatrix}.$$

For the sum to exist, the matrices **a** and **b** must be of the same type.

A matrix with all its elements zero is called a *zero matrix* **0**. When precision is necessary, the type may be indicated by suffices: thus

$$\mathbf{0} = \begin{pmatrix} 0 & 0 & 0 \\ 0 & 0 & 0 \end{pmatrix}$$

or, more precisely,

$$\mathbf{0}_{23} = \begin{pmatrix} 0 & 0 & 0 \\ 0 & 0 & 0 \end{pmatrix}.$$

By natural extension, we can define a finite *linear combination* of matrices,

$$p\mathbf{a} + q\mathbf{b} + r\mathbf{c} + \dots.$$

For example

$$p \begin{pmatrix} 1 & 2 \\ 3 & 4 \end{pmatrix} + q \begin{pmatrix} 3 & 4 \\ 5 & 6 \end{pmatrix} + r \begin{pmatrix} 5 & 6 \\ 7 & 8 \end{pmatrix}$$

$$= \begin{pmatrix} p+3q+5r & 2p+4q+6r \\ 3p+5q+7r & 4p+6q+8r \end{pmatrix};$$

again,
$$\begin{pmatrix} u & v & w \\ x & y & z \end{pmatrix} - \begin{pmatrix} u & v & w \\ x & y & z \end{pmatrix}$$

$$= \begin{pmatrix} u-u & v-v & w-w \\ x-x & y-y & z-z \end{pmatrix} = \begin{pmatrix} 0 & 0 & 0 \\ 0 & 0 & 0 \end{pmatrix}$$

$$= \mathbf{0}_{23}.$$

Exercise A

(The zero matrix $\mathbf{0}$ is to be taken of appropriate type.)

1. Prove that $\qquad\qquad \mathbf{a} + \mathbf{0} = \mathbf{0} + \mathbf{a} = \mathbf{a}.$

2. Prove that $\qquad\qquad \mathbf{a} + \mathbf{b} = \mathbf{0} \Leftrightarrow \mathbf{b} = -\mathbf{a}.$

3. Prove that, if $\mathbf{a}$ is a square matrix, $\mathbf{a} + \mathbf{a}^T$ is a symmetric matrix and $\mathbf{a} - \mathbf{a}^T$ is a skew-symmetric matrix.

4. Prove that a given matrix $\mathbf{a}$ can be written as a sum of matrices in the form $\mathbf{b} + \mathbf{c}$, where $\mathbf{b}$ is symmetric and $\mathbf{c}$ is skew symmetric.

2. Use in geometry

The standard notation of Cartesian geometry is modified here to allow the use of matrices. Let OX_1, OX_2 be two perpendicular *axes of coordinates* and P a point in the plane (Figure 192). The position of P determines, and is determined by, its distances (positive or negative) from the axes. It is customary to take p_1 as the distance in the direction $\overrightarrow{OX_1}$ and p_2 as the distance in the direction $\overrightarrow{OX_2}$. The two coordinates p_1, p_2 are then written in the form of a column matrix,

$$\mathbf{p} = \begin{pmatrix} p_1 \\ p_2 \end{pmatrix}.$$

For ease of printing, $\mathbf{p}$ is often written horizontally within braces { }:

$$\mathbf{p} = \{p_1, p_2\}.$$

Sometimes one uses the transposed version:

$$\mathbf{p}^T = (p_1, p_2),$$

the 'smooth' brackets being those of normal matrix notation.

Note the association of the matrix named $\mathbf{p}$ with the point named P. It is common to call $\mathbf{p}$ the *coordinate vector* (*position vector*) of P.

Most of the results of elementary coordinate geometry are assumed known. One result is worth establishing both for its own sake and also to illustrate procedure.

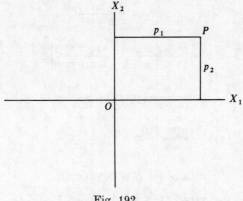

Fig. 192

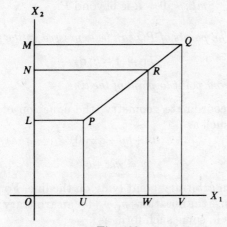

Fig. 193

Let PQ be a given segment and R the point dividing it in the ratio m/n, so that

$$\overrightarrow{PR}/\overrightarrow{RQ} = m/n;$$

then

$$\mathbf{r} = \frac{n\mathbf{p} + m\mathbf{q}}{n + m}.$$

Suppose that the lines through P, Q, R parallel to OX_2 meet OX_1 in U, V, W respectively (Figure 193). Then

$$\overrightarrow{PR}/\overrightarrow{RQ} = \overrightarrow{UW}/\overrightarrow{WV} = (r_1 - p_1)/(q_1 - r_1)$$

$$\Rightarrow \frac{r_1 - p_1}{q_1 - r_1} = \frac{m}{n}$$

$$\Rightarrow r_1 = \frac{np_1 + mq_1}{n + m}.$$

Similarly
$$r_2 = \frac{np_2 + mq_2}{n+m}.$$

Hence
$$\mathbf{r} = \left\{ \frac{np_1 + mq_1}{n+m}, \; \frac{np_2 + mq_2}{n+m} \right\}$$

$$= \frac{n}{(n+m)}\{p_1, p_2\} + \frac{m}{(n+m)}\{q_1, q_2\}$$

$$= \frac{n\mathbf{p} + m\mathbf{q}}{n+m}.$$

Note that:
$$m/n > 1 \Rightarrow R \text{ is beyond } Q;$$

$$0 < m/n < 1 \Rightarrow R \text{ is between } P \text{ and } Q;$$

$$m/n < 0 \Rightarrow R \text{ is beyond } P.$$

Corollary 1. *The points of PQ can be expressed in the form*

$$k\mathbf{p} + (1-k)\,\mathbf{q},$$

where k varies from point to point of the line.

In elementary coordinate geometry, the equation of a line is often given in forms such as

$$ax + by + c = 0,$$

$$y = mx + c,$$

where (x, y) is an arbitrary point lying on the line. For corresponding results, we now use the notation $\{p_1, p_2\}$ for an arbitrary point, and then the line appears in some such form as

$$a_1 p_1 + a_2 p_2 + c = 0,$$

$$p_2 = mp_1 + c.$$

For example, the equation

$$p_1 + 2p_2 + 3 = 0$$

represents a straight line which passes, say, through the points $\{-1, -1\}$ or $\{-3, 0\}$.

Exercise B

1. Prove that the line

$$p_1 = 2p_2$$

contains the points $\{0, 0\}$, $\{2, 1\}$, $\{-6, -3\}$.

2. Prove that the reflection of the point $\{3, -1\}$ in the line OX_1 is $\{3, 1\}$, and that the reflection of the point $\{4, 2\}$ in the line OX_2 is $\{-4, 2\}$.

3. Prove that, for all values of λ, the point $\{m\lambda, n\lambda\}$ lies on the line $np_1 - mp_2 = 0$.

4. Find equations, in the form $ap_1 + bp_2 + c = 0$, for the lines through the points

$$\text{(i)} \quad \{1, 0\}, \quad \{0, 2\},$$

$$\text{(ii)} \quad \{1, 1\}, \quad \{2, 3\},$$

$$\text{(iii)} \quad \{-1, 2\}, \quad \{3, -4\}.$$

5. Prove that the middle point of PQ has coordinate vector $\frac{1}{2}(\mathbf{p} + \mathbf{q})$.

6. Prove that, if P, Q, R are the vertices of a triangle, and if U is the middle point of QR, then the point G on PU such that $\overrightarrow{PG}/\overrightarrow{GU} = 2/1$ has coordinate vector

$$\acute{\mathbf{g}} = \tfrac{1}{3}(\mathbf{p} + \mathbf{q} + \mathbf{r}).$$

Deduce that the medians of a triangle are concurrent.

7. A straight line cuts the sides QR, RP, PQ of a triangle PQR in points L, M, N respectively. This line is taken as the axis OX_1, all points of which have their 'second' coordinate zero. Prove that

$$\overrightarrow{QL}/\overrightarrow{LR} = -q_2/r_2,$$

and deduce the *theorem of Menelaus*, that

$$(\overrightarrow{QL}/\overrightarrow{LR})\,(\overrightarrow{RM}/\overrightarrow{MP})\,(\overrightarrow{PN}/\overrightarrow{NQ}) = -1.$$

Deduce that the number of the points L, M, N lying on the line segments QR, RP, PQ is either 2 or 0.

8. The middle points of the sides AB, BC, CD, DA of a quadrilateral $ABCD$ are P, Q, R, S respectively, and U, V are the middle points of the diagonals AC, BD. Prove that the segments PR, QS, UV have the same middle point.

Deduce that $PQRS, PURV, QUSV$ are parallelograms.

3. Elementary transformations

Let a point $P\{p_1, p_2\}$ be subjected in turn to the transformations:

   (i) reflection in OX_1;

   (ii) reflection in OX_2;

   (iii) rotation about O through a half-turn.

Use the names x_1, x_2 for the lines which are the axes OX_1, OX_2 (Figure 194). Then, straight from the definitions, using the notation for operations explained in Section 1:

   (i) $P[\mathbf{x}_1] = \{p_1, -p_2\};$

   (ii) $P[\mathbf{x}_2] = \{-p_1, p_2\};$

   (iii) $P[\mathbf{O}_\pi] = \{-p_1, -p_2\}.$

[Since the notation may be unfamiliar, these results are given in words:

When P is the point with coordinates $\{p_1, p_2\}$

   (i) the reflection of P in OX_1 is $\{p_1, -p_2\}$,

  (ii) the reflection of P in OX_2 is $\{-p_1, p_2\}$,

 (iii) the rotation of P through a half-turn about O is $\{-p_1, -p_2\}$.]

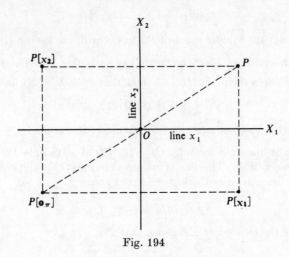

Fig. 194

Exercise C

The transform of a point P is often denoted by the symbol P', and the transform of P' by the symbol P''.

1. Prove that, if M is the middle point of PQ and M' the middle point of $P'Q'$ under the relevant transformation, then 'middle points transform to middle points'; that is,

$$M[\mathbf{x}_1] = M', \quad M[\mathbf{x}_2] = M', \quad M[\mathbf{O}_\pi] = M'.$$

2. Find all the *self-corresponding* points P such that

$$P[\mathbf{x}_1] = P, \quad P[\mathbf{x}_2] = P, \quad P[\mathbf{O}_\pi] = P.$$

3. By finding the lengths of $P'Q'$ in the three cases

$$\text{(i)} \quad (P'Q') = (PQ)[\mathbf{x}_1],$$

$$\text{(ii)} \quad (P'Q') = (PQ)[\mathbf{x}_2],$$

$$\text{(iii)} \quad (P'Q') = (PQ)[\mathbf{O}_\pi],$$

prove that these three transformations are *isometries*.

4. Prove that, if $[\mathbf{\dot{g}}(\mathbf{x}_1, \mathbf{k})]$ is the *glide reflection* of magnitude k in the direction $\overrightarrow{OX_1}$, then

$$P[\mathbf{\dot{g}}(\mathbf{x}_1, \mathbf{k})] = \{p_1 + k, -p_2\}.$$

Solve for this glide reflection the problems analogous to those of Questions 1, 2, 3.

5. Prove that $P[\mathbf{O}_{\frac{1}{2}\pi}] = \{-p_2, p_1\}$.

4. More general reflections

Let l be a line *through the origin* O making an angle α (in the counter-clockwise sense) with OX_1 (Figure 195). Let P be an arbitrary point of the plane and P' its reflection in l. Suppose that $OP = r$ and that OP makes an angle θ with OX_1. Then

(i) $OP' = OP = r$,

(ii) $\angle X_1 OP' = \angle X_1 OP + 2 \angle POl = \theta + 2(\alpha - \theta)$
$$= 2\alpha - \theta.$$

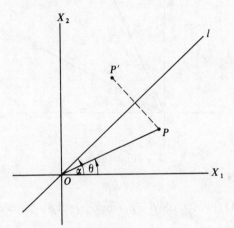

Fig. 195

Now, by elementary trigonometry,
$$p_1 = r \cos\theta, \quad p_2 = r \sin\theta;$$

$$p_1' = r \cos(2\alpha - \theta) = r \cos 2\alpha \cos\theta + r \sin 2\alpha \sin\theta$$
$$= p_1 \cos 2\alpha + p_2 \sin 2\alpha,$$

$$p_2' = r \sin(2\alpha - \theta) = r \sin 2\alpha \cos\theta - r \cos 2\alpha \sin\theta$$
$$= p_1 \sin 2\alpha - p_2 \cos 2\alpha.$$

Hence
$$P[1] = \{p_1 \cos 2\alpha + p_2 \sin 2\alpha, \; p_1 \sin 2\alpha - p_2 \cos 2\alpha\},$$

giving *the coordinates of the reflection of P in l.*

5. More general rotations

Let OP be rotated to OP' through a counterclockwise angle β *about the origin O* (Figure 196). Then, with the notation of Section 4,

$$p_1' = r \cos(\beta + \theta) = r \cos\beta \cos\theta - r \sin\beta \sin\theta$$

$$= p_1 \cos\beta - p_2 \sin\beta,$$

$$p_2' = r \sin(\beta + \theta) = r \sin\beta \cos\theta + r \sin\beta \sin\theta$$

$$= p_1 \sin\beta + p_2 \cos\beta.$$

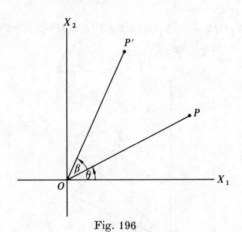

Fig. 196

Hence

$$P[\mathbf{O}_\beta] = \{p_1 \cos\beta - p_2 \sin\beta,\ p_1 \sin\beta + p_2 \cos\beta\},$$

giving *the coordinates of P after rotation about O through an angle β.*

Note. It is unfortunate that the formulae of Sections 4 and 5 are confusingly alike, but they are nevertheless quite distinct. In fact, identity of the transformations would require, *for all values of p_1 and p_2,*
  (i) first coordinates identical:

$$p_1 \cos 2\alpha + p_2 \sin 2\alpha \equiv p_1 \cos\beta - p_2 \sin\beta$$

$$\Rightarrow \cos 2\alpha = \cos\beta \text{ and } \sin 2\alpha = -\sin\beta;$$

  (ii) second coordinates identical:

$$p_1 \sin 2\alpha - p_2 \cos 2\alpha \equiv p_1 \sin\beta + p_2 \cos\beta$$

$$\Rightarrow \sin 2\alpha = \sin\beta \text{ and } -\cos 2\alpha = \cos\beta.$$

We should therefore need

$$\cos\beta = -\cos\beta, \quad \sin\beta = -\sin\beta;$$

but it is not possible to find a value of β to satisfy these equations simultaneously.

Exercise D

1. Solve for [1] and for $[\mathbf{O}_\beta]$ the problems analogous to those in Questions 1–3 of Exercise C, finding the self-corresponding points by *algebraic calculation*.

6. The 'shape' of the transformations

The formulae of Sections 3–5 can all be written as particular cases of a standard form

$$p_1' = \lambda p_1 + \mu p_2, \quad p_2' = \nu p_1 + \rho p_2,$$

where λ, μ, ν, ρ are numbers, not involving p_1 and p_2, which are characteristic of the various transformations. Thus, *writing λ, μ, ν, ρ as a 2×2 matrix in the form*

$$\begin{pmatrix} \lambda & \mu \\ \nu & \rho \end{pmatrix},$$

we have (inserting the numbers from Sections 3–5):

(i)   for $[\mathbf{x}_1]$, $\begin{pmatrix} 1 & 0 \\ 0 & -1 \end{pmatrix}$;

(ii)   for $[\mathbf{x}_2]$, $\begin{pmatrix} -1 & 0 \\ 0 & 1 \end{pmatrix}$;

(iii)   for $[\mathbf{O}_\pi]$, $\begin{pmatrix} -1 & 0 \\ 0 & -1 \end{pmatrix}$;

(iv)   for $[1]$, $\begin{pmatrix} \cos 2\alpha & \sin 2\alpha \\ \sin 2\alpha & -\cos 2\alpha \end{pmatrix}$;

(v)   for $[\mathbf{O}_\beta]$, $\begin{pmatrix} \cos\beta & -\sin\beta \\ \sin\beta & \cos\beta \end{pmatrix}$.

This concept leads directly to the important notion of 'matrix multiplication'. Consider for instance, the matrix corresponding to [1]. Under [1] the coordinate vector (matrix of type 2×1)

$$\mathbf{p} = \begin{pmatrix} p_1 \\ p_2 \end{pmatrix}$$

has been transformed to

$$\mathbf{p}' = \begin{pmatrix} p_1' \\ p_2' \end{pmatrix}$$

by means of the matrix (of type 2×2)

$$\mathbf{1} = \begin{pmatrix} \cos 2\alpha & \sin 2\alpha \\ \sin 2\alpha & -\cos 2\alpha \end{pmatrix}.$$

A sensible notation would have been to write

$$\mathbf{p}' = \mathbf{p}[\mathbf{1}],$$

that is, '$\mathbf{p}'$ is equal to $\mathbf{p}$ under the operation $[\mathbf{1}]$'; but *standard practice puts the matrix* $\mathbf{1}$ *first and the vector* $\mathbf{p}$ *after*, so that the generally accepted notation is

$$\mathbf{p}' = \mathbf{1p}.$$

The symbolism $P' = P[\mathbf{1}]$ of the earlier sections was useful, especially with product formulae such as $P[\mathbf{1m}]$ for the counterclockwise rotation $2 \triangle lUm$. There is little agreement about the order in which *operations* should be written, and we selected that which best suited our purpose. For *matrices*, however, there is much more agreement, and we adopt general practice. This is essentially the reason for using a distinctive symbol such as $[\mathbf{1}]$ for an operation in this section.

In detail, now,

$$\mathbf{p}' = \mathbf{1p}$$

$$\Rightarrow \begin{pmatrix} p_1' \\ p_2' \end{pmatrix} = \begin{pmatrix} \cos 2\alpha & \sin 2\alpha \\ \sin 2\alpha & -\cos 2\alpha \end{pmatrix} \begin{pmatrix} p_1 \\ p_2 \end{pmatrix},$$

and we have seen by calculation that

$$\begin{cases} p_1' = \cos 2\alpha \, . \, p_1 + \sin 2\alpha \, . \, p_2, \\ p_2' = \sin 2\alpha \, . \, p_1 + (-\cos 2\alpha) \, p_2. \end{cases}$$

The formula for p_1' (the *first* element of $\mathbf{p}'$) is found by 'running *along* the *first* row of $\mathbf{1}$ and *down* the column of $\mathbf{p}'$'; the formula for p_2' (the *second* element of $\mathbf{p}'$) is found by 'running *along* the *second* row of $\mathbf{1}$ and *down* the column of $\mathbf{p}'$'.

Exercise E

1. Trace this argument in similar form to deal with the transformation $[\mathbf{O}_\beta]$ given by

$$\mathbf{p}' = \mathbf{O}_\beta \mathbf{p}.$$

2. Repeat Question 1 for $[\mathbf{x}_1]$, $[\mathbf{x}_2]$, $[\mathbf{O}_\pi]$ and the corresponding matrix relations

$$\mathbf{p}' = \mathbf{x}_1\mathbf{p}, \quad \mathbf{p}' = \mathbf{x}_2\mathbf{p}, \quad \mathbf{p}' = \mathbf{O}_\pi\mathbf{p}.$$

7. Transformation products and matrix products: 'homogeneous' transformations

The five transformations given in Section 6 all assume the form

$$\mathbf{p}' = \mathbf{ap},$$

where $\mathbf{a}$ is a matrix of type 2×2. They are subject to one feature that ought to be emphasised explicitly:

$$\mathbf{p} = \mathbf{0} \Rightarrow \mathbf{p}' = \mathbf{0},$$

that is: the origin of coordinates is *self-corresponding* in the transformation $[\mathbf{a}]$. *We are therefore, temporarily, restricting attention to those transformations which have at least one self-corresponding point, and are taking the zero vector to be the vector of one such point.*

For ease of reference, we call such a transformation *homogeneous*. *This is a property of the coordinate system*; the matrix equation representing a given transformation may or may not be homogeneous, as we shall see.

Suppose, then, that $[\mathbf{a}]$, $[\mathbf{b}]$ are two homogeneous transformations and that

$$P' = P[\mathbf{a}], \quad P'' = P'[\mathbf{b}],$$

so that the transformation from P to P'' is

$$P'' = \{P[\mathbf{a}]\}[\mathbf{b}]$$
$$= P\{[\mathbf{a}][\mathbf{b}]\}.$$

In *matrix* terms, this requires the deduction

$$\mathbf{p}' = \mathbf{ap}, \quad \mathbf{p}'' = \mathbf{bp}'$$
$$\Rightarrow \mathbf{p}'' = \mathbf{b}(\mathbf{ap});$$

and we agree to write the last relation in the form

$$\mathbf{p}'' = (\mathbf{ba})\,\mathbf{p}.$$

The matrix $\mathbf{ba}$ is defined as the *product* of the matrices $\mathbf{a}$ and $\mathbf{b}$ in the order that $\mathbf{a}$ *acts first* and $\mathbf{b}$ *second*. (Thus $\mathbf{ab}$ is, usually, quite different from $\mathbf{ba}$.) The problem now is *to find a formula by means of which to express* $\mathbf{ba}$ *as a single matrix.*

In detail, the matrices are

$$\begin{pmatrix} b_{11} & b_{12} \\ b_{21} & b_{22} \end{pmatrix}, \quad \begin{pmatrix} a_{11} & a_{12} \\ a_{21} & a_{22} \end{pmatrix}.$$

To find an expression for the product, we trace the transformations in detail, following the pattern of Section 6:

$$\mathbf{p}' = \mathbf{a}\mathbf{p}$$

$$\Rightarrow \begin{cases} p_1' = a_{11}p_1 + a_{12}p_2, \\ p_2' = a_{21}p_1 + a_{22}p_2; \end{cases}$$

$$\mathbf{p}'' = \mathbf{b}\mathbf{p}';$$

$$\Rightarrow \begin{cases} p_1'' = b_{11}p_1' + b_{12}p_2', \\ p_2'' = b_{21}p_1' + b_{22}p_2'; \end{cases}$$

$$\Rightarrow \begin{cases} p_1'' = b_{11}(a_{11}p_1 + a_{12}p_2) + b_{12}(a_{21}p_1 + a_{22}p_2), \\ p_2'' = b_{21}(a_{11}p_1 + a_{12}p_2) + b_{22}(a_{21}p_1 + a_{22}p_2); \end{cases}$$

$$\Rightarrow \begin{cases} p_1'' = (b_{11}a_{11} + b_{12}a_{21})\,p_1 + (b_{11}a_{12} + b_{12}a_{22})\,p_2, \\ p_2'' = (b_{21}a_{11} + b_{22}a_{21})\,p_1 + (b_{21}a_{12} + b_{22}a_{22})\,p_2. \end{cases}$$

Hence
$$\mathbf{p}'' = \mathbf{c}\mathbf{p},$$

where
$$\mathbf{c} = \begin{pmatrix} b_{11}a_{11} + b_{12}a_{21} & b_{11}a_{12} + b_{12}a_{22} \\ b_{21}a_{11} + b_{22}a_{21} & b_{21}a_{12} + b_{22}a_{22} \end{pmatrix}.$$

In detail,

$$\begin{pmatrix} b_{11}a_{11} + b_{12}a_{21} & b_{11}a_{12} + b_{12}a_{22} \\ b_{21}a_{11} + b_{22}a_{21} & b_{21}a_{12} + b_{22}a_{22} \end{pmatrix} = \begin{pmatrix} b_{11} & b_{12} \\ b_{21} & b_{22} \end{pmatrix} \begin{pmatrix} a_{11} & a_{12} \\ a_{21} & a_{22} \end{pmatrix}.$$

The rule is exactly analogous to the one described in Section 6:

To find the element c_{ij} in the i-th row and j-th column of $\mathbf{ba}$, take row i of $\mathbf{b}$ and column j of $\mathbf{a}$. Multiply corresponding elements and add.

For example, c_{12} is found from the first row

$$b_{11} \quad b_{12}$$

of $\mathbf{b}$ and the second column

$$a_{12}$$
$$a_{22}$$

of $\mathbf{a}$. The sum of corresponding products is

$$b_{11}a_{12} + b_{12}a_{22},$$

which is precisely the element in row 1 and column 2 of $\mathbf{c}$.

Important note: The transformation of *points* given by

$$P' = P[\mathbf{a}]\,[\mathbf{b}],$$

is represented in *matrix language* by the relation

$$\mathbf{p}' = \mathbf{bap}.$$

In each case, the transformation [**a**], of matrix **a**, acts first, and the transformation [**b**], of matrix **b**, acts second.

The more general formula should be stated:

Let **a** be a matrix of type $m \times n$ and **b** a matrix of type $r \times s$. To find the element c_{ij} in row i and column j of $\mathbf{c} \equiv \mathbf{ba}$, take

(i) row i of **b**: $\{b_{i1}, b_{i2}, b_{i3}, ..., b_{in}\}$,

(ii) column j of **a**: $\{a_{1j}, a_{2j}, a_{3j}, ..., a_{rj}\}$.

Then $$c_{ij} = b_{i1}a_{1j} + b_{i2}a_{2j} + b_{i3}a_{3j} + \dots.$$

This product has a meaning only if the number of elements in a row of **b** is equal to the number of elements of a column of **a**: that is, if

$$n = r.$$

Then $$c_{ij} = \sum_{\lambda=1}^{n} b_{i\lambda}a_{\lambda j}.$$

There are m rows (m values of i) in **c** and s columns (s values of j). Hence **c** is of type $m \times s$. This is the *domino rule* for types:

'type $(m \times n)$' multiplied by 'type $(n \times s)$' is 'type $(m \times s)$',

or $$\underset{(m \times n)}{\mathbf{a}} \quad \underset{(n \times s)}{\mathbf{b}} = \underset{(m \times s)}{\mathbf{c}}.$$

When a matrix is multiplied by itself, the 'power' notation is used:

$$\mathbf{aa} = \mathbf{a}^2, \quad \mathbf{aaa} = \mathbf{a}^3.$$

The associative law. One tedious step must be faced. (The reader is advised, having faced it, to pass on.)

Given two matrices **a**, **b**, of types $m \times n$, $n \times p$, their product **ab**, of type $m \times p$, has been defined. Given a further matrix **c**, of type $p \times q$, the product $(\mathbf{ab})\mathbf{c}$, of type $m \times q$ can also be formed; and this process can be continued indefinitely.

What is not clear, though it is true, is that the product $(\mathbf{ab})\mathbf{c}$ can be calculated by the alternative process $\mathbf{a}(\mathbf{bc})$ to give the same answer. As a consequence, the brackets can be dropped and the symbol

$$\mathbf{abc}$$

used without ambiguity. (It is, of course, quite different from, say, **bca**, which might not even exist.)

We prove, then, that

$$(\mathbf{ab})\mathbf{c} = \mathbf{a}(\mathbf{bc});$$

or, to be more correct, we evaluate the left-hand side in detail and leave the reader to verify that the right-hand side gives the same answer.

By definition,

$$(\mathbf{ab}) = \begin{pmatrix} a_{11}\, a_{12} \\ a_{21}\, a_{22} \end{pmatrix} \begin{pmatrix} b_{11}\, b_{12} \\ b_{21}\, b_{22} \end{pmatrix}$$

$$= \begin{pmatrix} a_{11}b_{11}+a_{12}b_{21} & a_{11}b_{12}+a_{12}b_{22} \\ a_{21}b_{11}+a_{22}b_{21} & a_{21}b_{12}+a_{22}b_{22} \end{pmatrix}.$$

Then

$$(\mathbf{ab})\,\mathbf{c} = \begin{pmatrix} a_{11}b_{11}+a_{12}b_{21} & a_{11}b_{12}+a_{12}b_{22} \\ a_{21}b_{11}+a_{22}b_{21} & a_{21}b_{12}+a_{22}b_{22} \end{pmatrix} \begin{pmatrix} c_{11} & c_{12} \\ c_{21} & c_{21} \end{pmatrix}$$

$$= \begin{pmatrix} (a_{11}b_{11}+a_{12}b_{21})\,c_{11}+(a_{11}b_{12}+a_{12}b_{22})\,c_{21} \\ (a_{21}b_{11}+a_{22}b_{21})\,c_{11}+(a_{21}b_{12}+a_{22}b_{22})\,c_{21} \end{pmatrix}$$

$$\begin{matrix} (a_{11}b_{11}+a_{12}b_{21})\,c_{12}+(a_{11}b_{12}+a_{12}b_{22})\,c_{22} \\ (a_{21}b_{11}+a_{22}b_{21})\,c_{12}+(a_{21}b_{12}+a_{22}b_{22})\,c_{22} \end{matrix}.$$

Calculation of $\mathbf{a}(\mathbf{bc})$ may now be made, and the result checked.

Note, though, that a pattern has begun to emerge. If the result for $(\mathbf{ab})\,\mathbf{c}$ is written as

$$\mathbf{d} = \begin{pmatrix} d_{11} & d_{12} \\ d_{21} & d_{22} \end{pmatrix},$$

then each element of $\mathbf{d}$ is the sum, after removal of brackets, of *four* terms, each of which is the product of an a with a b with a c. More precisely, the term d_{12}, say, is the sum of four terms of the form

$$a_{1.}\, b_{..}\, c_{.2},$$

where the missing numbers are 1 or 2, fitted according to 'domino' rule, to give, as the total of possibilities,

$$a_{11}b_{11}c_{12}, \quad a_{12}b_{21}c_{12}, \quad a_{11}b_{12}c_{22}, \quad a_{12}b_{22}c_{22}.$$

The numbers d_{11}, d_{21}, d_{22} follow a similar pattern, which is precisely the same as that obtained for $\mathbf{a}(\mathbf{bc})$.

Illustration 1. *Change of axes.* Let the coordinates of a point P be $\{p_1, p_2\}$ referred to a rectangular coordinate system X_1OX_2 and $\{p_1', p_2'\}$ referred to a rectangular coordinate system U_1OU_2 in which $\measuredangle X_1OU_1 = \theta$ (Figure 197). It is required *to express p_1', p_2' in terms of* p_1, p_2, θ.

Rotate the system U_1OU_2, with P 'attached', through a *clockwise* angle θ so that OU_1 lies along OX_1. Let P assume the position P^*, whose coordinates referred to X_1OX_2 are now $\{p_1', p_2'\}$. Then, by the rotation formulae,

$$\mathbf{p}' = \mathbf{O}_{(-\theta)}\mathbf{p}$$

$$\Rightarrow \begin{pmatrix} p_1' \\ p_2' \end{pmatrix} = \begin{pmatrix} \cos(-\theta) & -\sin(-\theta) \\ \sin(-\theta) & \cos(-\theta) \end{pmatrix} \begin{pmatrix} p_1 \\ p_2 \end{pmatrix}$$

$$= \begin{pmatrix} \cos\theta & \sin\theta \\ -\sin\theta & \cos\theta \end{pmatrix} \begin{pmatrix} p_1 \\ p_2 \end{pmatrix}$$

$$\Rightarrow \begin{cases} p_1' = p_1\cos\theta + p_2\sin\theta, \\ p_2' = -p_1\sin\theta + p_2\cos\theta. \end{cases}$$

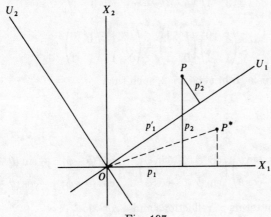

Fig. 197

Exercise F

1. Prove that

$$\begin{pmatrix} \cos\theta & \sin\theta \\ \sin\theta & -\cos\theta \end{pmatrix}^2 = \begin{pmatrix} 1 & 0 \\ 0 & 1 \end{pmatrix}.$$

2. Prove that

$$\begin{pmatrix} \cos\theta & -\sin\theta \\ \sin\theta & \cos\theta \end{pmatrix}^2 = \begin{pmatrix} \cos 2\theta & -\sin 2\theta \\ \sin 2\theta & \cos 2\theta \end{pmatrix}.$$

3. Prove that

$$\begin{pmatrix} 1 & 0 \\ 0 & 1 \end{pmatrix}\begin{pmatrix} a_{11} & a_{12} \\ a_{21} & a_{22} \end{pmatrix} = \begin{pmatrix} a_{11} & a_{12} \\ a_{21} & a_{2?} \end{pmatrix}\begin{pmatrix} 1 & 0 \\ 0 & 1 \end{pmatrix} = \begin{pmatrix} a_{11} & a_{12} \\ a_{21} & a_{22} \end{pmatrix}.$$

4. Prove that, if **a** and **b** are matrices of type 2×2 and **p** is a column vector of type 2×1, and if $\mathbf{a}^T$, $\mathbf{b}^T$, $\mathbf{p}^T$ are the corresponding transposes, then

$$(\mathbf{ap})^T = \mathbf{p}^T \mathbf{a}^T, \quad (\mathbf{ab})^T = \mathbf{b}^T \mathbf{a}^T.$$

5. Prove that, for the square $\mathbf{a}^2$ of a matrix **a** to have meaning, it is necessary that **a** is a square matrix.

6. Prove that $\mathbf{a}^T \mathbf{a}$ is a symmetric matrix.

7. Prove that

$$\begin{pmatrix} 3 & 5 \\ 1 & 2 \end{pmatrix} \begin{pmatrix} 2 & -5 \\ -1 & 3 \end{pmatrix} = \begin{pmatrix} 1 & 0 \\ 0 & 1 \end{pmatrix}.$$

8. Prove that, in general,

$$\begin{pmatrix} 1 & 2 \\ 3 & 4 \end{pmatrix} \begin{pmatrix} a & b \\ c & d \end{pmatrix} \neq \begin{pmatrix} a & b \\ c & d \end{pmatrix} \begin{pmatrix} 1 & 2 \\ 3 & 4 \end{pmatrix}$$

and that

$$\begin{pmatrix} 1 & 0 \\ 1 & 1 \end{pmatrix} \begin{pmatrix} 1 & 1 \\ 0 & 1 \end{pmatrix} \neq \begin{pmatrix} 1 & 1 \\ 0 & 1 \end{pmatrix} \begin{pmatrix} 1 & 0 \\ 1 & 1 \end{pmatrix}.$$

9. Find matrices **a**, **b** of type 2×2, such that
  (i) $\mathbf{ab} \neq \mathbf{ba}$;
  (ii) $\mathbf{ab} = \mathbf{ba}$.

10. Prove that

$$\begin{pmatrix} \cos\theta & \sin\theta \\ \sin\theta & -\cos\theta \end{pmatrix} \begin{pmatrix} \cos\phi & \sin\phi \\ \sin\phi & -\cos\phi \end{pmatrix} = \begin{pmatrix} \cos(\theta-\phi) & -\sin(\theta-\phi) \\ \cos(\theta-\phi) & \cos(\theta-\phi) \end{pmatrix}$$

and interpret in terms of reflections and a rotation.

11. Verify the associative law $\mathbf{a(bc)} = \mathbf{(ab)\,c}$ in the particular cases:

  (i) $\mathbf{a} = (1, 2)$, $\mathbf{b} = \begin{pmatrix} 1 & 3 \\ 0 & -2 \end{pmatrix}$, $\mathbf{c} = \begin{pmatrix} 1 & 2 & 3 \\ 3 & -2 & 1 \end{pmatrix}$;

  (ii) $\mathbf{a} = (x, y)$, $\mathbf{b} = \begin{pmatrix} 2 & -3 \\ -3 & 5 \end{pmatrix}$, $\mathbf{c} = \begin{pmatrix} x \\ y \end{pmatrix}$;

  (iii) $\mathbf{a} = \begin{pmatrix} 1 & 2 \\ 3 & 4 \end{pmatrix}$, $\mathbf{b} = \begin{pmatrix} 4 & 3 \\ 2 & 1 \end{pmatrix}$, $\mathbf{c} = \begin{pmatrix} 0 & 3 \\ 2 & 1 \end{pmatrix}$;

  (iv) $\mathbf{a} = \begin{pmatrix} 1 & 0 \\ 0 & 1 \end{pmatrix}$, $\mathbf{b} = \begin{pmatrix} p & q \\ r & s \end{pmatrix}$, $\mathbf{c} = \begin{pmatrix} 1 & 0 \\ 0 & 1 \end{pmatrix}$.

8. The transpose of a product

Let
$$\mathbf{c} = \mathbf{ab}$$

be a matrix which is the product of two matrices $\mathbf{a}$, $\mathbf{b}$ of types $m \times n$, $n \times p$. To prove that *the transpose of* $\mathbf{c}$ *is the product* $\mathbf{b}^T \mathbf{a}^T$, *in that order, of the transposed matrices* $\mathbf{b}^T$, $\mathbf{a}^T$ *of types* $p \times n$, $n \times m$:

The element in row i and column j of the transpose $\mathbf{c}^T$ is the element in row j and column i of $\mathbf{c}$, namely

$$\sum_{\lambda=1}^{n} a_{j\lambda} b_{\lambda i}.$$

But
$$a_{j\lambda} = a_{\lambda j}^T, \quad b_{\lambda i} = b_{i\lambda}^T,$$

where $a_{\lambda j}^T$, $b_{i\lambda}^T$ are elements of $\mathbf{a}^T$, $\mathbf{b}^T$; and so

$$a_{j\lambda} b_{\lambda i} = a_{\lambda j}^T b_{i\lambda}^T$$
$$= b_{i\lambda}^T a_{\lambda j}^T,$$

so that the element in row i and column j of $\mathbf{c}^T$ is

$$\sum_{\lambda=1}^{n} b_{i\lambda}^T a_{\lambda j}^T,$$

which is the element in row i and column j of $\mathbf{b}^T \mathbf{a}^T$. Hence

$$\mathbf{c}^T = \mathbf{b}^T \mathbf{a}^T.$$

Exercise G

Verify the result $\mathbf{c}^T = \mathbf{b}^T \mathbf{a}^T$ in the following cases:

1. $\mathbf{a} = \begin{pmatrix} 1 & 2 \\ 3 & 4 \end{pmatrix}$, $\mathbf{b} = \begin{pmatrix} p & q \\ r & s \end{pmatrix}$.

2. $\mathbf{a} = \begin{pmatrix} 1 & 2 \\ 3 & 4 \end{pmatrix}$, $\mathbf{b} = \begin{pmatrix} p & q & x \\ r & s & y \end{pmatrix}$.

3. $\mathbf{a} = \begin{pmatrix} 1 & 3 \\ 3 & 4 \end{pmatrix}$, $\mathbf{b} = \begin{pmatrix} p \\ q \end{pmatrix}$.

4. $\mathbf{a} = \begin{pmatrix} 3 & 1 \\ 5 & 2 \end{pmatrix}$, $\mathbf{b} = \begin{pmatrix} 2 & -1 \\ -5 & 3 \end{pmatrix}$.

5. $\mathbf{a} = (1 \quad 2)$, $\mathbf{b} = \begin{pmatrix} p & q \\ r & s \end{pmatrix}$.

9. Unit and inverse

Unit. The questions in Exercise G have indicated that a matrix like

$$\begin{pmatrix} 1 & 0 \\ 0 & 1 \end{pmatrix}$$

acts as a unit for multiplication in the sense that any matrix that can be multiplied by it remains unaltered.

More generally, the $n \times n$ matrix

$$I_n = \begin{pmatrix} 1 & 0 & 0 & \dots & 0 \\ 0 & 1 & 0 & \dots & 0 \\ \multicolumn{5}{c}{\dotfill} \\ 0 & 0 & 0 & \dots & 1 \end{pmatrix},$$

where $a_{ij} = 1$ when $i = j$ and $a_{ij} = 0$ when $i \neq j$, is called the *unit matrix of order* n. The suffix n is often omitted when the meaning is clear, and the unit is then written I.

Exercise H

1. Prove that, if **c** is a matrix of type $m \times n$, then

$$I_m c = c I_n = c.$$

2. Prove that

$$\begin{pmatrix} 0 & -1 \\ 1 & 0 \end{pmatrix}^2 = -I.$$

(So there is a matrix whose square is the negative of the unit matrix.)

3. Prove that, if **ua** = **a**, where

$$a = \begin{pmatrix} 1 & 2 \\ 3 & 4 \end{pmatrix},$$

then **u** must be the unit matrix **I**.

4. Prove that, if **ua** = **a**, where

$$a = \begin{pmatrix} 1 & 2 \\ 3 & 6 \end{pmatrix},$$

then **u** must be a matrix of the form

$$\begin{pmatrix} 1-3\lambda, & \lambda \\ 1-3\mu, & \mu \end{pmatrix},$$

where λ and μ are arbitrary.

Inverse. One essential step in matrix theory is to establish a process analogous to division. In essence, division by a matrix **a** requires the existence of some matrix that can be allotted, reasonably, a notation $\mathbf{a}^{-1}$. Then *multiplication* by $\mathbf{a}^{-1}$ can take the place occupied by *division* in elementary algebra.

Such a matrix $\mathbf{a}^{-1}$, when it exists (and there are matrices **a** for which it does not), is called the *inverse* of **a**. A matrix which does have an inverse is said to be *invertible* or, somewhat oddly, *non-singular*.

A matrix $\mathbf{a}^{-1}$ will be required, by definition, to satisfy the relations

$$\mathbf{a}^{-1}\mathbf{a} = \mathbf{a}\mathbf{a}^{-1} = \mathbf{I}.$$

Note that *the inverse of a matrix* **a**, *when it exists, is unique:* Suppose that, on the contrary, there were two inverses, **x** and **y**. Then

$$\mathbf{xa} = \mathbf{ax} = \mathbf{I}, \quad \mathbf{ya} = \mathbf{ay} = \mathbf{I}.$$

From the first, $\qquad\qquad \mathbf{xay} = \mathbf{Iy} = \mathbf{y};$

from the second, $\qquad\quad \mathbf{xay} = \mathbf{xI} = \mathbf{x}.$

Hence $\qquad\qquad\qquad \mathbf{x} = \mathbf{y}.$

Illustration 2. Consider, for example, the 'rotation' matrix

$$\mathbf{a} = \begin{pmatrix} \cos\theta & -\sin\theta \\ \sin\theta & \cos\theta \end{pmatrix}$$

and the transformation from P to P' given by

$$\mathbf{p}' = \mathbf{a}\mathbf{p}.$$

If $\mathbf{a}^{-1}$ exists, we can '*solve*' *for* **p** *in terms of* $\mathbf{p}'$ in the form

$$\mathbf{a}^{-1}\mathbf{p}' = \mathbf{a}^{-1}(\mathbf{a}\mathbf{p}) = (\mathbf{a}^{-1}\mathbf{a})\,\mathbf{p} = \mathbf{I}\mathbf{p}$$
$$= \mathbf{p},$$

so that $\qquad\qquad \mathbf{p}' = \mathbf{a}\mathbf{p} \Leftrightarrow \mathbf{p} = \mathbf{a}^{-1}\mathbf{p}',$

and we observe the interchange of roles between $\mathbf{p}'$, **p** and between $\mathbf{a}, \mathbf{a}^{-1}$.

Consider, then, the details of the relation $\mathbf{p}' = \mathbf{a}\mathbf{p}$:

$$\mathbf{p}' = \mathbf{a}\mathbf{p}$$

$$\Rightarrow \begin{pmatrix} p_1' \\ p_2' \end{pmatrix} = \begin{pmatrix} \cos\theta & -\sin\theta \\ \sin\theta & \cos\theta \end{pmatrix} \begin{pmatrix} p_1 \\ p_2 \end{pmatrix}$$

$$\Rightarrow \begin{cases} p_1' = p_1\cos\theta - p_2\sin\theta, \\ p_2' = p_1\sin\theta + p_2\cos\theta \end{cases}$$

$$\Rightarrow \begin{cases} p_1' \cos\theta + p_2' \sin\theta = p_1, \\ -p_1' \sin\theta + p_2' \cos\theta = p_2 \end{cases}$$

$$\Rightarrow \begin{cases} p_1 = p_1' \cos\theta + p_2' \sin\theta, \\ p_2 = -p_1' \sin\theta + p_2' \cos\theta \end{cases}$$

$$\Rightarrow \mathbf{p} = \begin{pmatrix} \cos\theta & \sin\theta \\ -\sin\theta & \cos\theta \end{pmatrix} \mathbf{p}'.$$

This is to be equivalent to the relation, obtained above,

$$\mathbf{p} = \mathbf{a}^{-1}\mathbf{p}',$$

and so
$$\mathbf{a}^{-1} = \begin{pmatrix} \cos\theta & \sin\theta \\ -\sin\theta & \cos\theta \end{pmatrix},$$

an explicit expression for the inverse of $\mathbf{a}$.

The formula can also be seen directly from the isometry: The operation of the matrix

$$\mathbf{a} = \begin{pmatrix} \cos\theta & -\sin\theta \\ \sin\theta & \cos\theta \end{pmatrix}$$

rotates a ray OP through an angle θ, and the inverse $\mathbf{a}^{-1}$ may therefore be expected to rotate it back again, replacing θ by $-\theta$. Then

$$\mathbf{a}^{-1} = \begin{pmatrix} \cos\theta & \sin\theta \\ -\sin\theta & \cos\theta \end{pmatrix}.$$

It is easy to check that, indeed,

$$\begin{pmatrix} \cos\theta & -\sin\theta \\ \sin\theta & \cos\theta \end{pmatrix} \begin{pmatrix} \cos\theta & \sin\theta \\ -\sin\theta & \cos\theta \end{pmatrix} = \begin{pmatrix} 1 & 0 \\ 0 & 1 \end{pmatrix}.$$

Illustration 3. Consider now, with an eye to non-invertible cases, the matrix

$$\mathbf{a} = \begin{pmatrix} 1 & 2 \\ 3 & k \end{pmatrix},$$

where k is any number.

Start, as in Illustration 2, with the relation

$$\mathbf{p}' = \mathbf{a}\mathbf{p}$$

$$\Rightarrow \begin{pmatrix} p_1' \\ p_2' \end{pmatrix} = \begin{pmatrix} 1 & 2 \\ 3 & k \end{pmatrix} \begin{pmatrix} p_1 \\ p_2 \end{pmatrix}$$

$$\Rightarrow \begin{cases} p_1' = p_1 + 2p_2, \\ p_2' = 3p_1 + kp_2 \end{cases}$$

$$\Rightarrow \begin{cases} kp_1' - 2p_2' = (k-6)\,p_1, \\ -3p_1' + p_2' = (k-6)\,p_2 \end{cases}$$

$$\Rightarrow (k-6)\begin{pmatrix} p_1 \\ p_2 \end{pmatrix} = \begin{pmatrix} k & -2 \\ -3 & 1 \end{pmatrix}\begin{pmatrix} p_1' \\ p_2' \end{pmatrix}.$$

If, now, k has *any value except* 6, we can 'solve' for **p** in the form

$$\begin{pmatrix} p_1 \\ p_2 \end{pmatrix} = \frac{1}{k-6}\begin{pmatrix} k & -2 \\ -3 & 1 \end{pmatrix}\begin{pmatrix} p_1' \\ p_2' \end{pmatrix}.$$

For example, if $k = 8$, the relation

$$\mathbf{p}' = \mathbf{ap},$$

with

$$\mathbf{a} = \begin{pmatrix} 1 & 2 \\ 3 & 8 \end{pmatrix},$$

leads to the 'inverse' relation

$$\mathbf{p} = \mathbf{a}^{-1}\mathbf{p}'$$

with

$$\mathbf{a}^{-1} = \tfrac{1}{2}\begin{pmatrix} 8 & -2 \\ -3 & 1 \end{pmatrix}$$

$$= \begin{pmatrix} 4 & -1 \\ -\tfrac{3}{2} & \tfrac{1}{2} \end{pmatrix};$$

and it is easy to check that, indeed,

$$\begin{pmatrix} 4 & -1 \\ -\tfrac{3}{2} & \tfrac{1}{2} \end{pmatrix}\begin{pmatrix} 1 & 2 \\ 3 & 8 \end{pmatrix} = \begin{pmatrix} 1 & 0 \\ 0 & 1 \end{pmatrix}.$$

For a general value of $k\,(\neq 6)$, we have, similarly,

$$\mathbf{a}^{-1} = \frac{1}{k-6}\begin{pmatrix} k & -2 \\ -3 & 1 \end{pmatrix}.$$

On the other hand, *when $k = 6$*, the relation

$$(6-6)\begin{pmatrix} p_1 \\ p_2 \end{pmatrix} = \begin{pmatrix} 6 & -2 \\ -3 & 1 \end{pmatrix}\begin{pmatrix} p_1' \\ p_2' \end{pmatrix}$$

cannot be 'solved' for $\mathbf{p}$: the coefficient of $\mathbf{p}$ is zero, and what we have obtained is

$$\begin{pmatrix} 0 \\ 0 \end{pmatrix} = \begin{pmatrix} 6 & -2 \\ -3 & 1 \end{pmatrix} \begin{pmatrix} p_1' \\ p_2' \end{pmatrix},$$

a relation which tells us nothing about $\mathbf{p}$. Thus, *in the case $k = 6$, $\mathbf{a}^{-1}$ does not exist.*

Check. We might also proceed as follows (generally, but restricting attention here to the case $k = 6$):

If
$$\mathbf{a}^{-1} = \begin{pmatrix} a & b \\ c & d \end{pmatrix},$$

then
$$\begin{pmatrix} a & b \\ c & d \end{pmatrix} \begin{pmatrix} 1 & 2 \\ 3 & 6 \end{pmatrix} = \begin{pmatrix} 1 & 0 \\ 0 & 1 \end{pmatrix}$$

$$\Rightarrow \begin{pmatrix} a+3b & 2a+6b \\ c+3d & 2c+6d \end{pmatrix} = \begin{pmatrix} 1 & 0 \\ 0 & 1 \end{pmatrix}$$

$$\Rightarrow \begin{cases} a+3b = 1, & 2a+6b = 0, \\ c+3d = 0, & 2c+6d = 1, \end{cases}$$

equations which are incompatible.

Finally, a remark in terms of transformations may be useful.

Consider a transformation

$$\mathbf{p}' = \mathbf{a}\mathbf{p},$$

where
$$\mathbf{a} = \begin{pmatrix} 1 & 2 \\ 3 & 6 \end{pmatrix}.$$

This gives
$$p_1' = p_1 + 2p_2,$$
$$p_2' = 3p_1 + 6p_2.$$

Immediately,
$$p_1' - 3p_2' = 0,$$

so that *the transform of P always lies on the line whose equation is*

$$p_1' - 3p_2' = 0.$$

For example, as in Figure 198,

$$P\{1, 0\} \to P'\{1, 3\},$$
$$Q\{0, 1\} \to Q'\{2, 6\},$$
$$R\{1, 1\} \to R'\{3, 9\}.$$

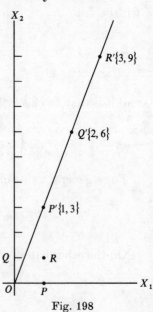

Fig. 198

To find a point U, say, from which a given point U' arises, *there is thus no answer unless U' lies on the specific straight line.* In other words, the plane as a whole cannot be inverted, and so $\mathbf{a}^{-1}$ cannot exist.

These examples cover the essentials of what we require in this context, but a calculation for the general case of 2×2 matrices seems desirable to prepare for some developments that are to come later.

Let

$$\mathbf{a} = \begin{pmatrix} a_{11} & a_{12} \\ a_{21} & a_{22} \end{pmatrix}$$

be a given matrix, and consider the transformation

$$\mathbf{p}' = \mathbf{a}\mathbf{p}$$

$$\Rightarrow \begin{pmatrix} p_1' \\ p_2' \end{pmatrix} = \begin{pmatrix} a_{11} & a_{12} \\ a_{21} & a_{22} \end{pmatrix} \begin{pmatrix} p_1 \\ p_2 \end{pmatrix}$$

$$\Rightarrow \begin{cases} p_1' = a_{11}\, p_1 + a_{12}\, p_2, \\ p_2' = a_{21}\, p_1 + a_{22}\, p_2 \end{cases}$$

$$\Rightarrow \begin{cases} a_{22}\, p_1' - a_{12}\, p_2' = (a_{11} a_{22} - a_{12} a_{21})\, p_1, \\ -a_{21}\, p_1' + a_{11}\, p_2' = (a_{11} a_{22} - a_{12} a_{21})\, p_2. \end{cases}$$

The expression

$$a_{11} a_{22} - a_{12} a_{21}$$

assumes considerable importance in the theory and is called the *determinant of the matrix* $\mathbf{a}$, written

$$|\mathbf{a}| \quad \text{or} \quad \det \mathbf{a}.$$

Thus

$$|\mathbf{a}| = \det \mathbf{a} = \begin{vmatrix} a_{11} & a_{12} \\ a_{21} & a_{22} \end{vmatrix} = a_{11} a_{22} - a_{12} a_{21}.$$

The relations just obtained are

$$\begin{cases} |\mathbf{a}|\, p_1 = a_{22} p_1' - a_{12}\, p_2', \\ |\mathbf{a}|\, p_2 = a_{21} p_1' + a_{11}\, p_2'. \end{cases}$$

(i) When $|\mathbf{a}| \neq 0$, we have

$$\mathbf{p} = \mathbf{a}^{-1}\mathbf{p}',$$

where

$$\mathbf{a}^{-1} = \frac{1}{|\mathbf{a}|} \begin{pmatrix} a_{22} & -a_{12} \\ -a_{21} & a_{11} \end{pmatrix}.$$

(ii) When $|\mathbf{a}| = 0$, $\mathbf{p}$ cannot be expressed in terms of $\mathbf{p'}$. There are therefore the two alternatives:

(i) $|\mathbf{a}| \neq 0 \Rightarrow \mathbf{a}^{-1} = \dfrac{1}{|\mathbf{a}|} \begin{pmatrix} a_{22} & -a_{12} \\ a_{21} & a_{11} \end{pmatrix}$,

(ii) $|\mathbf{a}| = 0 \Rightarrow \mathbf{a}^{-1}$ does not exist.

With the language defined earlier,

$$\det \mathbf{a} \neq 0 \Leftrightarrow \mathbf{a} \text{ is invertible (non-singular)};$$

$$\det \mathbf{a} = 0 \Leftrightarrow \mathbf{a} \text{ is non-invertible (singular)}.$$

Exercise I

1. Find the inverses of the following matrices:

(i) $\begin{pmatrix} 1 & 0 \\ 1 & 1 \end{pmatrix}$, (ii) $\begin{pmatrix} 1 & 0 \\ 1 & -1 \end{pmatrix}$, (iii) $\begin{pmatrix} 1 & 0 \\ -4 & 3 \end{pmatrix}$, (iv) $\begin{pmatrix} 1 & 2 \\ 0 & -1 \end{pmatrix}$.

2. Prove that each of the following matrices is non-invertible and find, in each case, the equation of the line containing the transforms by it of the points of a plane:

(i) $\begin{pmatrix} 1 & 2 \\ 2 & 4 \end{pmatrix}$, (ii) $\begin{pmatrix} \cos\theta & \sin\theta \\ -\cos\theta & -\sin\theta \end{pmatrix}$, (iii) $\begin{pmatrix} 2 & -1 \\ -4 & 2 \end{pmatrix}$.

3. *The Cayley–Hamilton theorem for 2×2 non-invertible matrices:*

(i) Prove that, if $\qquad \mathbf{a} = \begin{pmatrix} a_{11} & a_{12} \\ a_{21} & a_{22} \end{pmatrix}$,

then $\qquad |\mathbf{a}|\,\mathbf{a}^{-1} = \begin{pmatrix} a_{22} & -a_{12} \\ -a_{21} & a_{22} \end{pmatrix}$

and show that $\qquad |\mathbf{a}|\,\mathbf{a}^{-1} + \mathbf{a} = (a_{11} + a_{22})\,\mathbf{I}$.

Deduce that $\qquad \mathbf{a}^2 - (a_{11} + a_{22})\,\mathbf{a} + |\mathbf{a}|\,\mathbf{I} = \mathbf{0}$.

(ii) Prove that

$$\det(\mathbf{a} - \lambda\mathbf{I}) = \lambda^2 - (a_{11} + a_{22})\,\lambda + |\mathbf{a}|,$$

so that $\quad \det(\mathbf{a} - \lambda\mathbf{I}) = 0 \Rightarrow \lambda^2 - (a_{11} + a_{22})\,\lambda + |\mathbf{a}| = 0$.

(The formal identity of the equations in (i) and (ii) establishes this very special case of a general result known as the *Cayley–Hamilton theorem*.)

4. Prove that $\qquad\qquad \det\mathbf{I} = 1$.

5. Prove that, if $\mathbf{a}$ is a matrix of type 2×2, then

$$\det(k\mathbf{a}) = k^2 \det\mathbf{a}.$$

6. Examine geometrically, as in the text, the transformations

$$\mathbf{p}' = \mathbf{a}\mathbf{p}$$

when **a** is

(i) $\begin{pmatrix} 1 & 2 \\ -2 & -4 \end{pmatrix}$, (ii) $\begin{pmatrix} 3 & 1 \\ 6 & 2 \end{pmatrix}$, (iii) $\begin{pmatrix} 0 & 0 \\ 1 & 2 \end{pmatrix}$, (iv) $\begin{pmatrix} 0 & -1 \\ 0 & 2 \end{pmatrix}$.

7. Prove that, if

$$\mathbf{a} = \begin{pmatrix} 1 & 3 \\ 2 & 7 \end{pmatrix},$$

then $\det \mathbf{a} = 1$,

$$\mathbf{a}^{-1} = \begin{pmatrix} 7 & -3 \\ -2 & 1 \end{pmatrix}.$$

(i) Write down other matrices with the property $\det \mathbf{a} = 1$ and give their inverses.

(ii) Write down matrices with the property $\det \mathbf{a} = -1$ and give their inverses.

10. The determinant of a product

It is a general result that, *if* **a**, **b** *are matrices of type* $n \times n$, *then*

$$\det \mathbf{a}\mathbf{b} = (\det \mathbf{a})(\det \mathbf{b}).$$

We prove this result for $n = 2$.

For ease of reading, write

$$\mathbf{a} = \begin{pmatrix} p & q \\ r & s \end{pmatrix}, \quad \mathbf{b} = \begin{pmatrix} \lambda & \mu \\ \nu & \rho \end{pmatrix}.$$

Then
$$\mathbf{a}\mathbf{b} = \begin{pmatrix} p\lambda + q\nu & p\mu + q\rho \\ r\lambda + s\nu & r\mu + s\rho \end{pmatrix},$$

so that
$$\det \mathbf{a}\mathbf{b} = (p\lambda + q\nu)(r\mu + s\rho) - (p\mu + q\rho)(r\lambda + s\nu).$$

Collect terms in pr, ps, qr, qs:

$$\det \mathbf{a}\mathbf{b} = pr(\lambda\mu - \mu\lambda) + ps(\lambda\rho - \mu\nu) + qr(\nu\mu - \rho\lambda) + qs(\nu\rho - \rho\nu)$$

$$= ps(\lambda\rho - \mu\nu) - qr(\lambda\rho - \mu\nu)$$

$$= (ps - qr)(\lambda\rho - \mu\nu)$$

$$= (\det \mathbf{a})(\det \mathbf{b}).$$

Exercise J

1. Evaluate explicitly, for each of the following pairs of determinants **a**, **b**, (i) the product **ab**, (ii) the product **ba**, (iii) the determinants det **a**, det **b**, det (**ab**), det (**ba**):

(*a*) $\mathbf{a} = \begin{pmatrix} 1 & 2 \\ 3 & 4 \end{pmatrix}$, $\mathbf{b} = \begin{pmatrix} 0 & 1 \\ -2 & 3 \end{pmatrix}$,

(*b*) $\mathbf{a} = \begin{pmatrix} 1 & 2 \\ 3 & 6 \end{pmatrix}$, $\mathbf{b} = \begin{pmatrix} 4 & -3 \\ 2 & -1 \end{pmatrix}$,

(*c*) $\mathbf{a} = \begin{pmatrix} 3 & -2 \\ -1 & 0 \end{pmatrix}$, $\mathbf{b} = \begin{pmatrix} 5 & 5 \\ 5 & 10 \end{pmatrix}$.

11. The inverse of a product

Let $$\mathbf{ab}$$

be the product of two invertible (*non-singular*) matrices **a**, **b**, *each of type* $m \times m$. To prove that *the inverse of* **ab** *is the product* $\mathbf{b}^{-1}\mathbf{a}^{-1}$.

Since **a**, **b** are invertible, the inverses $\mathbf{a}^{-1}$, $\mathbf{b}^{-1}$ exist, so that $\mathbf{b}^{-1}\mathbf{a}^{-1}$ exists also (the types of $\mathbf{a}^{-1}$, $\mathbf{b}^{-1}$ being $m \times m$). Consider the product

$$(\mathbf{b}^{-1}\mathbf{a}^{-1})(\mathbf{ab}) = \mathbf{b}^{-1}(\mathbf{a}^{-1}\mathbf{a})\mathbf{b} = \mathbf{b}^{-1}\mathbf{Ib} = \mathbf{b}^{-1}\mathbf{b}$$
$$= \mathbf{I};$$

and the product

$$(\mathbf{ab})(\mathbf{b}^{-1}\mathbf{a}^{-1}) = \mathbf{a}(\mathbf{bb}^{-1})\mathbf{a}^{-1} = \mathbf{aIa}^{-1} = \mathbf{aa}^{-1}$$
$$= \mathbf{I}.$$

The two relations just proved give

$$(\mathbf{b}^{-1}\mathbf{a}^{-1})(\mathbf{ab}) = (\mathbf{ab})(\mathbf{b}^{-1}\mathbf{a}^{-1}) = \mathbf{I},$$

so that $\mathbf{b}^{-1}\mathbf{a}^{-1}$ is indeed the inverse of **ab**.

Exercise K

1. Prove that, when the matrices exist,

$$(\mathbf{abc})^{-1} = \mathbf{c}^{-1}\mathbf{b}^{-1}\mathbf{a}^{-1}.$$

2. The matrix $\mathbf{a} = \begin{pmatrix} 1 & 2 \\ 2 & 4 \end{pmatrix}$

is not invertible. Let

$$\mathbf{b} = \begin{pmatrix} p & q \\ r & s \end{pmatrix}$$

be any other matrix. Form the products

$$\mathbf{ab}, \quad \mathbf{ba}$$

and verify that neither of these is invertible.

3. Verify the formula $(\mathbf{ab})^{-1} = \mathbf{b}^{-1}\mathbf{a}^{-1}$ in the following cases:

(i) $\mathbf{a} = \begin{pmatrix} \cos\theta & \sin\theta \\ -\sin\theta & \cos\theta \end{pmatrix}$, $\mathbf{b} = \begin{pmatrix} \cos\phi & \sin\phi \\ -\sin\phi & \cos\phi \end{pmatrix}$;

(ii) $\mathbf{a} = \begin{pmatrix} \cos\theta & \sin\theta \\ -\sin\theta & \cos\theta \end{pmatrix}$, $\mathbf{b} = \begin{pmatrix} \cos\theta & \sin\theta \\ \sin\theta & -\cos\theta \end{pmatrix}$.

12. The equation cp = 0, where all the matrices are of type 2×2

Let $\mathbf{c}$ be a given matrix and consider the equation

$$\mathbf{cp} = \mathbf{0}.$$

The solution $\mathbf{p} = \mathbf{0}$ is trivial, and we search for non-zero solutions.

(i) If $\mathbf{c}$ *is invertible* (*non-singular*), then $\mathbf{c}^{-1}$ exists, so that the equation gives

$$\mathbf{c}^{-1}\mathbf{cp} = \mathbf{c}^{-1}\mathbf{0} = \mathbf{0}$$

$$\Rightarrow \mathbf{p} = \mathbf{0}.$$

Hence *the existence of non-zero solutions requires the condition*

$$\det \mathbf{c} = 0,$$

or

$$c_{11}c_{22} - c_{12}c_{21} = 0.$$

(ii) *If* $\mathbf{c}$ *is not invertible* (*that is, if* $\mathbf{c}$ *is singular*), then

$$c_{11}c_{22} - c_{12}c_{21} = 0.$$

The matrix equation, on expansion, gives

$$c_{11}p_1 + c_{12}p_2 = 0,$$

$$c_{21}p_1 + c_{22}p_2 = 0.$$

Let us clear aside first the cases that can happen when one or more of the coefficients c_{ij} is zero.

(i) *All four coefficients zero.* The equation is

$$\mathbf{0p} = \mathbf{0}$$

and is, trivially, satisfied for all values of $\mathbf{p}$.

(ii) *Three coefficients zero.* The element p_1 or p_2 multiplying the surviving coefficient must be zero, and the other is unrestricted. The solutions are therefore

$$\mathbf{p} = \begin{pmatrix} \lambda \\ 0 \end{pmatrix} \quad \text{or} \quad \begin{pmatrix} 0 \\ \lambda \end{pmatrix} \quad (\lambda \text{ arbitrary})$$

as the case may be.

(iii) *Two coefficients zero.* Since $\det \mathbf{c} = 0$, the possibilities are

$$c_{11} = 0, \quad c_{12} = 0;$$
$$c_{11} = 0, \quad c_{21} = 0;$$
$$c_{22} = 0, \quad c_{12} = 0;$$
$$c_{22} = 0, \quad c_{21} = 0.$$

These give immediately the respective possibilities:

$$\mathbf{p} = \begin{pmatrix} c_{22}\lambda \\ -c_{21}\lambda \end{pmatrix},$$

$$\mathbf{p} = \begin{pmatrix} \lambda \\ 0 \end{pmatrix},$$

$$\mathbf{p} = \begin{pmatrix} 0 \\ \lambda \end{pmatrix},$$

$$\mathbf{p} = \begin{pmatrix} -c_{12}\lambda \\ c_{11}\lambda \end{pmatrix},$$

for arbitrary λ. In other words, the solutions are, under the respective conditions, multiples of

$$\begin{pmatrix} c_{22} \\ -c_{21} \end{pmatrix}, \quad \begin{pmatrix} 1 \\ 0 \end{pmatrix}, \quad \begin{pmatrix} 0 \\ 1 \end{pmatrix}, \quad \begin{pmatrix} -c_{12} \\ c_{11} \end{pmatrix}.$$

(iv) *One coefficient zero.* This case cannot arise, since the relation

$$c_{11}c_{22} - c_{12}c_{21} = 0$$

cannot be satisfied when one, and only one coefficient is zero.

(v) *All coefficients non-zero.* This is the major case, and can be set out with reasonable simplicity once zero coefficients have been excluded. The equations are

$$c_{11}p_1 + c_{12}p_2 = 0, \quad c_{21}p_1 + c_{22}p_2 = 0.$$

The first equation gives

$$\frac{p_1}{p_2} = -\frac{c_{12}}{c_{11}},$$

and the second gives

$$\frac{p_1}{p_2} = -\frac{c_{22}}{c_{21}},$$

these two ratios being *the same* by virtue of the relation $\det \mathbf{c} = 0$. Hence the general solution can be expressed in either of the equivalent forms

$$\mathbf{p} = \lambda \begin{pmatrix} -c_{12} \\ c_{11} \end{pmatrix}, \quad \mathbf{p} = \lambda \begin{pmatrix} c_{22} \\ -c_{21} \end{pmatrix},$$

for arbitrary values of λ.

Exercise L

1. Prove that, if

$$\mathbf{c} = \begin{pmatrix} 5 & 7 \\ 15 & 21 \end{pmatrix},$$

then the equation

$$\mathbf{cp} = \mathbf{0}$$

is satisfied by

$$\mathbf{p} = \lambda \begin{pmatrix} 7 \\ -5 \end{pmatrix}$$

for all values of λ.

2. Find the value of k for which the equation $\mathbf{cp} = \mathbf{0}$ has a non-zero solution, where

$$\mathbf{c} = \begin{pmatrix} 3 & 2 \\ 9 & k \end{pmatrix},$$

and solve the equation in that case.

3. There are two values of k for which the equation

$$\mathbf{cp} = k\mathbf{p}$$

has a non-zero solution, where

$$\mathbf{c} = \begin{pmatrix} 5 & 8 \\ 1 & 3 \end{pmatrix}.$$

Prove that these values satisfy the relation

$$(5 - k)(3 - k) = 8.$$

Hence find them, and the corresponding values of $\mathbf{p}$.

4. Solve the equations $\mathbf{cp} = \mathbf{0}$ when $\mathbf{c}$ is

(i) $\begin{pmatrix} 1 & 0 \\ 0 & 0 \end{pmatrix}$, (ii) $\begin{pmatrix} 1 & 2 \\ 3 & 0 \end{pmatrix}$, (iii) $\begin{pmatrix} 1 & 2 \\ 3 & 4 \end{pmatrix}$, (iv) $\begin{pmatrix} 1 & 1 \\ 2 & 2 \end{pmatrix}$, (v) $\begin{pmatrix} 2 & 0 \\ 0 & 3 \end{pmatrix}$.

5. Prove that, if $\mathbf{a}$ is an invertible matrix and if $\mathbf{b}$ is a matrix such that

$$\mathbf{ab} = \mathbf{0},$$

where all matrices are of type 2×2, then $\mathbf{b}$ must be the zero matrix.

13. Length and angle in terms of coordinates

As in Section 2, let P, Q be two points whose coordinate vectors are

$$P = \{p_1, p_2\}, \quad Q = \{q_1, q_2\}.$$

Let the line through P parallel to the axis OX_1 meet the line through Q parallel to the axis OX_2 in U (Figure 199). Then

$$\mathbf{u} = \{p_1, q_2\}.$$

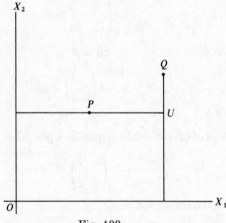

Fig. 199

Hence, numerically,

$$PU = q_1 - p_1, \quad UQ = q_2 - p_2.$$

By the theorem of Pythagoras, $PQ^2 = PU^2 + UQ^2$, so that

$$PQ^2 = (q_1 - p_1)^2 + (q_2 - p_2)^2.$$

This result can be expressed in matrix form:

$$\mathbf{q} - \mathbf{p} = \{q_1 - p_1, q_2 - p_2\},$$

so that $\qquad\qquad (\mathbf{q}-\mathbf{p})^T = (q_1 - p_1, q_2 - p_2).$

Hence $\qquad (\mathbf{q}-\mathbf{p})^T(\mathbf{q}-\mathbf{p}) = (q_1 - p_1, q_2 - p_2)\begin{pmatrix} q_1 - p_1 \\ q_2 - p_2 \end{pmatrix}$

$$= (q_1 - p_1)^2 + (q_2 - p_2)^2$$

$$= PQ^2.$$

Thus the formula for length is

$$PQ^2 = (\mathbf{q}-\mathbf{p})^T(\mathbf{q}-\mathbf{p}).$$

Corollary 2. *The length of OP is given by the relation*

$$OP^2 = \mathbf{p}^T\mathbf{p}.$$

The magnitude OP $(\geqslant 0)$ is often denoted by

$$|\mathbf{p}|,$$

so that $\qquad\qquad\qquad |\mathbf{p}|^2 = \mathbf{p}^T\mathbf{p}.$

The angle θ between OP and OQ is given by the trigonometrical relation

$$PQ^2 = OP^2 + OQ^2 - 2OP \cdot OQ\cos\theta,$$

so that $\qquad (\mathbf{q}-\mathbf{p})^T(\mathbf{q}-\mathbf{p}) = \mathbf{p}^T\mathbf{p} + \mathbf{q}^T\mathbf{q} - 2|\mathbf{p}|\,|\mathbf{q}|\cos\theta,$

or $\qquad (\mathbf{q}^T - \mathbf{p}^T)(\mathbf{q}-\mathbf{p}) = \mathbf{p}^T\mathbf{p} + \mathbf{q}^T\mathbf{q} - 2|\mathbf{p}|\,|\mathbf{q}|\cos\theta,$

or (after multiplying the terms on the left),

$$\mathbf{q}^T\mathbf{p} + \mathbf{p}^T\mathbf{q} = 2|\mathbf{p}|\,|\mathbf{q}|\cos\theta.$$

Now $\qquad\qquad \mathbf{q}^T\mathbf{p} = q_1 p_1 + q_2 p_2 = \mathbf{p}^T\mathbf{q},$

so that *the angle θ is given by the relation*

$$\mathbf{p}^T\mathbf{q} = |\mathbf{p}|\,|\mathbf{q}|\cos\theta.$$

Corollary 3. $\qquad\qquad OP \perp OQ \Leftrightarrow \mathbf{p}^T\mathbf{q} = 0.$

Exercise M

1. Prove that, if $OP = OQ = PQ$, then $\angle POQ = \tfrac{1}{3}\pi$.

2. Prove that, if H is a point such that $PH \perp OQ$, then $(\mathbf{p}-\mathbf{h})^T\mathbf{q} = 0$. Deduce that

$$\left.\begin{array}{l} PH \perp OQ \\ QH \perp OP \end{array}\right\} \Rightarrow OH \perp PQ.$$

13

MATRICES: ISOMETRY AND OTHER TRANSFORMATIONS

1. The distance between two points

Let $P\{p_1, p_2\}$ and $Q\{q_1, q_2\}$ be two given points. Then (cf. Chapter 12, Section 13)

$$PQ^2 = (p_1 - q_1)^2 + (p_2 - q_2)^2.$$

Now $\quad \mathbf{p} - \mathbf{q} = \begin{pmatrix} p_1 - q_1 \\ p_2 - q_2 \end{pmatrix}, \quad \mathbf{p}^T - \mathbf{q}^T = (p_1 - q_1, p_2 - q_2),$

so that, by normal matrix multiplication,

$$(\mathbf{p} - \mathbf{q})^T (\mathbf{p} - \mathbf{q}) = (p_1 - q_1)^2 + (p_2 - q_2)^2$$
$$= PQ^2.$$

That is, *the square of the distance between two points P, Q is equal to $(\mathbf{p} - \mathbf{q})^T (\mathbf{p} - \mathbf{q})$.*

Note the order. The product $(\mathbf{p} - \mathbf{q})(\mathbf{p} - \mathbf{q})^T$ is *very different*, being a matrix of type 2×2.

Exercise A

Use the above formula

1. Prove that, if $\mathbf{p} = \{4, 7\}$, $\mathbf{q} = \{1, 3\}$, then $PQ = 5$.

2. Prove that, if $\mathbf{a} = \{1, 0\}$, $\mathbf{b} = \{0, 1\}$, then

$$PA^2 + PB^2 = 4 \Rightarrow p_1^2 + p_2^2 - p_1 - p_2 - 1 = 0$$

$$\Rightarrow (\mathbf{p} - \mathbf{c})^T (\mathbf{p} - \mathbf{c}) = \tfrac{3}{2},$$

where $\quad\quad\quad\quad \mathbf{c} = \{\tfrac{1}{2}, \tfrac{1}{2}\}.$

2. The (homogeneous) transform of the length of a segment

Let points $P\{p_1, p_2\}$, $Q\{q_1, q_2\}$ be subjected to a homogeneous transformation of matrix $\mathbf{a}$, giving

$$\mathbf{p}' = \mathbf{ap}, \quad \mathbf{q}' = \mathbf{aq},$$

so that $\qquad\qquad (\mathbf{p}')^T = \mathbf{p}^T\mathbf{a}^T, \quad (\mathbf{q}')^T = \mathbf{q}^T\mathbf{a}^T.$

Then $\qquad\qquad\begin{aligned}(P'Q')^2 &= (\mathbf{q}' - \mathbf{p}')^T\,(\mathbf{q}' - \mathbf{p}')\\ &= (\mathbf{aq} - \mathbf{ap})^T\,(\mathbf{aq} - \mathbf{ap})\\ &= [\mathbf{a}(\mathbf{q} - \mathbf{p})]^T\,[\mathbf{a}(\mathbf{q} - \mathbf{p})]\\ &= (\mathbf{q} - \mathbf{p})^T\,\mathbf{a}^T\mathbf{a}(\mathbf{q} - \mathbf{p}).\end{aligned}$

Write $\mathbf{q} - \mathbf{p} = \mathbf{r}$. Then

$$PQ^2 = \mathbf{r}^T\mathbf{r}, \quad (P'Q')^2 = \mathbf{r}^T(\mathbf{a}^T\mathbf{a})\,\mathbf{r}.$$

Comment. Suppose that the matrix $\mathbf{a}$ corresponds to a transformation

$$\mathbf{p}' = \mathbf{ap}.$$

Since $\mathbf{p} = \mathbf{0} \Rightarrow \mathbf{p}' = \mathbf{0}$, the origin is self-corresponding, and so the transformation is one of the types that have at least one self-corresponding point. Consider, as an example, the case of a similarity; there must then be a constant k such that

$$(P'Q')^2 = k^2 PQ^2$$

for all line segments PQ. Hence we need the relation, *true for all values of* $\mathbf{r}$:

$$\mathbf{r}^T(\mathbf{a}^T\mathbf{a})\,\mathbf{r} = k^2\mathbf{r}^T\mathbf{r}.$$

(When the transformation is an isometry, $k = \pm 1$.)

The relation is easily seen to be satisfied when

$$\mathbf{a}^T\mathbf{a} = k^2\mathbf{I},$$

but this must not lead to false conclusions. Special properties of a matrix of the form $\mathbf{a}^T\mathbf{a}$ are involved; it is, in general, *not true* that

$$\mathbf{r}^T\mathbf{u}\mathbf{r} = k^2\mathbf{r}^T\mathbf{r} \Rightarrow \mathbf{u} = k^2\mathbf{I}.$$

Exercise B

1. Prove that $\mathbf{r}^T\mathbf{u}\mathbf{r} = \mathbf{r}^T\mathbf{r}$ in the following cases, although $\mathbf{u}$ is *not* the unit matrix:

(i) $\mathbf{u} = \begin{pmatrix} 1 & 3 \\ -3 & 1 \end{pmatrix}$, (ii) $\mathbf{u} = \begin{pmatrix} 1 & -1 \\ 1 & 1 \end{pmatrix}$, (iii) $\mathbf{u} = \begin{pmatrix} 1 & -2 \\ 2 & 1 \end{pmatrix}$.

The next section supplies the missing criterion.

3. The relation $\mathbf{r}^T\mathbf{u}\mathbf{r} = \mathbf{r}^T\mathbf{r}$

To find necessary and sufficient conditions on a matrix $\mathbf{u}$ *to ensure that, for all values of* $\mathbf{r}$, $\qquad\qquad \mathbf{r}^T\mathbf{u}\mathbf{r} = \mathbf{r}^T\mathbf{r}.$

(i) If the relation does hold, then

$$(r_1, r_2) \begin{pmatrix} u_{11} & u_{12} \\ u_{21} & u_{22} \end{pmatrix} \begin{pmatrix} r_1 \\ r_2 \end{pmatrix} \equiv (r_1, r_2) \begin{pmatrix} r_1 \\ r_2 \end{pmatrix}$$

$$\Rightarrow (r_1, r_2) \begin{pmatrix} u_{11} r_1 + u_{12} r_2 \\ u_{21} r_1 + u_{22} r_2 \end{pmatrix} \equiv r_1^2 + r_2^2$$

$$\Rightarrow r_1(u_{11} r_1 + u_{12} r_2) + r_2(u_{21} r_1 + u_{22} r_2) \equiv r_1^2 + r_2^2$$

$$\Rightarrow u_{11} r_1^2 + (u_{12} + u_{21}) r_1 r_2 + u_{22} r_2^2 \equiv r_1^2 + r_2^2$$

and this, to be identically true for all r_1, r_2, requires

$$u_{11} = 1, \quad u_{22} = 1, \quad u_{12} + u_{21} = 0.$$

Hence *a necessary condition is that* **u** *should be of the form*

$$\mathbf{u} \equiv \begin{pmatrix} 1 & \alpha \\ -\alpha & 1 \end{pmatrix}$$

for some constant α.

(ii) The condition is also *sufficient*, since then

$$\mathbf{r}^T \mathbf{u} \mathbf{r} = (r_1, r_2) \begin{pmatrix} 1 & \alpha \\ -\alpha & 1 \end{pmatrix} \begin{pmatrix} r_1 \\ r_2 \end{pmatrix}$$

$$= (r_1, r_2) \begin{pmatrix} r_1 + \alpha r_2 \\ -\alpha r_1 + r_2 \end{pmatrix}$$

$$= r_1(r_1 + \alpha r_2) + r_2(-\alpha r_1 + r_2)$$

$$= r_1^2 + r_2^2$$

$$= \mathbf{r}^T \mathbf{r}.$$

Corollary 1. *If* **u** *is a symmetric matrix such that*

$$\mathbf{r}^T \mathbf{u} \mathbf{r} \equiv \mathbf{r}^T \mathbf{r}$$

for all **r**, *then, necessarily,* **u** = **I**.

This follows at once from the condition $\alpha = 0$. That is, the condition '**u** symmetrical' must be established when we wish to deduce from $\mathbf{r}^T \mathbf{u} \mathbf{r} \equiv \mathbf{r}^T \mathbf{r}$ that **u** is the unit matrix.

We may now return to the relation (Section 2)

$$\mathbf{r}^T (\mathbf{a}^T \mathbf{a}) \mathbf{r} = k^2 \mathbf{r}^T \mathbf{r},$$

simplified to the form

$$\mathbf{r}^T (\mathbf{b}^T \mathbf{b}) \mathbf{r} = \mathbf{r}^T \mathbf{r}$$

by writing $\mathbf{a} = k\mathbf{b}$. It is to be observed that, whatever the matrix $\mathbf{b}$ may be, the product $\mathbf{b}^T\mathbf{b}$ is necessarily symmetrical, since

$$(\mathbf{b}^T\mathbf{b})^T = \mathbf{b}^T(\mathbf{b}^T)^T = \mathbf{b}^T\mathbf{b}.$$

Corollary 1 then shows that

$$\mathbf{b}^T\mathbf{b} = \mathbf{I}.$$

Hence *the matrix $\mathbf{a}$ of the similarity transformation*

$$\mathbf{p}' = \mathbf{a}\mathbf{p}$$

satisfies the relation

$$\mathbf{a}^T\mathbf{a} = k^2\mathbf{I}.$$

Note: *the matrix of any homogeneous isometry* has the property

$$\mathbf{a}^T\mathbf{a} = \mathbf{I}.$$

Definition. A matrix $\mathbf{a}$ with the property

$$\mathbf{a}^T\mathbf{a} = \mathbf{I}$$

is said to be *orthogonal*.

Exercise C

1. The matrices

$$\begin{pmatrix} \cos\theta & -\sin\theta \\ \sin\theta & \cos\theta \end{pmatrix}, \quad \begin{pmatrix} \cos\theta & \sin\theta \\ \sin\theta & -\cos\theta \end{pmatrix}$$

are both orthogonal.

2. $\left.\begin{array}{l} \mathbf{u} \text{ orthogonal} \\ \mathbf{v} \text{ orthogonal} \end{array}\right\} \Rightarrow \mathbf{u}\mathbf{v}$ orthogonal.

3. Find values of p and k if the matrix

$$k\begin{pmatrix} 1 & p \\ 2 & 1 \end{pmatrix}$$

is orthogonal.

4. Find all the orthogonal matrices of type 2×2 that have one zero element.

5. Prove that *the transpose and the inverse of an orthogonal matrix are both orthogonal.*

6. Prove that, for real numbers, all elements of an orthogonal matrix are numerically less than 1.

7. Give examples of two matrices $\mathbf{u}$, $\mathbf{v}$, neither of which is orthogonal, which have an orthogonal product $\mathbf{u}\mathbf{v}$.

4. Properties of orthogonal matrices

Let $\mathbf{a}$ be a given orthogonal matrix, of type 2×2 (though several of the results are more general), so that

$$\mathbf{a}^T\mathbf{a} = \mathbf{I}.$$

(i) By the result of Chapter 12, Section 10,

$$\det{(\mathbf{a}^T)}\det{(\mathbf{a})} = \det{(\mathbf{a}^T\mathbf{a})} = \det \mathbf{I}$$
$$= 1.$$

But the value of a determinant is unaltered by transposition. That is, $\det{(\mathbf{a}^T)} = \det{(\mathbf{a})}$. Hence the relation gives

$$\{\det{(\mathbf{a})}\}^2 = 1$$

$$\Rightarrow \det \mathbf{a} = 1 \quad \text{or} \quad \det \mathbf{a} = -1.$$

Both possibilities can happen. For example, $\mathbf{I}$ itself is orthogonal and $\det \mathbf{I} = 1$; the matrix

$$\mathbf{J} = \begin{pmatrix} 1 & 0 \\ 0 & -1 \end{pmatrix}$$

is orthogonal, and $\det \mathbf{J} = -1$.

(ii) In particular, $\det \mathbf{a} \neq 0$, so that $\mathbf{a}$ is invertible and $\mathbf{a}^{-1}$ exists. Thus

$$\mathbf{a}^T\mathbf{a} = \mathbf{I}$$

$$\Rightarrow \mathbf{a}^T\mathbf{a}\mathbf{a}^{-1} = \mathbf{I}\mathbf{a}^{-1} = \mathbf{a}^{-1}$$

$$\Rightarrow \mathbf{a}^T\mathbf{I} = \mathbf{a}^{-1}$$

$$\Rightarrow \mathbf{a}^T = \mathbf{a}^{-1}.$$

Hence *the transpose of an orthogonal matrix is equal to its inverse.*

(iii) *The product of two orthogonal matrices is orthogonal.* Let $\mathbf{a}$, $\mathbf{b}$ be two given orthogonal matrices, so that

$$\mathbf{a}^T\mathbf{a} = \mathbf{I}, \quad \mathbf{b}^T\mathbf{b} = \mathbf{I}.$$

Then $\quad (\mathbf{ab})^T(\mathbf{ab}) = (\mathbf{b}^T\mathbf{a}^T)(\mathbf{ab}) = \mathbf{b}^T(\mathbf{a}^T\mathbf{a})\mathbf{b} = \mathbf{b}^T\mathbf{b}$

$$= \mathbf{I},$$

as required.

5. The two general forms of an orthogonal 2×2 matrix

Let $\quad\quad\quad\quad\quad\quad\quad\quad \mathbf{a} = \begin{pmatrix} p & q \\ r & s \end{pmatrix}$

be an orthogonal matrix. Then

$$\mathbf{a}^T\mathbf{a} = \mathbf{I}$$

$$\Rightarrow \begin{pmatrix} p & r \\ q & s \end{pmatrix} \begin{pmatrix} p & q \\ r & s \end{pmatrix} = \begin{pmatrix} 1 & 0 \\ 0 & 1 \end{pmatrix}$$

$$\Rightarrow \begin{cases} p^2 + r^2 = 1, & pq + rs = 0, \\ qp + sr = 0, & q^2 + s^2 = 1. \end{cases}$$

Since $p^2 + r^2 = 1$, there exists an angle θ such that (whatever the signs of p and r)

$$p = \cos\theta, \quad r = \sin\theta.$$

Similarly there exists an angle ϕ such that

$$q = \cos\phi, \quad s = \sin\phi.$$

Then
$$pq + rs = 0$$

$$\Rightarrow \cos(\theta - \phi) = 0$$

$$\Rightarrow \theta - \phi = (k + \tfrac{1}{2})\pi \quad (k \text{ integer})$$

$$\Rightarrow \phi = \theta - (k + \tfrac{1}{2})\pi$$

$$\Rightarrow \begin{cases} \cos\phi = \cos\theta \cos(k + \tfrac{1}{2})\pi + \sin\theta \sin(k + \tfrac{1}{2})\pi, \\ \sin\phi = \sin\theta \cos(k + \tfrac{1}{2})\pi - \cos\theta \sin(k + \tfrac{1}{2})\pi \end{cases}$$

$$\Rightarrow \begin{cases} \cos\phi = \sin\theta \sin(k + \tfrac{1}{2})\pi, \\ \sin\phi = -\cos\theta \sin(k + \tfrac{1}{2})\pi \end{cases}$$

$$\Rightarrow \begin{cases} \cos\phi = \pm\sin\theta, \\ \sin\phi = \mp\cos\theta \end{cases}$$

since $\sin(k + \tfrac{1}{2})\pi$ is either $+1$ or -1.

Hence **a** assumes one or other of the forms

$$\begin{pmatrix} \cos\theta & \sin\theta \\ \sin\theta & -\cos\theta \end{pmatrix}, \quad \begin{pmatrix} \cos\theta & -\sin\theta \\ \sin\theta & \cos\theta \end{pmatrix}.$$

We have seen (Chapter 12, Sections 4–6) that

$$\begin{pmatrix} \cos\theta & \sin\theta \\ \sin\theta & -\cos\theta \end{pmatrix}$$

is the matrix for a *reflection* in the line

$$p_2 = p_1 \tan\tfrac{1}{2}\theta;$$

the determinant of this matrix is -1, and it is symmetrical.

Also
$$\begin{pmatrix} \cos\theta & -\sin\theta \\ \sin\theta & \cos\theta \end{pmatrix}$$

is the matrix for *rotation* about the origin through an angle θ; the determinant of this matrix is $+1$, and it is not symmetrical.

These are the two homogeneous isometries (that is, having at least one fixed point), and they are entirely distinct.

Exercise D

1. Prove the formula
$$\begin{pmatrix} \cos\phi & \sin\phi \\ \sin\phi & -\cos\phi \end{pmatrix} \begin{pmatrix} \cos\theta & \sin\theta \\ \cos\theta & -\cos\theta \end{pmatrix} = \begin{pmatrix} \cos(\phi-\theta) & -\sin(\phi-\theta) \\ \sin(\phi-\theta) & \cos(\phi-\theta) \end{pmatrix}.$$

Deduce that reflection in the line l_θ followed by reflection in the line l_ϕ is equivalent to rotation about an angle $\phi-\theta$, where the lines l_θ, l_ϕ through the origin make angles $\tfrac{1}{2}\theta$, $\tfrac{1}{2}\phi$ with the axis OX_1.
What happens when $\phi = \pi + \theta$?

2. Prove the formula
$$\begin{pmatrix} \cos\theta & \sin\theta \\ \sin\theta & -\cos\theta \end{pmatrix} \begin{pmatrix} \cos\phi & -\sin\phi \\ \sin\phi & \cos\phi \end{pmatrix} = \begin{pmatrix} \cos(\theta-\phi) & \sin(\theta-\phi) \\ \sin(\theta-\phi) & -\cos(\theta-\phi) \end{pmatrix}$$

and interpret it as the result of a rotation followed by a reflection.

Discuss what happens to the product matrix and to the resulting transformations when the order of the matrices on the left-hand side is interchanged.

3. Prove the formula
$$\begin{pmatrix} \cos\theta & -\sin\theta \\ \sin\theta & \cos\theta \end{pmatrix} \begin{pmatrix} \cos\phi & -\sin\phi \\ \sin\phi & \cos\phi \end{pmatrix} = \begin{pmatrix} \cos(\theta+\phi) & -\sin(\theta+\phi) \\ \sin(\theta+\phi) & \cos(\theta+\phi) \end{pmatrix}$$

and interpret it in terms of transformations.

4. Prove that, if $\mathbf{p}' = \mathbf{a}\mathbf{p}$ is the matrix equation of a reflection in the line l, then
    (i) the matrix $\mathbf{I} + \mathbf{a}$ is not invertible,
    (ii) the transformation $\mathbf{p}' = (\mathbf{I} + \mathbf{a})\mathbf{p}$ is not an isometry,
    (iii) the transformation $\mathbf{p}' = (\mathbf{I} + \mathbf{a})\mathbf{p}$ transforms every point P into a point P' on l.
Find the corresponding results for the matrix $\mathbf{I} - \mathbf{a}$.
Illustrate your two sets of results geometrically.

5. Prove that, if $\mathbf{p}' = \mathbf{a}\mathbf{p}$ is the matrix equation of a rotation through an angle θ about the origin O, then $\mathbf{p}' = (\mathbf{I} + \mathbf{a})\,\mathbf{p}$ represents a spiral similarity of ratio $2\cos\tfrac{1}{2}\theta$ and angle $\tfrac{1}{2}\theta$.

Prove also that, if $\mathbf{p}' = \mathbf{a}\mathbf{p}$ is the matrix equation for a spiral similarity, then $\mathbf{p}' = (\mathbf{I} + \mathbf{a})\,\mathbf{p}$ also represents a spiral similarity.

6. Describe geometrically the transformations given by the particular orthogonal matrices:

(i) $\begin{pmatrix} \dfrac{1}{\sqrt{2}} & \dfrac{1}{\sqrt{2}} \\[2mm] \dfrac{1}{\sqrt{2}} & \dfrac{-1}{\sqrt{2}} \end{pmatrix}$, (ii) $\begin{pmatrix} \dfrac{1}{\sqrt{2}} & \dfrac{1}{\sqrt{2}} \\[2mm] \dfrac{-1}{\sqrt{2}} & \dfrac{1}{\sqrt{2}} \end{pmatrix}$, (iii) $\begin{pmatrix} \dfrac{1}{2} & \dfrac{-\sqrt{3}}{2} \\[2mm] \dfrac{\sqrt{3}}{2} & \dfrac{1}{2} \end{pmatrix}$.

(iv) $\begin{pmatrix} \dfrac{\sqrt{3}}{2} & \dfrac{1}{2} \\[2mm] \dfrac{1}{2} & \dfrac{-\sqrt{3}}{2} \end{pmatrix}$, (v) $\begin{pmatrix} \dfrac{-1}{\sqrt{2}} & \dfrac{-1}{\sqrt{2}} \\[2mm] \dfrac{-1}{\sqrt{2}} & \dfrac{1}{\sqrt{2}} \end{pmatrix}$, (vi) $\begin{pmatrix} 1 & 0 \\ 0 & -1 \end{pmatrix}$.

6. Stretch reflection and spiral similarity

We return to the equation

$$\mathbf{r}^T(\mathbf{a}^T\mathbf{a})\,\mathbf{r} = k^2\mathbf{r}^T\mathbf{r},$$

equivalent to $(P'Q')^2 = k^2 PQ^2$, as in Section 2. Writing

$$\mathbf{a} = k\mathbf{b}$$

as in Section 3, we have the relation

$$\mathbf{b}^T\mathbf{b} = \mathbf{I},$$

with $\mathbf{b}$ an orthogonal matrix.

Since $\mathbf{b}$ is either

$$\begin{pmatrix} \cos\theta & \sin\theta \\ \sin\theta & -\cos\theta \end{pmatrix},$$

for reflection; or

$$\begin{pmatrix} \cos\theta & -\sin\theta \\ \sin\theta & \cos\theta \end{pmatrix},$$

for rotation, the matrix $\mathbf{a}$ assumes one or other of the forms

$$k\begin{pmatrix} \cos\theta & \sin\theta \\ \sin\theta & -\cos\theta \end{pmatrix}, \quad k\begin{pmatrix} \cos\theta & -\sin\theta \\ \sin\theta & \cos\theta \end{pmatrix},$$

the former corresponding to *stretch reflection* and the latter to *spiral similarity* (Chapter 11, Sections 5, 1). The case $\theta = 0$ in the second matrix gives an enlargement.

Exercise E

1. Express each of the matrices

$$\begin{pmatrix} a & b \\ b & -a \end{pmatrix}, \quad \begin{pmatrix} a & b \\ -b & a \end{pmatrix}$$

in similarity form (corresponding to stretch-reflection or spiral similarity as the case may be).

2. Describe geometrically the similarities given by the matrices:

(i) $\begin{pmatrix} 1 & 1 \\ 1 & -1 \end{pmatrix}$, (ii) $\begin{pmatrix} 1- & \sqrt{3} \\ \sqrt{3} & 1 \end{pmatrix}$, (iii) $\begin{pmatrix} 5 & 0 \\ 0 & -5 \end{pmatrix}$,

(iv) $\begin{pmatrix} 3 & \sqrt{3} \\ \sqrt{3} & -3 \end{pmatrix}$, (v) $\begin{pmatrix} -2\sqrt{2} & -2\sqrt{2} \\ -2\sqrt{2} & 2\sqrt{2} \end{pmatrix}$.

7. The shear

It may be useful, though perhaps not strictly relevant, to give here a brief account, with matrix calculation, of the transformation called the *shear*, which is seen, for example, when a pack of cards is pushed to the position shown in Figure 200. The result is that a point P is transformed to a point P' at the same 'level' through a distance proportional to its 'height'. Thus if P is the point with position vector $\mathbf{p} = \{p_1, p_2\}$ referred to axes $OX_1\, OX_2$ (Figure 201) then P' is given by $\mathbf{p}' = \{p'_1, p'_2\}$, where $p'_2 = p_2$ and $p'_1 - p_1 = kp_2$ for a given shear constant k.

Assuming that a matrix transformation is implied, we have

$$\mathbf{p}' = \mathbf{a}\mathbf{p}$$

$$\Rightarrow \begin{pmatrix} p'_1 \\ p'_2 \end{pmatrix} = \begin{pmatrix} a_{11} & a_{12} \\ a_{21} & a_{22} \end{pmatrix} \begin{pmatrix} p_1 \\ p_2 \end{pmatrix}$$

$$\Rightarrow \begin{cases} p'_1 = a_{11}\, p_1 + a_{12}\, p_2, \\ p'_2 = a_{21}\, p_1 + a_{22}\, p_2. \end{cases}$$

Now $p'_2 = p_2$ *for all points* P, and so, as an identity,

$$p_2 \equiv a_{21}p_1 + a_{22}p_2,$$

so that

$$a_{21} = 0, \quad a_{22} = 1.$$

Further, $p'_1 - p_1 = kp_2$, so that, *for all points* P,

$$p_1 + kp_2 \equiv a_{11}p_1 + a_{12}p_2.$$

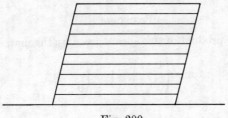

Fig. 200

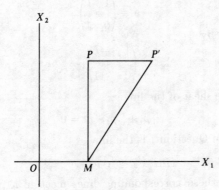

Fig. 201

Hence $\qquad\qquad a_{11} = 1, \quad a_{12} = k.$

The matrix of transformation is thus

$$\mathbf{a} = \begin{pmatrix} 1 & k \\ 0 & 1 \end{pmatrix}.$$

To see what points are self-corresponding, consider the relation

$$\mathbf{p}' = \mathbf{a}\mathbf{p},$$

with $\mathbf{p}' = \mathbf{p}$. Then

$$\begin{pmatrix} p_1 \\ p_2 \end{pmatrix} = \begin{pmatrix} 1 & k \\ 0 & 1 \end{pmatrix} \begin{pmatrix} p_1 \\ p_2 \end{pmatrix},$$

so that $\qquad\qquad p_1 = p_1 + kp_2, \quad p_2 = p_2.$

The first equation shows that $p_2 = 0$, since the alternative $k = 0$ would reduce the transformation to identity; and the two equations together are satisfied by $p = \{\lambda, 0\}$ for any value of λ. That is *the coordinate axis OX_1 is a line of self-corresponding points.*

The line OX_1 may be called the *axis* of the shear and the constant k its *ratio*.

Exercise F

1. Prove that the product of two shears given by the matrices

$$\mathbf{a} \equiv \begin{pmatrix} 1 & k \\ 0 & 1 \end{pmatrix}, \quad \mathbf{b} \equiv \begin{pmatrix} 1 & 1 \\ 0 & 1 \end{pmatrix},$$

is another shear.

2. Prove that the inverse of the shear given by

$$\mathbf{a} \equiv \begin{pmatrix} 1 & k \\ 0 & 1 \end{pmatrix}$$

is the shear given by

$$\begin{pmatrix} 1 & -k \\ 0 & 1 \end{pmatrix}.$$

3. Prove that the shear of the line

$$l_1 p_1 + l_2 p_2 + m = 0$$

by the matrix **a** of Question 1 is the line

$$l_1 p_1 + (l_2 - k l_1) p_2 + m = 0,$$

and verify that these corresponding lines meet in a point of the self-corresponding line $p_2 = 0$.

Discuss the case $l_1 = 0$.

4. Prove that if P, Q are two given points whose transforms in a shear are P', Q', then $PQ \cap P'Q'$ is on the axis of the shear, and the middle point of PQ transforms to the middle point of $P'Q'$.

5. A shear transforms an arbitrary point P to P_1; it transforms P_1 to P_2; and P_2 to P_3; …. Prove that, for any positive integer n, the points $P_1, P_2, \ldots, P_{n-1}$ divide the segment PP_n into n equal parts.

Prove also that, if the given shear has matrix

$$\begin{pmatrix} 1 & k \\ 0 & 1 \end{pmatrix},$$

then the transformation $p \to p_n$ can be expressed by the matrix

$$\begin{pmatrix} 1 & nk \\ 0 & 1 \end{pmatrix}.$$

6. A line l and two points A, A' are given such that $AA' \parallel l$ (Figure 202). A transformation $P \to P'$ is defined by the construction:

$AP \cap l = U$; the line through P parallel to l meets $A'U$ in P'.

Prove that the transformation is a shear.

[Thus a shear is defined by its axis and one pair of corresponding points.]

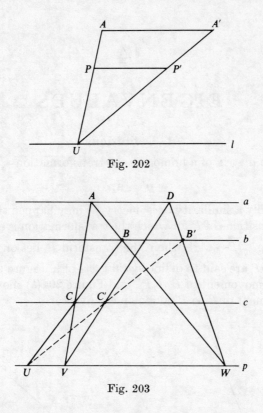

Fig. 202

Fig. 203

7. Four parallel lines a, b, c, p are given (Figure 203). Points A, D are taken on a; B is taken on b; and C is taken on c. The lines BC, CA, AB meet p in U, V, W; the line DV meets c in C', and the line DW meets b in B'. Prove that the line $B'C'$ passes through U.

8. Prove that the shears with a given axis form a group.

14

EIGENVALUES

1. Definitions

Let **a** be the matrix of a homogeneous transformation

$$\mathbf{p}' = \mathbf{ap},$$

not necessarily a similarity or isometry. It may happen that there are *particular* positions of P for which the transformation is equivalent to a 'stretching' $\overrightarrow{OP} \rightarrow \overrightarrow{OP'}$, where the transform P' lies on the line OP. Such lines $\overrightarrow{OP}$ are said to define *eigenvectors* of **a**. Figure 204 (*a*) shows the general movement of P to P', and Figure 204 (*b*) shows the particular movement of P to P' along an eigenvector.

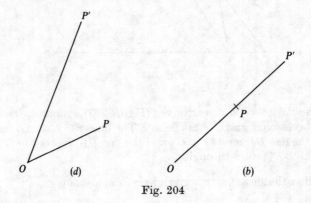

Fig. 204

Since **p**′ is a scalar multiple of **p** for an eigenvector, there exists a scalar λ such that

$$\mathbf{p}' = \lambda \mathbf{p} \quad \text{or} \quad \mathbf{ap} = \lambda \mathbf{p},$$

and this definitive relation can be written in the form

$$(\mathbf{a} - \lambda \mathbf{I}) \mathbf{p} = \mathbf{0}.$$

It is implicit that **p** *is not the zero vector*, otherwise the analysis has little significance.

Now it was proved in Chapter 12, Section 11, that the existence of a relation $\mathbf{cp} = \mathbf{0}$ for non-zero **p** requires **c** to be non-invertible (singular), since the existence of $\mathbf{c}^{-1}$ would involve the relation $\mathbf{c}^{-1}(\mathbf{c}\mathbf{p}) = \mathbf{0}$, giving $\mathbf{I}\mathbf{p} = \mathbf{0}$ and thus $\mathbf{p} = \mathbf{0}$. It was also shown that the condition for the non-existence of $\mathbf{c}^{-1}$ is that $\det \mathbf{c} = 0$.

In the present case, the relation

$$(\mathbf{a} - \lambda \mathbf{I})\,\mathbf{p} = \mathbf{0} \quad (\mathbf{p} \neq \mathbf{0})$$

requires the condition

$$\det(\mathbf{a} - \lambda \mathbf{I}) \equiv |\mathbf{a} - \lambda \mathbf{I}| = 0.$$

Illustration 1. Consider first the particular example

$$\mathbf{a} = \begin{pmatrix} 3 & 1 \\ 8 & 5 \end{pmatrix}.$$

Then
$$|\mathbf{a} - \lambda \mathbf{I}| = 0$$

$$\Rightarrow \begin{vmatrix} 3 - \lambda & 1 \\ 8 & 5 - \lambda \end{vmatrix} = 0$$

$$\Rightarrow \lambda^2 - 8 + 7 = 0$$

$$\Rightarrow \lambda = 7 \quad \text{or} \quad \lambda = 1.$$

(i) *The case $\lambda = 7$.* Write $\mathbf{p} = \{p_1, p_2\}$, $\mathbf{p}' = \{p_1', p_2'\}$. Then

$$\mathbf{p}' = \mathbf{a}\mathbf{p}$$

$$\Rightarrow \begin{pmatrix} p_1' \\ p_2' \end{pmatrix} = \begin{pmatrix} 3 & 1 \\ 8 & 5 \end{pmatrix} \begin{pmatrix} p_1 \\ p_2 \end{pmatrix}$$

$$= \begin{pmatrix} 3p_1 + p_2 \\ 8p_1 + 5p_2 \end{pmatrix}.$$

This is the same as $7\mathbf{p}$ (that is, $\lambda \mathbf{p}$ with $\lambda = 7$) if

$$3p_1 + p_2 = 7p_1, \quad 8p_1 + 5p_2 = 7p_2$$

and each of these relations gives

$$4p_1 = p_2.$$

Hence *the eigenvector* $\mathbf{p}$ assumes the form

$$\begin{pmatrix} \rho \\ 4\rho \end{pmatrix},$$

where ρ is any arbitrary non-zero scalar multiplier.

(ii) *The case* $\lambda = 1$. Similar argument gives the relations

$$3p_1 + p_2 = p_1, \quad 8p_1 + 5p_2 = p_2,$$

so that $$p_2 = -2p_1.$$

Hence *this eigenvector* **p** assumes the form

$$\begin{pmatrix} \sigma \\ -2\sigma \end{pmatrix},$$

where σ is an arbitrary non-zero scalar multiplier.

Note that, for $\lambda = 7$,
$$\mathbf{p}' = 7\mathbf{p}$$
but that, for $\lambda = 1$,
$$\mathbf{p}' = \mathbf{p}.$$

Thus in the first case $\overrightarrow{OP'} = 7\overrightarrow{OP}$, so that the eigenvector is a line each point of which corresponds to some *other* point on it; whereas in the second case $\overrightarrow{OP'} = \overrightarrow{OP}$, so that the eigenvector is a line of *self-corresponding* points.

More generally, if

$$\mathbf{a} = \begin{pmatrix} a_{11} & a_{12} \\ a_{21} & a_{22} \end{pmatrix},$$

the relation giving λ is

$$\begin{vmatrix} a_{11} - \lambda & a_{12} \\ a_{21} & a_{22} - \lambda \end{vmatrix} = 0,$$

or $$\lambda^2 - (a_{11} + a_{22})\lambda + (a_{11}a_{22} - a_{12}a_{21}) = 0.$$

There are therefore two possible values for λ, *and these may be real and distinct, or 'coincident', or complex.*

When the value of λ is known, the corresponding vector **p** can be calculated from the relation

$$(\mathbf{a} - \lambda\mathbf{I})\mathbf{p} = \mathbf{0}$$

$$\Rightarrow \begin{pmatrix} a_{11} - \lambda & a_{12} \\ a_{21} & a_{22} - \lambda \end{pmatrix} \begin{pmatrix} p_1 \\ p_2 \end{pmatrix} = \mathbf{0}$$

$$\Rightarrow \begin{cases} (a_{11} - \lambda)p_1 + a_{12}p_2 = 0 \\ \text{and} \quad a_{21}p_1 + (a_{22} - \lambda)p_2 = 0. \end{cases}$$

Thus the ratio p_1/p_2 assumes either of the forms

$$-a_{12}/(a_{11} - \lambda), \quad -(a_{22} - \lambda)/a_{21},$$

these being the same by virtue of the relation

$$(a_{11} - \lambda)(a_{22} - \lambda) - a_{12}a_{21} = 0.$$

Definition. Generalising, let $\mathbf{a}$ be any square matrix of type $n \times n$. The equation

$$\det(\mathbf{a} - \lambda\mathbf{I}) = 0, \quad \text{or} \quad |\mathbf{a} - \lambda\mathbf{I}| = 0,$$

is called the *characteristic equation* of $\mathbf{a}$. It has n roots, not necessarily distinct, called *eigenvalues* of $\mathbf{a}$ (characteristic values, latent roots). With each eigenvalue λ_i $(i = 1, 2, ..., n)$ is associated an *eigenvector* $\mathbf{p}_i$ such that $\mathbf{a}\mathbf{p}_i = \lambda_i\mathbf{p}_i$, where $\mathbf{p}_i \neq \mathbf{0}$; an eigenvector is undetermined to the extent of a non-zero scalar factor, since

$$\mathbf{a}\mathbf{p} = \lambda\mathbf{p} \Rightarrow \mathbf{a}(k\mathbf{p}) = \lambda(k\mathbf{p}).$$

Exercise A

1. Find the eigenvalues and corresponding eigenvectors of the matrices:

(i) $\begin{pmatrix} 2 & 3 \\ 4 & 3 \end{pmatrix}$, (ii) $\begin{pmatrix} 2 & -2 \\ -6 & 3 \end{pmatrix}$, (iii) $\begin{pmatrix} 1 & 0 \\ 3 & 2 \end{pmatrix}$, (iv) $\begin{pmatrix} 3 & 2 \\ 6 & 4 \end{pmatrix}$,

(v) $\begin{pmatrix} 1 & 1 \\ 5 & -3 \end{pmatrix}$, (vi) $\begin{pmatrix} 3 & 5 \\ 4 & 5 \end{pmatrix}$, (vii) $\begin{pmatrix} 1 & 2 \\ -2 & 5 \end{pmatrix}$, (viii) $\begin{pmatrix} 1 & 2 \\ 0 & 5 \end{pmatrix}$.

2. Prove that, if the matrix $\mathbf{a}$ has an eigenvalue λ with corresponding eigenvector $\mathbf{p}$, then $\mathbf{a}^2$ has an eigenvalue λ^2 and $\mathbf{a}^3$ has an eigenvalue λ^3, each with eigenvector $\mathbf{p}$.

Verify these results for three of the matrices of Question 1.

3. Find the eigenvalues and corresponding eigenvectors for the matrices:

(i) reflection, $\begin{pmatrix} \cos\theta & \sin\theta \\ \sin\theta & -\cos\theta \end{pmatrix}$,

(ii) rotation, $\begin{pmatrix} \cos\theta & -\sin\theta \\ \sin\theta & \cos\theta \end{pmatrix}$,

(iii) stretch reflection, $\begin{pmatrix} a & b \\ b & -a \end{pmatrix}$,

(iv) shear $\begin{pmatrix} 1 & n^2 \\ 0 & 1 \end{pmatrix}$.

2. The eigenvalues of a real orthogonal matrix

The importance of orthogonal matrices was established in Chapter 13. We consider here an orthogonal matrix of type $n \times n$, with real elements, subject to the defining condition

$$\mathbf{a}^T \mathbf{a} = \mathbf{I}.$$

(i) To prove that, *if an eigenvalue λ is real, then $\lambda = +1$ or $\lambda = -1$.*

Lemma 1. *If $\mathbf{p}$ is a non-zero column vector*

$$\mathbf{p} \equiv \{p_1, p_2, ..., p_n\}$$

and if $\bar{\mathbf{p}}$ is the vector whose elements are the complex conjugates of $\mathbf{p}$, then

$$\mathbf{p}^T \mathbf{p} > 0.$$

[The complex conjugate of $x + iy$ is $x - iy$. The number $x + iy$ is equal to its complex conjugate when it is real – that is, when $y = 0$.]

By definition,

$$\bar{\mathbf{p}}^T \mathbf{p} = (\bar{p}_1, \bar{p}_2, ..., \bar{p}_n) \begin{pmatrix} p_1 \\ p_2 \\ \vdots \\ p_n \end{pmatrix}$$

$$= (\bar{p}_1 p_1 + \bar{p}_2 p_2 + ... + \bar{p}_n p_n).$$

If now $\qquad\qquad p_k = x_k + iy_k \quad (x_k, y_k \text{ real})$

then $\qquad\qquad \bar{p}_k p_k = (x_k - iy_k)(x_k + iy_k)$

$$= x_k^2 + y_k^2,$$

which is greater than zero since x_k, y_k are real, with equality to zero only when $x_k = y_k = 0$.

Thus $\bar{\mathbf{p}}^T \mathbf{p}$ is, excluding the forbidden case $\mathbf{p} = \mathbf{0}$, the sum of positive elements not all of which are zero. It is therefore itself greater than zero.

Returning to the main result:

$$\mathbf{a}\mathbf{p} = \lambda \mathbf{p}$$

$$\Rightarrow \mathbf{p}^T \mathbf{a}^T = \lambda \mathbf{p}^T$$

$$\Rightarrow (\mathbf{p}^T \mathbf{a}^T)(\mathbf{a}\mathbf{p}) = \lambda^2 \mathbf{p}^T \mathbf{p}$$

$$\Rightarrow \mathbf{p}^T \mathbf{I} \mathbf{p} = \lambda^2 \mathbf{p}^T \mathbf{p}$$

$$\Rightarrow \mathbf{p}^T \mathbf{p} = \lambda^2 \mathbf{p}^T \mathbf{p}$$

$$\Rightarrow (\lambda^2 - 1) \mathbf{p}^T \mathbf{p} = 0.$$

Now $\mathbf{a}$ has real elements (given) and λ is real (by assumption). The elements of $\mathbf{p}$ are found from the matrix equation $(\mathbf{a} - \lambda\mathbf{I})\mathbf{p} = \mathbf{0}$, giving

$$(a_{11} - \lambda)p_1 + a_{12}p_2 + \ldots + a_{1n}p_n = 0$$
$$\ldots\ldots\ldots\ldots\ldots\ldots\ldots\ldots\ldots\ldots\ldots\ldots\ldots\ldots\ldots\ldots\ldots$$
$$a_{n1}p_1 + a_{n2}p_2 + \ldots + (a_{nn} - \lambda)p_n = 0,$$

and $p_1, p_2, \ldots, p_n$ (found by solving these equations) are therefore real. It follows also from Lemma 1 that $\mathbf{p}^T\mathbf{p}$ cannot be zero. Hence

$$\lambda^2 - 1 = 0,$$

as required.

Remark. The statement, '$p_1, p_2, \ldots, p_n$ are therefore real' is not strictly true. It was shown in Illustration 1 that these elements are undetermined to the extent of a factor (called ρ or σ in Illustration 1) and that factor might be chosen to be complex. Since the result is easily seen to be true when (as here) the *ratios* are real, the complication may safely be ignored.

(ii) To prove that, *if an eigenvalue λ is complex, then its modulus is equal to* 1; *that is,* $|\lambda| = 1$.

The previous result $\lambda = \pm 1$ is included in this, but the two cases are perhaps best kept separate.

The equation for λ is

$$|\mathbf{a} - \lambda\mathbf{I}| = 0$$

which, on expansion, is a polynomial equation in λ of degree n whose coefficients are real. It is a standard result in the theory of algebraic equations that the complex conjugate $\overline{\lambda}$ is also a root. Informally, complex roots occur in conjugate pairs.

Further, the calculation from λ to the corresponding eigenvector $\mathbf{p}$ is identical with the calculation from $\overline{\lambda}$ to its corresponding eigenvector $\overline{\mathbf{p}}$ save that i must be replaced by $-i$ throughout. An example may help:

Illustration 2. Let

$$\mathbf{a} = \begin{pmatrix} \cos\theta & -\sin\theta \\ \sin\theta & \cos\theta \end{pmatrix}.$$

The characteristic equation is

$$\lambda^2 - 2\lambda\cos\theta + 1 = 0,$$

so that

$$\lambda = \cos\theta + i\sin\theta,$$

$$\overline{\lambda} = \cos\theta - i\sin\theta.$$

Then **p** is given by the equations

$$(-i\sin\theta)\,p_1 + (-\sin\theta)\,p_2 = 0 \quad \text{and} \quad (\sin\theta)\,p_1 + (-i\sin\theta)\,p_2 = 0,$$

so that we may take

$$\mathbf{p} = \begin{pmatrix} 1 \\ -i \end{pmatrix}.$$

Similarly, $\bar{\mathbf{p}}$ is given by the equations

$$(i\sin\theta)\,\bar{p}_1 + (-\sin\theta)\,\bar{p}_2 = 0 \quad \text{and} \quad (\sin\theta)\,\bar{p}_1 + (i\sin\theta)\,\bar{p}_2 = 0,$$

so that we may take

$$\bar{\mathbf{p}} = \begin{pmatrix} 1 \\ i \end{pmatrix}.$$

Returning to the main theme, the relations are

$$\mathbf{a}\mathbf{p} = \lambda\mathbf{p}, \quad \mathbf{a}\bar{\mathbf{p}} = \bar{\lambda}\bar{\mathbf{p}},$$

the matrix **a** with real coefficients being unaffected by the change in the sign of i. As before,

$$(\bar{\mathbf{p}}^T\mathbf{a}^T)\,(\mathbf{a}\mathbf{p}) = \lambda\bar{\lambda}\bar{\mathbf{p}}^T\mathbf{p}$$

$$\Rightarrow (\lambda\bar{\lambda} - 1)\,\bar{\mathbf{p}}^T\mathbf{p} = \mathbf{0},$$

where, by Lemma 1, $\bar{\mathbf{p}}^T\mathbf{p}$ is not zero. Hence

$$\lambda\bar{\lambda} = 1,$$

so that

$$|\lambda^2| = 1$$

or

$$|\lambda| = 1$$

since the modulus is, by definition, positive.

3. The Cayley–Hamilton theorem (elementary case)

In Chapter 12, Exercise I, we gave a theorem that is now becoming more pressing. Let **a** be a matrix of type 2×2, whose characteristic equation is

$$\begin{vmatrix} a_{11} - \lambda & a_{12} \\ a_{21} & a_{22} - \lambda \end{vmatrix} = 0,$$

or

$$\lambda^2 - (a_{11} + a_{22})\lambda + (a_{11}a_{22} - a_{12}a_{21}) = 0.$$

We are to prove the Cayley–Hamilton theorem (true for matrices of type $n \times n$ generally) that *the square matrix* **a** *satisfies its characteristic equation*, in the sense that

$$\mathbf{a}^2 - (a_{11} + a_{22})\,\mathbf{a} + (a_{11}a_{22} - a_{12}a_{21})\,\mathbf{I} = \mathbf{0}.$$

[This proof, which does not extend to values of n beyond 2, is also restricted to invertible (non-singular) matrices.]

Write
$$\Delta = \det \mathbf{a} \neq 0.$$

Then (Chapter 12, Section 9)

$$\mathbf{a}^{-1} = \Delta^{-1}\begin{pmatrix} a_{22} & -a_{12} \\ -a_{21} & a_{11} \end{pmatrix},$$

so that
$$\mathbf{a} + \Delta\mathbf{a}^{-1} = \begin{pmatrix} a_{11} + a_{22} & 0 \\ 0 & a_{11} + a_{22} \end{pmatrix}$$

$$= (a_{11} + a_{22})\,\mathbf{I}.$$

Multiply by **a**; then
$$\mathbf{a}^2 - (a_{11} + a_{22})\,\mathbf{a} + \Delta\mathbf{I} = \mathbf{0}.$$

4. The homogeneous isometry $\mathbf{p}' = \mathbf{ap}$ with equal eigenvalues

Since the eigenvalues are the roots of a quadratic equation with real coefficients, they must be real if they are equal, and so their ('coincident') values are $+1, +1$ or $-1, -1$. Suppose them to be $+1, +1$.

The characteristic equation is then

$$\lambda^2 - 2\lambda + 1 = 0,$$

so that, by the Cayley–Hamilton theorem,

$$\mathbf{a}^2 - 2\mathbf{a} + \mathbf{I} = \mathbf{0}.$$

Multiply by $\mathbf{a}^T$ and use the fact that, for an isometry, $\mathbf{a}^T\mathbf{a} = \mathbf{I}$. Then

$$\mathbf{a} + \mathbf{a}^T = 2\mathbf{I}.$$

Write
$$\mathbf{b} = \mathbf{a} - \mathbf{I},$$

so that
$$\mathbf{b}^T = \mathbf{a}^T - \mathbf{I}.$$

Then
$$\mathbf{b}^T\mathbf{b} = (\mathbf{a}^T - \mathbf{I})\,(\mathbf{a} - \mathbf{I})$$

$$= \mathbf{a}^T\mathbf{a} - \mathbf{a} - \mathbf{a}^T + \mathbf{I}$$

$$= 2\mathbf{I} - \mathbf{a} - \mathbf{a}^T$$

$$= \mathbf{0}.$$

Suppose, finally, that

$$\mathbf{b} = \begin{pmatrix} \alpha & \beta \\ \gamma & \delta \end{pmatrix}.$$

Then

$$\mathbf{b}^T\mathbf{b} = \begin{pmatrix} \alpha & \gamma \\ \beta & \delta \end{pmatrix}\begin{pmatrix} \alpha & \beta \\ \gamma & \delta \end{pmatrix}$$

$$= \begin{pmatrix} \alpha^2+\gamma^2 & \alpha\beta+\gamma\delta \\ \beta\alpha+\delta\gamma & \beta^2+\delta^2 \end{pmatrix}.$$

Since this is zero,

$$\alpha^2+\gamma^2 = 0 \quad \text{and} \quad \beta^2+\delta^2 = 0$$

for *real* α, β, γ, δ. Hence $\alpha = \gamma = 0$ and $\beta = \delta = 0$, giving

$$\mathbf{b} = \mathbf{0},$$

so that

$$\mathbf{a} = \mathbf{I}.$$

Thus *the only isometry with eigenvalues* 1, 1 *is the identity.*

Exercise B

1. Prove similarly that *the only isometry with eigenvalues* -1, -1 *is the half-turn about the origin.*

5. The homogeneous isometry with eigenvalues $+1$, -1

Let the isometry be

$$\mathbf{p}' = \mathbf{a}\mathbf{p} \quad (\mathbf{a}^T\mathbf{a} = \mathbf{I})$$

with eigenvalues $+1$, -1.

Take any eigenvector $\mathbf{u}$ corresponding to $+1$, so that

$$\mathbf{a}\mathbf{u} = \mathbf{u}.$$

Then all the points with coordinate vectors $\mathbf{x}$ of the form $\rho\mathbf{u}$ are self-corresponding, since

$$\mathbf{a}(\rho\mathbf{u}) = \rho\mathbf{u},$$

and so there is a line l of self-corresponding points.

Consider next an eigenvector $\mathbf{v}$ corresponding to -1, so that

$$\mathbf{a}\mathbf{v} = -\mathbf{v}.$$

The points with coordinate vectors $\mathbf{y}$ of the form $\sigma\mathbf{v}$ lie on a line m, but this time the transform of $\mathbf{y}$ is given by

$$\mathbf{y}' = \mathbf{a}(\sigma\mathbf{v}) = -\sigma\mathbf{v} = -\mathbf{y},$$

so that the corresponding points Y, Y' define a segment whose middle point is the origin O.

The two lines l, m are in fact perpendicular:

It was shown in Chapter 12, Section 13, that

$$OU \perp OV \Leftrightarrow \mathbf{u}^T\mathbf{v} = 0.$$

Here, $$\mathbf{au} = \mathbf{u}, \; \mathbf{av} = -\mathbf{v}$$

$$\Rightarrow \mathbf{u}^T\mathbf{v} = (\mathbf{u}^T\mathbf{a}^T)(-\mathbf{av})$$

$$= -\mathbf{u}^T(\mathbf{a}^T\mathbf{a})\mathbf{v}$$

$$= -\mathbf{u}^T\mathbf{v} \qquad (\mathbf{a}^T\mathbf{a} = \mathbf{I}).$$

Hence $$\mathbf{u}^T\mathbf{v} = 0$$

$$\Rightarrow l \perp m.$$

The isometry is the *reflection* with l as axis.

6. The homogeneous isometry with complex eigenvalues

It was proved in Chapter 13, Section 5, that an orthogonal matrix assumes one or other of the forms

$$\begin{pmatrix} \cos\theta & \sin\theta \\ \sin\theta & -\cos\theta \end{pmatrix}, \; \begin{pmatrix} \cos\theta & -\sin\theta \\ \sin\theta & \cos\theta \end{pmatrix}.$$

It is easily checked that the eigenvalues of the former are ± 1, discussed in Section 5.

Consider then the second form

$$\mathbf{a} = \begin{pmatrix} \cos\theta & -\sin\theta \\ \sin\theta & \cos\theta \end{pmatrix}.$$

The characteristic equation is

$$\lambda^2 - 2\lambda\cos\theta + 1 = 0,$$

so that, by the Cayley–Hamilton theorem,

$$\mathbf{a}^2 - 2\mathbf{a}\cos\theta + \mathbf{I} = \mathbf{0}$$

or, since $\mathbf{a}^T\mathbf{a} = \mathbf{I}$,

$$\mathbf{a} + \mathbf{a}^T = 2\mathbf{I}\cos\theta.$$

This result may be illustrated by confirming that *the transformation is a rotation about the origin O:*

Let P be transformed to Q by the matrix $\mathbf{a}$, so that

$$\mathbf{q} = \mathbf{ap},$$

and suppose that $\angle POQ = \alpha$ (Figure 205). Then

$$PQ^2 = OP^2 + OQ^2 - 2OP \cdot OQ \cos\alpha$$

$$\Rightarrow (\mathbf{q}-\mathbf{p})^T(\mathbf{q}-\mathbf{p}) = \mathbf{p}^T\mathbf{p} + \mathbf{q}^T\mathbf{q} - 2OP \cdot OQ \cos\alpha$$

$$\Rightarrow \mathbf{q}^T\mathbf{p} + \mathbf{p}^T\mathbf{q} = 2OP \cdot OQ \cos\alpha$$

on expanding the left-hand side.

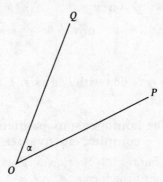

Fig. 205

But $$\mathbf{q}^T = \mathbf{p}^T\mathbf{a}^T,$$

so that $$\mathbf{p}^T\mathbf{a}^T\mathbf{p} + \mathbf{p}^T\mathbf{a}\mathbf{p} = 2OP \cdot OQ \cos\alpha$$

$$\Rightarrow \mathbf{p}^T(\mathbf{a}^T + \mathbf{a})\,\mathbf{p} = 2OP \cdot OQ \cos\alpha$$

$$\Rightarrow \mathbf{p}^T(2\mathbf{I}\cos\theta)\,\mathbf{p} = 2OP \cdot OQ \cos\alpha,$$

as above. Hence

$$\mathbf{p}^T\mathbf{p}\cos\theta = 2OP \cdot OQ \cos\alpha.$$

Finally, $$OQ^2 = \mathbf{q}^T\mathbf{q} = \mathbf{p}^T\mathbf{a}^T\mathbf{a}\mathbf{p}$$

$$= \mathbf{p}^T\mathbf{p}$$

$$= OP^2,$$

so that $OP = OQ = +\sqrt{(\mathbf{p}^T\mathbf{p})}$.

It follows that

$$\cos\alpha = \cos\theta$$

$$= \text{constant determined by } \mathbf{a},$$

so that *the transformation is a rotation about O through the angle θ.*

7. Reflections; an alternative treatment

Let l be a given line through the origin of coordinates and making a counterclockwise angle α with the axis OX_1 (Figure 206). Take the point U on l such that $\overrightarrow{OU}$ is of unit length. The position vector of U is thus $\mathbf{u}$, where

$$\mathbf{u} = \begin{pmatrix} \cos\alpha \\ \sin\alpha \end{pmatrix}.$$

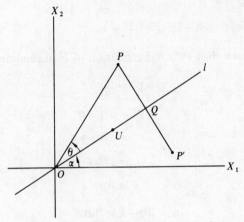

Fig. 206

Let P be an arbitrary point with coordinate vector $\mathbf{p}$. Let Q, with coordinate vector $\mathbf{q}$, be the foot of the perpendicular from P to l and denote by θ the angle $\triangle QOP$. Then, by Chapter 12, Section 13,

$$\mathbf{u}^T\mathbf{p} = OU . OP \cos\theta$$
$$= OP \cos\theta \qquad (OU = 1)$$
$$= OQ,$$

so that
$$\mathbf{q} = \mathbf{u}(OQ)$$
$$= \mathbf{u}(\mathbf{u}^T\mathbf{p})$$
$$= (\mathbf{u}\mathbf{u}^T)\,\mathbf{p}.$$

Hence *the projection of P on the line l joining O to U (where $\overrightarrow{OU} = 1$) is given by the formula*
$$\mathbf{q} = \mathbf{b}\mathbf{p},$$
where
$$\mathbf{b} = \mathbf{u}\mathbf{u}^T.$$

Note that $\mathbf{b}$ is of type 2×2 and is very different from the scalar $\mathbf{u}^T\mathbf{u}$.

Exercise C

Prove the relations:

1. det $\mathbf{b} = 0$.

2. $\mathbf{b}^T = \mathbf{b}$; $\mathbf{b}^2 = \mathbf{b}$.

3. $\mathbf{c}^2 = \mathbf{c}$, where $\mathbf{c} = \mathbf{I} - \mathbf{b}$.

4. $\mathbf{b}^T\mathbf{c} = \mathbf{c}^T\mathbf{b} = 0$.

5. $(2\mathbf{b} - \mathbf{I})^2 = \mathbf{I}$; $(2\mathbf{b} - \mathbf{I})^T (2\mathbf{b} - \mathbf{I}) = \mathbf{I}$.

Suppose now that P' is the reflection of P in the line l. Then

$$\mathbf{p} + \mathbf{p}' = 2\mathbf{q}$$
$$\Rightarrow \mathbf{p}' = 2\mathbf{q} - \mathbf{p}$$
$$= 2\mathbf{bp} - \mathbf{p}$$
$$= (2\mathbf{b} - \mathbf{I})\,\mathbf{p}$$
$$= \mathbf{ap},$$

where $$\mathbf{a} = 2\mathbf{b} - \mathbf{I} = 2\mathbf{u}\mathbf{u}^T - \mathbf{I}.$$

We have therefore derived the matrix $\mathbf{a}$ of the reflection in the line l.

Exercise D

Eigenvalues for a shear

Eigenvalues and eigenvectors for shears. Compare Chapter 13, Section 7.

1. Prove that the eigenvalues of the shear matrix

$$\begin{pmatrix} 1 & k \\ 0 & 1 \end{pmatrix}$$

both have value 1, and find the corresponding eigenvector.
  Interpret geometrically.

2. A shear has its axis as the line $p_2 = p_1 \tan \beta$ referred to coordinate axes OX_1, OX_2. By rotating the coordinate system to a new one with the axis OY_1 along the axis of the shear, or otherwise, obtain the equation of the shear in the form

$$\mathbf{p}' = \mathbf{dp},$$

where ($\mathbf{p}'$ and $\mathbf{p}$ being expressed relative to the new axes OY_1, OY_2)

$$\mathbf{d} = \begin{pmatrix} \cos\beta & -\sin\beta \\ \sin\beta & \cos\beta \end{pmatrix} \begin{pmatrix} 1 & d \\ 0 & 1 \end{pmatrix} \begin{pmatrix} \cos\beta & \sin\beta \\ -\sin\beta & \cos\beta \end{pmatrix}$$

$$= \begin{pmatrix} 1 - d\sin\beta\cos\beta & d\cos^2\beta \\ -d\sin^2\beta & 1 + d\sin\beta\cos\beta \end{pmatrix}.$$

3. By finding the eigenvalues of $\mathbf{d}$, prove that *every shear has each of its eigenvalues equal to* 1.

4. Find the product of the shears

$$\begin{pmatrix} 1 & a \\ 0 & 1 \end{pmatrix}, \quad \begin{pmatrix} 1 & 0 \\ b & 1 \end{pmatrix}$$

with perpendicular axes, and, using Question 3, prove that it cannot be a shear.

15

THE NON-HOMOGENEOUS
SIMILARITIES

We recall that a homogeneous similarity is one in which *the origin of coordinates* is self-corresponding. The words *homogeneous, non-homogeneous* are properties of the algebra rather than of the basic geometry.

1. The matrix form of equation

Denote by $[\mathbf{T}]$ a given similarity and choose a coordinate system in which *the origin O is not a self-corresponding point*. Let $O[\mathbf{T}]$ be the point O'.

Subject an arbitrary point P of the plane to the similarity transformation $[\mathbf{T}]$ and then to the translation $\overrightarrow{O'O}$. The operation retains similarity, *but now the point O is self-corresponding*, having been sent to O' by $[\mathbf{T}]$ and returned to O by $\overrightarrow{O'O}$. This product can therefore be expressed homogeneously with matrix $\mathbf{a}$ where, if the similarity ratio is k, Chapter 13, Section 3, gives the condition

$$\mathbf{a}^T\mathbf{a} = k^2\mathbf{I}.$$

If $\overrightarrow{OO'} = \mathbf{b} \,(\neq \mathbf{0})$ and if $\mathbf{p}'$ corresponds to $\mathbf{p}$ in the original transformation, then $\mathbf{p}' - \mathbf{b}$ corresponds to $\mathbf{p}$ in the new similarity, so that

$$\mathbf{p}' - \mathbf{b} = \mathbf{a}\mathbf{p}.$$

Hence
$$\mathbf{p}' = \mathbf{a}\mathbf{p} + \mathbf{b},$$

where $\mathbf{a}^T\mathbf{a} = k^2\mathbf{I}$, $\mathbf{b} \neq \mathbf{0}$. This is *the form of equation for a non-homogeneous similarity*, and it represents an isometry when $k^2 = 1$.

Exercise A

1. Prove that a translation can be expressed in the form
$$\mathbf{p}' = \mathbf{p} + \mathbf{b}.$$

2. Prove that a glide-reflection, whose axis is the line through the origin making a counterclockwise angle α with OX_1 and whose glide is of length k, can be expressed in the form
$$\mathbf{p}' = \mathbf{a}\mathbf{p} + k\mathbf{b},$$

where
$$\mathbf{a} = \begin{pmatrix} \cos 2\alpha & \sin 2\alpha \\ \sin 2\alpha & -\cos 2\alpha \end{pmatrix}, \quad \mathbf{b} = \begin{pmatrix} \cos \alpha \\ \sin \alpha \end{pmatrix}.$$

3. Prove that, if $\mathbf{a}$ is the matrix of a half-turn, then the transformation
$$\mathbf{p}' = \mathbf{a}\mathbf{p} + \mathbf{b}$$
is a half-turn.

2. The similarity $\mathbf{p}' = \mathbf{a}\mathbf{p} + \mathbf{b}$

Consider a given similarity
$$\mathbf{p}' = \mathbf{a}\mathbf{p} + \mathbf{b} \quad (\mathbf{a}^T\mathbf{a} = k^2\mathbf{I}, \ \mathbf{b} \neq \mathbf{0}).$$

(i) We prove first that, *if*
$$|\mathbf{a} - \mathbf{I}| = 0,$$
then $k^2 = 1$ and $\mathbf{a}$ is orthogonal.

Write $\mathbf{a} = k\mathbf{c}$. Then
$$\mathbf{a}^T\mathbf{a} = k^2\mathbf{I} \Rightarrow \mathbf{c}^T\mathbf{c} = \mathbf{I},$$
so that $\mathbf{c}$ is orthogonal. Further,
$$|\mathbf{a} - \mathbf{I}| = |k\mathbf{c} - \mathbf{I}| = k^2|\mathbf{c} - k^{-1}\mathbf{I}|$$
(on 'taking out' the factor k from each of the two rows of the determinant). Hence
$$|\mathbf{a} - \mathbf{I}| = 0 \Rightarrow |\mathbf{c} - k^{-1}\mathbf{I}| = 0$$
$$\Rightarrow k^{-1} \text{ is an eigenvalue of } \mathbf{c}.$$
But $\mathbf{c}$ is orthogonal, and so $k^{-1} = \pm 1$, that is,
$$k^2 = 1.$$

(ii) Consider next the case $k^2 \neq 1$, so that *the similarity is not an isometry.* Then
$$|\mathbf{a} - \mathbf{I}| \neq 0,$$
so that $\mathbf{a} - \mathbf{I}$ is invertible, and the relation
$$\mathbf{h} = \mathbf{a}\mathbf{h} + \mathbf{b} \quad \text{or} \quad (\mathbf{I} - \mathbf{a})\mathbf{h} = \mathbf{b},$$
has a solution for $\mathbf{h}$, given by
$$\mathbf{h} = (\mathbf{I} - \mathbf{a})^{-1}\mathbf{b}.$$
That is, *the similarity has a self-corresponding point $\mathbf{h}$ not at the origin.*

Further, this self-corresponding point is *unique*, since
$$\left.\begin{array}{l}(\mathbf{I} - \mathbf{a})\mathbf{h}_1 = \mathbf{b} \\ (\mathbf{I} - \mathbf{a})\mathbf{h}_2 = \mathbf{b}\end{array}\right\} \Rightarrow (\mathbf{I} - \mathbf{a})(\mathbf{h}_1 - \mathbf{h}_2) = 0$$
$$\Rightarrow \mathbf{h}_1 - \mathbf{h}_2 = 0$$
since $(\mathbf{I} - \mathbf{a})^{-1}$ exists.

Hence *the equation*

$$\mathbf{p}' = \mathbf{ap} + \mathbf{b} \quad (\mathbf{a}^T\mathbf{a} = k^2\mathbf{I},\ k^2 \neq 1,\ \mathbf{b} \neq \mathbf{0})$$

defines a non-isometric similarity with a unique self-corresponding point.
Writing the relation in the form

$$\mathbf{p}' - \mathbf{h} = \mathbf{a}(\mathbf{p} - \mathbf{h}),$$

which follows from the equation $\mathbf{h} = \mathbf{ah} + \mathbf{b}$, we see that *the similarity
is* either *a spiral similarity with centre H* or *a stretch reflection with
centre H*.

These two similarities were studied in Chapter 11 and given a brief
mention in Chapter 13, Section 6. It may be convenient to follow with
a treatment leading from the equation to the underlying geometry.

3. Geometrical treatment; the spiral similarity

Suppose that the relation

$$\mathbf{p}' = \mathbf{ap} + \mathbf{b} \quad (\mathbf{a}^T\mathbf{a} = k^2\mathbf{I},\ \mathbf{b} \neq \mathbf{0})$$

represents a spiral similarity. This can be taken in two stages:
  (i) the spiral similarity

$$\mathbf{p}_1 = \mathbf{ap},$$

which has the origin O as a self-corresponding point;
  (ii) the translation

$$\mathbf{p}' = \mathbf{p}_1 + \mathbf{b}.$$

Let B be the point for which $\overrightarrow{OB} = \mathbf{b}$; and denote by α the counterclockwise angle of the spiral similarity $\mathbf{p}_1 = \mathbf{ap}$ (Figure 207).
An arbitrary point P is transformed by two stages:
  (i) the ray $\overrightarrow{OP}$ is rotated to $\overrightarrow{OP_2}$ so that $\triangle POP_2 = \alpha$, and then
P_1 is taken on OP_2 so that $\overrightarrow{OP_1} = k\overrightarrow{OP_2}$;
  (ii) the point P_1 is translated to P' so that $\overrightarrow{P_1P'} = \overrightarrow{OB} = \mathbf{b}$.
Note that the triangle OPP_1 is constant in shape, since

$$\triangle POP_1 = \alpha = \text{constant and } OP_1/OP = \text{constant.}$$

There is therefore one particular *size* of this triangle for which
$P_1P = OB$; this may be referred to as a 'constant-sized triangle
OQQ_1'.

Let the constant-sized triangle OQQ_1 be rotated round O till Q_1Q is
parallel to OB. In that position, the lines $\overrightarrow{Q_1Q}$, $\overrightarrow{OB}$ are equal and
parallel. For reference, denote this position of the triangle by OHH_1.

Then *the point H is self-corresponding in the given transformation* $\mathbf{p}' = \mathbf{ap} + \mathbf{b}$; for, from the definitions,

$$\mathbf{h}_1 = \mathbf{ah},$$

and then

$$\mathbf{h}_1 + \mathbf{b} = \mathbf{h}$$

so that

$$\mathbf{h} = \mathbf{ah} + \mathbf{b}.$$

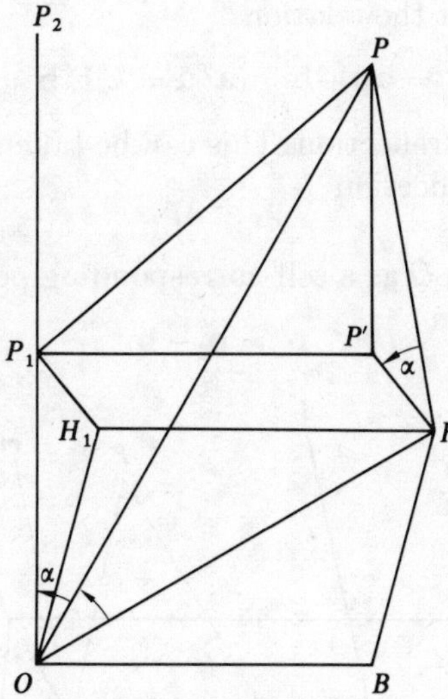

Fig. 207

We now prove that *the given transformation is equivalent to a spiral similarity about H with angle α and ratio k:*

The spiral similarity $\mathbf{p}_1 = \mathbf{ap}$ gives

$$P \rightarrow P_1, \quad H \rightarrow H_1$$

so that the angle between $\overrightarrow{HP}$ and $\overrightarrow{H_1P_1}$ is the angle α. But, by parallelograms,

$$H_1P_1 \parallel HP',$$

so that

$$\triangle PHP' = \alpha.$$

Further, the triangles HOP, H_1OP_1 are similar, since

$$\triangle HOP = \triangle HOH_1 - \triangle POH_1 = \alpha - \triangle POH_1 = \triangle H_1OP_1$$

and the sides OH_1, OP_1 are kOH, kOP respectively. It follows that $H_1P_1 = kHP$, so that

$$HP' = kHP.$$

The two relations

$$\triangle PHP' = \alpha, \quad HP' = kHP$$

confirm that *the transformation is the spiral similarity about H with angle α and ratio k.*

4. Geometrical treatment; the stretch reflection

Suppose next that the relation

$$\mathbf{p'} = \mathbf{ap} + \mathbf{b} \quad (\mathbf{a}^T\mathbf{a} = k^2\mathbf{I}, \ \mathbf{b} \neq \mathbf{0})$$

represents a stretch reflection. This can be taken in two stages:
   (i) the stretch reflection

$$\mathbf{p_1} = \mathbf{ap},$$

which has the origin O as a self-corresponding point;
   (ii) the translation

$$\mathbf{p'} = \mathbf{p_1} + \mathbf{b}.$$

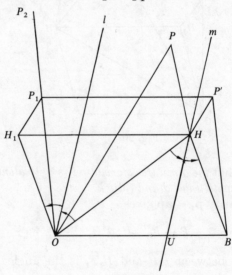

Fig. 208

Let B be the point for which $\overrightarrow{OB} = \mathbf{b}$; and denote by l the axis of the stretch reflection $\mathbf{p_1} = \mathbf{ap}$ (Figure 208) constructed by bisecting $\triangle POP_1$ for any position of P.

An arbitrary point P is transformed by two stages:
   (i) the point P is reflected in l to P_2 and then P_1 is taken on OP_2 such that $\overrightarrow{OP_1} = k\overrightarrow{OP_2}$;
   (ii) the point P_1 is translated to P' so that $\overrightarrow{P_1P'} = \overrightarrow{OB} = \mathbf{b}$.

In order to locate the self-corresponding point H geometrically, we analyse the position resulting when H is *assumed* to be known. Then $\overrightarrow{H_1H} = \overrightarrow{OB}$ determines the position of H_1, which, in its turn, arises also by stretch reflection from H. Thus l bisects the angle $\measuredangle HOH_1$ and $OH_1 = kOH$.

Let the line m be drawn through the (assumed) position of H parallel to l. Since $OBHH_1$ is a parallelogram, it follows quickly that m bisects the angle $\measuredangle OHB$, and also that $BH = kOH$.

At this stage it may be convenient to recall the results of Chapter 10, Section 7:

If the internal bisector of the angle H of a triangle BHO (Figure 209) meets the line OB in U, while the external bisector meets it in V, then U, V are the two fixed points for which

$$\frac{BU}{UO} = \frac{BH}{OH} = k, \quad \frac{BV}{VO} = \frac{BH}{OH} = k,$$

and H lies on the fixed circle having UV as a diameter.

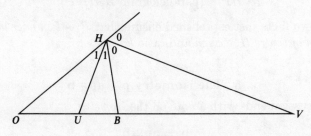

Fig. 209

For the present problem, in which $BH/OH = k$:

(i) The point U is determined, and $m \parallel l$, where l is a fixed line; the line UH is thus determined.

(ii) H lies on the circle, just described, passing through U and V.

Taken together, these two facts mean that H is at the intersection other than U of the fixed line m with the fixed circle, and so H can be constructed.

We now prove that *the given transformation is equivalent to a stretch reflection with H as vertex and m as axis of reflection.*

Let P be any point of the plane, with P_1 and P' defined, as before, by reference to O and the line l.

Under the stretch reflection $\mathbf{p_1} = \mathbf{ap}$, the points H, P give rise to H_1, P_1 respectively, so that the triangle OP_1H_1 is similar to the triangle OPH, with similarity ratio k.

9

Hence, *first*,

$$\triangle OHP = \triangle P_1 H_1 O \quad \text{(reversed orientation)}$$

so that
$$\triangle UHP = \triangle UHO + \triangle OHP$$

$$= \triangle BHU + \triangle P_1 H_1 O$$

$$= \triangle P_1 H_1 O + \triangle BHU.$$

But the triangles $OP_1 H_1$, $BP'H$ are congruent under the translation **b**, so that, in all,

$$\triangle UHP = \triangle P'HB + \triangle BHU$$

$$= \triangle P'HU.$$

It follows that

$$\triangle (PH, m) = \triangle (m, HP'),$$

so that m bisects the angle $P'HP$.

Second,

$$kHP = H_1 P_1 \quad \text{(triangles } OPH, OP_1 H_1 \text{ similar)}$$

$$= HP' \quad \text{(parallelogram } H_1 HP'P).$$

The two facts just established ensure that $P \to P'$ *under the stretch reflection of centre H, axis m and ratio k.*

5. The isometry $\mathbf{p}' = a\mathbf{p} + \mathbf{b}$

The discussion ends with a note on the *isometry*

$$\mathbf{p}' = a\mathbf{p} + \mathbf{b},$$

where $\mathbf{a}^T \mathbf{a} = \mathbf{I}$ and $\mathbf{b} \neq \mathbf{0}$. The former condition confirms the transformation $\mathbf{p}_1 = a\mathbf{p}$ as an *isometry* and the subsequent relation $\mathbf{p}' = \mathbf{p}_1 + \mathbf{b}$ defines a *translation* following the isometry.

The two results which follow give geometrical treatments for the cases

(i) $\mathbf{p}_1 = a\mathbf{p}$, a rotation,

(ii) $\mathbf{p}_1 = a\mathbf{p}$, a reflection.

(i) *Rotation followed by translation.* Let the rotation

$$\mathbf{p}_1 = a\mathbf{p}$$

have centre O and angle α; also let B be the point such that

$$\overrightarrow{OB} = \mathbf{b}.$$

The result of rotating B to B_1 and then translating B_1 to B' is a *rhombus* $OBB'B_1$, since $\overrightarrow{OB} = \overrightarrow{B_1B'} = \mathbf{b}$ and $OB = OB_1$ by the rotation (Figure 210).

Thus B transforms by the given isometry to B'.

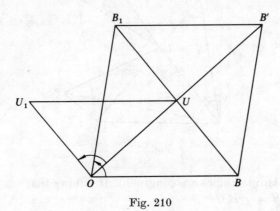

Fig. 210

Suppose now that the isometry has a self-corresponding point U. Then OU rotates to OU_1, where $\angle UOU_1 = \alpha$, and $\overrightarrow{U_1U} = \overrightarrow{OB}$. Thus $OBUU_1$ is a parallelogram, and the 'triangle of rotation' OUU_1 is similar to the 'triangle of rotation' OBB_1. Hence

$$\angle OBU = \angle UU_1O \quad \text{(by the parallelogram)}$$

$$= \angle BB_1O \quad \text{(similar triangles)}$$

$$= \angle OBB_1 \quad (OB = OB_1).$$

That is, U lies on the diagonal BB_1. It is located there by the fact that $UO = UB$, each being equal to U_1O (rotation and parallelogram respectively), so that U is the point where BB_1 meets the mediator of OB.

By the symmetry of the rhombus about BB_1, it follows further that $B'U = UO = UB$.

It is now possible to prove that *the transformation* $\mathbf{p}' = a\mathbf{p} + \mathbf{b}$ *is in fact equivalent to a rotation about U through an angle* α.

Let P be an arbitrary point; rotation about O gives P_1 and translation then gives P' (Figure 211).

Under the transformation $\mathbf{p}' = a\mathbf{p} + \mathbf{b}$, then, there are three correspondences:

$$U \to U, \quad B \to B', \quad P \to P',$$

so that $$\triangle UBP \to \triangle UB'P'.$$

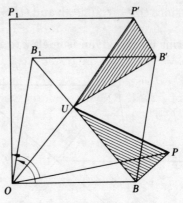

Fig. 211

Hence these two triangles are congruent. It follows that
    (a) $\triangle BUP = \triangle B'UP'$,

so that
$$\triangle PUP' = \triangle PUB' + \triangle B'UP'$$
$$= \triangle PUB' + \triangle BUP$$
$$= \triangle BUB'$$
$$= \alpha$$

since the isosceles triangles BUB', BOB_1 are similar, being equiangular;
    (b) $UP = UP'$.

These two results confirm that P' can be obtained from P by rotation through the angle α.

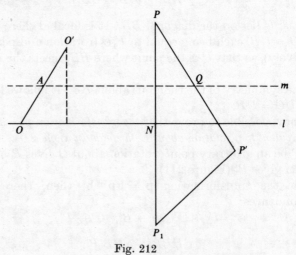

Fig. 212

(ii) *Reflection followed by translation.* Let a reflection $\mathbf{p}_1 = a\mathbf{p}$ have axis l, and let it be followed by a translation $\mathbf{b} = \overrightarrow{OO'}$ measured from the origin O, which necessarily lies on l (Figure 212).

Select any point P. Let P_1 be the result of reflecting in l and P' the result of translating P_1 so that $\overrightarrow{P_1P'} = \overrightarrow{OO'}$. The line PP_1 meets l in N, the middle point of PP_1; let Q be the middle point of PP' and A the middle point of OO'. Then

$$\left. \begin{array}{l} PN = NP_1 \\ PQ = QP' \end{array} \right\} \Rightarrow \overrightarrow{NQ} = \tfrac{1}{2}\overrightarrow{P_1P'} = \tfrac{1}{2}\overrightarrow{OO'} = \overrightarrow{OA},$$

so that $AQ \parallel l$. Hence Q lies on the *fixed* line m through A parallel to l. Also, since $\overrightarrow{P_1P'} = \overrightarrow{OO'}$, the projection of P_1P' on m is equal to the *fixed* projection of OO' on m. Hence *the isometry from P to P' is a glide reflection of axis m and length of glide equal to the projection of $\overrightarrow{OO'}$ on m.*

MISCELLANEOUS EXERCISE

1. In the square $EFGH$, points X on the side EF and Y on the side GH are such that $EX = GY$. Prove that the triangles HEX, FGY are congruent and that the lines HX, FY are parallel.   [C.]

2. $ABCD$ is a parallelogram and X is the middle point of BC (Figure 213). The line AX produced meets DC produced at Q. The parallelogram $ABPQ$ is completed. Prove that
  (i) the triangles ABX, QCX are congruent,
  (ii) $DC = CQ = QP$,
  (iii) the area of the parallelogram $ABCD$ is equal to the area of the triangle BCP.   [C.]

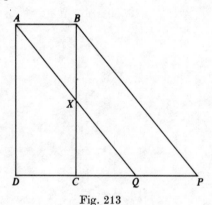

Fig. 213

3. In a quadrilateral $ABCD$, the diagonals AC, BD are equal. The middle points of the sides AB, BC, CD, DA are P, Q, R, S respectively. Prove that $PQRS$ is a rhombus and hence that $PR \perp QS$.   [C.]

4. In Figure 214, APC and AQB are straight lines; CQT and AT are tangents to the circle PAQ. Prove that $TA \parallel BC$ and that $CB = CQ$.   [C.]

5. $ABCD$ is a parallelogram; E is the middle point of AB; F is a point on DE such that $DE = 3FE$. Prove that A, F, C are collinear and that F is a point of trisection of AC.   [S.]

6. Two lines l, m meet in a point O, and P is an arbitrary point of the plane. First, P is reflected in l to give a point V, and V is reflected in m to give a point W; second, P is reflected in m to give a point Q, and Q is reflected in l

to give a point R. Prove that P, V, W, Q, R lie on a circle whose centre is O, and that $PW = PR$.   [C.J.E.]

7. Write down the coordinates of the reflection of the point $\{4, 3\}$ in the line whose equation is $p_1 = p_2$.   [C.]

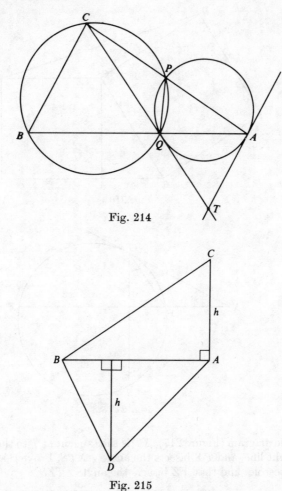

Fig. 214

Fig. 215

8. In the diagram (Figure 215), $\angle BAC = \frac{1}{2}\pi$ and the perpendicular distance from D to BA is equal to AC. State clearly two geometrical transformations which, if combined, will map the triangle ABD on the triangle ABC.

[They are not both isometries.]   [C.]

9. ABC is a triangle in which $AB \perp AC$. Squares are constructed on the sides BC and AC, then the corners D, E are joined (Figure 216).

When the triangle ABC is rotated about C in the *clockwise* sense through $\frac{1}{2}\pi$, the point A is mapped on A'. Prove that the points A', C, E lie on a straight line.

Hence prove that the triangles ABC, DCE are equal in area.   [C.]

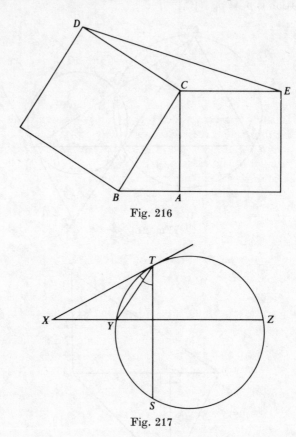

Fig. 216

Fig. 217

10. In the diagram (Figure 217), XT is the tangent at T to the circle, XYZ is a straight line, and TY bisects the angle $\angle XTS$. Prove that the triangle YTS is isosceles and that YZ bisects the angle $\angle TZS$.

11. In the triangle ABC, the middle point of BC is D, and G is any point on AD. Through C a line is drawn parallel to GB to meet AD produced at H. Prove that the triangles GDB, HDC are congruent and that $GC \parallel BH$.   [C.]

12. Points A, B, C, D are taken on a circle; AD meets BC in P and AB meets CD in Q. The bisector of the angle APB meets the circle in U and V. By reflection in the line PUV, the points A, B, C, D, Q become A', B', C', D', Q' respectively. State why

   (i) A', B', C', D', U, V lie on a circle equal to the given circle;

(ii) QQ' is perpendicular to UV;

(iii) $A'B'$ meets AB in a point L of UV and $C'D'$ meets CD in a point M of UV.

Give reasons for the two statements

$$\angle QCB = \angle B'AB = \angle B'A'B$$

and deduce that $A'B' \parallel CD$.

Show that $QLQ'M$ is a rhombus and hence that QQ' is the bisector of the angle BQC. [C.]

13. Two circles intersect in A and B. [A convenient figure is obtained by taking the radii to be approximately 5 units, 4 units and the distance between the centres to be approximately 6 units.] A line through A cuts the first circle again in P and the second in Q. Prove that the triangle PBQ is constant in shape for all positions of the line through A.

The line through B parallel to PAQ cuts the first circle again in R and the second in S. Prove that the points P, Q, S, R are at the vertices of a parallelogram, two of whose sides are of length AB.

Give a construction for the chord PAQ if the parallelogram is to be a rhombus. [It may be assumed that the dimensions of the figure are such that this construction is possible.] [C.J.E.]

14. Two circles intersect in distinct points A, B. A variable chord through A meets one circle again in P and the other in Q. Find that position of the chord for which the length of PQ is greatest. [C.J.E.]

15. ABC is a triangle with vertices ordered in the counterclockwise sense. Show that the resultant of counterclockwise rotations of angles $\pi - A$ about $A, \pi - B$ about $B, \pi - C$ about C (in the order mentioned) is a translation of the plane in the direction AC, through a distance equal to the perimeter of the triangle. [C.J.E.]

16. Investigate the effect of the following matrices upon the triangle with vertices $\{0, 0\}, \{2, 1\}, \{1, 2\}$:

(i) $\begin{pmatrix} -2 & 0 \\ 0 & -2 \end{pmatrix}$;   (ii) $\begin{pmatrix} \frac{1}{2}\sqrt{3} & -\frac{1}{2} \\ \frac{1}{2} & \frac{1}{2}\sqrt{3} \end{pmatrix}$;

(iii) $\begin{pmatrix} 1 & 2 \\ 0 & 1 \end{pmatrix}$;   (iv) $\begin{pmatrix} 1 & 0 \\ 0 & 3 \end{pmatrix}$.   [S.]

17. The position vectors of the vertices A, B, C, D of a square are

$$\mathbf{a} = \{1, 2\}, \quad \mathbf{b} = \{4, 2\}, \quad \mathbf{c} = \{4, 5\}, \quad \mathbf{d} = \{1, 5\}.$$

They are transformed by the matrix $\mathbf{u}$, where

$$\mathbf{u} = \begin{pmatrix} 0 & 1 \\ 1 & 1 \end{pmatrix},$$

to the points P, Q, R, S given, in similar notation, by the relations

$$\mathbf{p} = \mathbf{ua}, \quad \mathbf{q} = \mathbf{ub}, \quad \mathbf{r} = \mathbf{uc}, \quad \mathbf{s} = \mathbf{ud}.$$

Draw a diagram in which the points A, B, C, D and P, Q, R, S are clearly labelled.

More generally, points A, B, C, D are now taken to be the vertices of a parallelogram, where

$$\mathbf{a} = \{\alpha_1, \alpha_2\}, \quad \mathbf{b} = \{\beta_1, \beta_2\}, \quad \mathbf{c} = \{\gamma_1, \gamma_2\}, \quad \mathbf{d} = \{\delta_1, \delta_2\},$$

and the same matrix of transformation $\mathbf{u}$ is again applied to give the vertices P, Q, R, S of a quadrilateral, where

$$\mathbf{p} = \mathbf{ua}, \quad \mathbf{q} = \mathbf{ub}, \quad \mathbf{r} = \mathbf{uc}, \quad \mathbf{s} = \mathbf{ud}.$$

Prove that $PQRS$ is also a parallelogram.   [C.]

18. $ABCD$ is a rectangle 6 units by 2 units with the origin at its centre and its sides parallel to the two axes of coordinates

$$(AB \,\|\, CD \,\|\, OX_1, \quad BC \,\|\, AD \,\|\, OX_2).$$

Examine the effect on the rectangle of multiplication of coordinate vectors by the matrix

$$\begin{pmatrix} 2 & 0 \\ 0 & -2 \end{pmatrix}. \quad \text{[S.I.E.]}$$

19. Discuss the geometrical significance of the mapping

$$\mathbf{p}' = \mathbf{ap}$$

in each of the cases:

(i) $\mathbf{a} = \begin{pmatrix} 1 & 0 \\ 0 & -0 \end{pmatrix}$,   (ii) $\mathbf{a} = \begin{pmatrix} 1/\sqrt{2} & -1/\sqrt{2} \\ 1/\sqrt{2} & 1/\sqrt{2} \end{pmatrix}$,

(iii) $\mathbf{a} = \begin{pmatrix} 0 & -1 \\ -1 & 1 \end{pmatrix}$,   (iv) $\mathbf{a} = \begin{pmatrix} 0 & -\frac{1}{3} \\ -\frac{1}{3} & 0 \end{pmatrix}$.   [S.I.E.]

20. Show that the images of the points $\{1, 0\}$, $\{0, 1\}$ under the transformation given by the matrix

$$\begin{pmatrix} a_{11} & a_{12} \\ a_{21} & a_{22} \end{pmatrix}$$

are $\{a_{11}, a_{21}\}$, $\{a_{12}, a_{22}\}$ respectively.

Find transformation matrices $\mathbf{a}$, $\mathbf{b}$, $\mathbf{c}$ which have the following effects on the plane $X_1 O X_2$:

   $\mathbf{a}$ reflects the plane in the line $p_1 = p_2$,

   $\mathbf{b}$ rotates the plane through $\frac{1}{3}\pi$ clockwise,

   $\mathbf{c}$ reflects the plane in the line $p_1 \tan \frac{1}{3}\pi = p_2$.

Evaluate $\mathbf{ab}$ and $\mathbf{ba}$.

Find the image of the square with vertices $\{0,0\}, \{1,0\}, \{1,1\}, \{0,1\}$ under each of the transformation matrices

$$\begin{pmatrix} 1 & 2 \\ 2 & 6 \end{pmatrix}, \quad \begin{pmatrix} 1 & 2 \\ 3 & 6 \end{pmatrix}.$$

Illustrate your answer and comment briefly on the results.   [S.I.E.]

21. Write down the images of the points $\{3, -3\}, \{0,0\}, \{4, -4\}$ under the transformation $\mathbf{p'} = \mathbf{ap}$, where

$$\mathbf{a} = \begin{pmatrix} 12 & 14 \\ -7 & -9 \end{pmatrix}.$$

Show that points on any line through the origin $O\{0,0\}$, are transformed by $[\mathbf{a}]$ into points on another line through the origin.

Show that there are 2 lines through the origin that are transformed into themselves under $[\mathbf{a}]$, and find their equations. Describe how points on these lines are transformed by $[\mathbf{a}]$.

In what important respects do the transformations with matrices

$$\mathbf{b} = \begin{pmatrix} 3 & 6 \\ 1 & 2 \end{pmatrix}, \quad \mathbf{c} = \begin{pmatrix} 3 & 6 \\ -1 & 2 \end{pmatrix}$$

differ from $[\mathbf{a}]$?   [M.A.]

22. The points $A\{0,0\}, B\{3,0\}, C\{3,3\}, D\{0,3\}$ determine a square. What are the coordinates of the images A', B', C', D' under the transformation $\{p_1, p_2\} \to \{p_1 - \frac{3}{2}, p_2 - \frac{3}{2}\}$?

Comment on any invariant properties.   [C.I.E.]

23. Find the image of the circle whose equation is

$$p_1^2 + p_2^2 - 2p_1 + 6p_2 + 1 = 0$$

under the transformation $\mathbf{p} \to 3\mathbf{p}$.

Find the centre of the image circle and the image of the centre of the original circle.   [C.I.E.]

24. The points A, B, C, D have coordinates $\{2,0\}, \{2,1\}, \{0,1\}, \{0,0\}$ respectively. A mapping is defined by

$$\mathbf{p'} = \mathbf{ap},$$

where $\mathbf{a} = \begin{pmatrix} 2 & 5 \\ 1 & 3 \end{pmatrix}.$

Find the images A', B', C', D' of the points A, B, C, D.

A further mapping is defined by

$$\mathbf{p}'' = \mathbf{b}\mathbf{p}',$$

where

$$\mathbf{b} = \begin{pmatrix} 3 & -5 \\ -1 & 2 \end{pmatrix}.$$

Find the images of the points A', B', C', D'. What deductions can be made about the product $\mathbf{ab}$? Represent your work geometrically and comment. [S.I.E.]

25. The set of all points on the line $p_1 - p_2 + 1 = 0$ is transformed under the matrix

$$\begin{pmatrix} 2 & 0 \\ 0 & 1 \end{pmatrix}.$$

Find the coordinates of the self-corres-ponding (invariant) point P. [C.]

26. In the diagram (Figure 218) $OA = AC$, $DA = 2AB$, $BD \perp OC$. The triangle OAB can be transformed into the triangle OCD by the following operations performed in succession:

   (i) an enlargement, centre O;
   (ii) a reflection;
   (iii) a shear.

Give the scale factor for (i), the axis for (ii), and the direction of the shear for (iii). [C.]

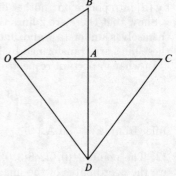

Fig. 218

27. Define a group. Let $G = \{\mathbf{I}, \mathbf{a}, \mathbf{b}, \mathbf{c}\}$, where

$$\mathbf{I} = \begin{pmatrix} 1 & 0 \\ 0 & 1 \end{pmatrix}, \quad \mathbf{a} = \begin{pmatrix} 0 & 1 \\ -1 & 0 \end{pmatrix}, \quad \mathbf{b} = \begin{pmatrix} -1 & 0 \\ 0 & -1 \end{pmatrix}, \quad \mathbf{c} = \begin{pmatrix} 0 & -1 \\ 1 & 0 \end{pmatrix}.$$

Show that the set G with the operation multiplication forms a group. Determine whether the group is Abelian. [S.I.E.]

28. Show that, if $G = \{\mathbf{I}, \mathbf{p}, \mathbf{q}, \mathbf{r}\}$, where

$$\mathbf{I} = \begin{pmatrix} 1 & 0 \\ 0 & 1 \end{pmatrix}, \quad \mathbf{p} = \begin{pmatrix} -1 & 0 \\ 0 & -1 \end{pmatrix}, \quad \mathbf{q} = \begin{pmatrix} 1 & 0 \\ 0 & -1 \end{pmatrix}, \quad \mathbf{r} = \begin{pmatrix} -1 & 0 \\ 0 & 1 \end{pmatrix},$$

then the set G with the operation multiplication forms a group. Determine whether the set G forms a group under addition. [S.I.E.]

29. Two perpendicular straight lines l, m meet in U. Prove that $\mathbf{lm} = \mathbf{U}_\pi$, and that the four transformations $\mathbf{l}$, $\mathbf{m}$, $\mathbf{U}_\pi$, $\mathbf{I}$ form a group under the operation of combination of transformations. [C., adapted.]

30. Give an example of two transformations, neither of which is an isometry, with the property that their product is an isometry other than the identity. [C.]

31. Points $A, B, C, \ldots$ are represented by their position vectors $\mathbf{a}, \mathbf{b}, \mathbf{c}, \ldots$ referred to an origin O. The half-turn with centre A is denoted by $\mathbf{H_a}$ and the translation $O \to C$ is denoted by $\mathbf{T_c}$. Show that

$$\mathbf{T_a\,T_b} = \mathbf{T_{(a+b)}}, \quad \mathbf{H_a\,T_b} = \mathbf{H_{(a-\frac{1}{2}b)}}, \quad \mathbf{H_b\,H_a} = \mathbf{T_{2(b-a)}}.$$

(*Note.* $\mathbf{FG}$ means that the transformation $\mathbf{G}$ acts first and is then followed by $\mathbf{F}$.)

Write down the inverses of $\mathbf{H_a}$ and $\mathbf{T_c}$ and deduce that the set of all translations and half-turns forms a group.

Prove that $\mathbf{H_a\,H_b\,H_c}$ is a half-turn. Hence, or otherwise, prove that

$$\mathbf{H_a\,H_b\,H_c} = \mathbf{H_c\,H_b\,H_a}. \quad [C.]$$

32. Prove that, if a, b are elements of a group, then

$$ab = ba \Rightarrow ba^2 = a^2b.$$

Show that the converse is false by taking a to be an element of order 2 in the group of symmetries of an equilateral triangle (so that $a^2 = $ the identity). [S.M.P.]

33. Let $\mathbf{T}$ be a translation and $\mathbf{M}$ a reflection. Prove that there is a translation $\mathbf{S}$ such that $\mathbf{MT} = \mathbf{SM}$. If we can take $\mathbf{S} = \mathbf{T}$, what can we say about the relation between $\mathbf{T}$ and $\mathbf{M}$?

The pattern P illustrated below (Figure 219) consists of the (whole) axis OX_1, together with a line, for every integer n, of slope $(-1)^n$ and length 1 having its right-hand end-point at $\{n, 0\}$. If $\mathbf{T}$ is the translation

$$\{0, 0\} \to \{1, 0\}$$

and $\mathbf{M}$ is reflection in the axis OX_1, show that every isometry transformation that maps P onto itself is of the form $(\mathbf{TM})^k$ for some integer k. [S.M.P.]

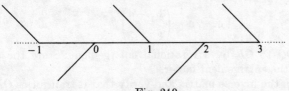

Fig. 219

34. S_3 is the group of all permutations of the set $\{1, 2, 3\}$ of three elements. The elements of S_3 may be listed as follows:

$$\rho_0 = \begin{pmatrix} 1 & 2 & 3 \\ 1 & 2 & 3 \end{pmatrix}, \quad \rho_1 = \begin{pmatrix} 1 & 2 & 3 \\ 2 & 3 & 1 \end{pmatrix}, \quad \rho_2 = \begin{pmatrix} 1 & 2 & 3 \\ 3 & 1 & 2 \end{pmatrix},$$

$$\mu_1 = \begin{pmatrix} 1 & 2 & 3 \\ 1 & 3 & 2 \end{pmatrix}, \quad \mu_2 = \begin{pmatrix} 1 & 2 & 3 \\ 3 & 2 & 1 \end{pmatrix}, \quad \mu_3 = \begin{pmatrix} 1 & 2 & 3 \\ 2 & 1 & 3 \end{pmatrix}.$$

Using the symbol $\tau\sigma$ to stand for 'σ followed by τ', express the elements of S_3 in terms of ρ_1 and μ_1.

Explain why this group has the same structure as the group of isometry transformations of an equilateral triangle under rotations and reflections, and specify which permutations in S_3 correspond to which transformations of the triangle.

Is S_3 Abelian? How many proper subgroups has S_3, and are these subgroups Abelian?   [S.M.P.]

35. Each of the following matrices, when used to pre-multiply column position vectors, gives a transformation in the plane. In each case describe the transformation geometrically and illustrate it by a sketch showing the image of the unit square $OPQR$, where O is $\{0,0\}$, P is $\{1,0\}$, Q is $\{1,1\}$, R is $\{0,1\}$.

(i) $\begin{pmatrix} 3 & 0 \\ 0 & 1 \end{pmatrix}$;   (ii) $\begin{pmatrix} 0 & 0 \\ 0 & 1 \end{pmatrix}$;   (iii) $\begin{pmatrix} -1 & 0 \\ 0 & 1 \end{pmatrix}$;

(iv) $\begin{pmatrix} 0 & -1 \\ -1 & 0 \end{pmatrix}$;   (v) $\begin{pmatrix} 1 & 0 \\ 0 & 2 \end{pmatrix}$;   (vi) $\begin{pmatrix} 1 & 0 \\ 0 & 0 \end{pmatrix}$.

Choose matrices $\mathbf{a}$, $\mathbf{b}$ from these six satisfying

(a) $\mathbf{ab} = \mathbf{ba} \neq \mathbf{0}$;   (b) $\mathbf{ab} \neq \mathbf{ba}$;   (c) $\mathbf{ab} = \mathbf{0}$.   [S.M.P.]

36. The set $\{1,2,3,4,5,6\}$ forms a group under multiplication modulo 7 (that is, a product ab is taken to be the remainder after division by 7, so that $3 \times 5 = 1$, $6 \times 2 = 5$). Write out the combination table for this group.

Describe briefly in geometrical terms a symmetry group which is isomorphic to this group. Identify two subgroups, one of order 2 and one of order 3.   [S.M.P.]

37. Given two points $Q\{1,1\}$ and $R\{-1,7\}$, prove that the matrix

$$\mathbf{a} = \begin{pmatrix} 3 & -4 \\ 4 & 3 \end{pmatrix}$$

transforms OQ to OR by a rotational enlargement. State the angle of rotation and the enlargement factor.

Write down the inverse matrix and verify that it transforms OR to OQ. [S.M.P.]

38. Write down the inverse of $\begin{pmatrix} 5 & 7 \\ 2 & 3 \end{pmatrix}$.

Solve the equation $\begin{pmatrix} 5 & 7 \\ 2 & 3 \end{pmatrix} \begin{pmatrix} x \\ y \end{pmatrix} = \begin{pmatrix} 5 \\ 2 \end{pmatrix}$.

Solve the equation $\begin{pmatrix} 5 & 7 \\ 2 & 3 \end{pmatrix} \begin{pmatrix} x & z \\ y & t \end{pmatrix} = \begin{pmatrix} 5 & 2 \\ 2 & 1 \end{pmatrix}$.   [S.M.P.]

39. A, B, C are three points on a circle centre O. The image of O under reflection in AC is R. Explain why $AOCR$ is a rhombus and state a relation between the sizes of the angles $\angle OAC$, $\angle OAR$.

The image of O under reflection in AB is Q. State a similar relation between the angles $\angle OAB$, $\angle OAQ$ and hence obtain a relation between the angles $\angle BAC$, $\angle QAR$.

If $\mathbf{T}$ is the translation that maps A on O, name, with reasons, the images of R and Q under $\mathbf{T}$. Deduce a relation between the angles $\angle BAC$, $\angle BOC$. [S.M.P.]

40. Under a shear which leaves the origin invariant, $\{1, 2\}$ is mapped to $\{1, 4\}$. Find the matrix $\mathbf{a}$ representing this shear.

Show that the transformation given by the matrix product $\mathbf{ab}$, where

$$\mathbf{b} = \begin{pmatrix} 1 & 2 \\ -2 & -3 \end{pmatrix},$$

is a shear, and describe it fully. [S.M.P.]

41. A plane transformation consists of a counterclockwise rotation of $\frac{1}{4}\pi$ about O, followed by a shear in the direction $\overrightarrow{OX_1}$ with scale factor 2. Find the matrix of the transformation. [S.M.P.]

42. Two equal circles C_1, C_2 intersect in O and A. Prove that there is a rotation about O that takes C_1 to C_2. Prove also that, if P on C_1 goes to Q on C_2, then PAQ is a straight line.

Four points O, A, B, C are such that the circles OBC, OCA, OAB are equal and a point P is taken on the circle OBC; PC meets the circle OCA again in Q; QA meets the circle OAB again in R. Prove that the line RP passes through B. [C.]

43. Given that $\mathbf{a} = \begin{pmatrix} 2 & 0 \\ 2 & 2 \end{pmatrix}$, find the matrix product $\mathbf{ap}$, where $\mathbf{p} = \{p_1, p_2\}$.

$OABC$ is a square whose corners are the points $\{0, 0\}, \{1, 0\}, \{1, 1\}, \{0, 1\}$. Under the transformation $\mathbf{a}$ the square is mapped on $ODEF$. Find the coordinates of D, E, F. Hence prove that $ODEF$ is a parallelogram and find its area. [C.]

44. If P is the point $\{3, 7\}$, write down the coordinates of the point obtained by reflecting P in the line $p_1 - p_2 = 0$, and the coordinates of the point obtained by rotating P through $\frac{1}{2}\pi$ in the counterclockwise sense about the origin.

Give the matrices corresponding to these transformations. [S.M.P.]

45. Find the eigenvalues and eigenvectors of the matrix

$$\begin{pmatrix} 1 & 4 \\ 4 & -5 \end{pmatrix}$$

and show that the eigenvectors are orthogonal. [S.I.E.]

46. Give a list of the three isometries, other than the identity, which are rotations in its own plane mapping a square $ABCD$ onto itself. State a binary operation under which these isometries, with the identity, form a group and prove that it is a group.

Give a similar list for reflections. Do they form a group in the same way as the rotations?

Determine any modifications required in your answer to the problem in the first paragraph if the square $ABCD$ is replaced by a rectangle which is not a square. [C.]

47. The foot of the perpendicular from a point A to a line l is the point B. Prove that reflection in l followed by a half-turn about A is equivalent to a translation $2\overrightarrow{BA}$ followed by reflection in the line AB. [C.]

48. (a) Define the inverse $\mathbf{a}^{-1}$ of a square invertible matrix $\mathbf{a}$. Prove that

$$(\mathbf{a}^T)^{-1} = (\mathbf{a}^{-1})^T.$$

(b) The matrix
$$\begin{pmatrix} \cos 2\theta & \sin 2\theta \\ \sin 2\theta & -\cos 2\theta \end{pmatrix}$$

represents a reflection of the plane in the line $p_2 = p_1 \tan \theta$.

(i) Write down the matrix that represents a half-turn about the origin, and find the matrix $\mathbf{b}$ representing reflection in the line $p_2 = p_1 \tan \theta$ followed by a half-turn about the origin.

(ii) What single transformation of the plane is represented by $\mathbf{b}$? [C.I.E.]

49. Write down the characteristic equation of

$$\mathbf{a} = \begin{pmatrix} 2 & 1 \\ 3 & 4 \end{pmatrix}.$$

Find the eigenvalues and associated eigenvectors. Illustrate your result geometrically. [S.I.E.]

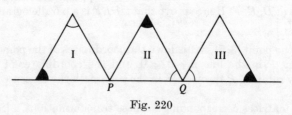

Fig. 220

50. A prism whose cross-section is an equilateral triangle with two differently marked corners lies on a table in position I (Figure 220). It is rotated about the edge through P into position II, then about the edge through Q into position III. Identify a transformation that could describe the mapping I → III. [S.M.P.]

51. $\mathbf{M}$ is the set of matrices of the form $\begin{pmatrix} b & a \\ 0 & b \end{pmatrix}$, where a and b are positive integers. A relation $\mathbf{R}$ is defined on $\mathbf{M}$ by

$$\mathbf{M}_1 \, \mathbf{R} \, \mathbf{M}_2 \Leftrightarrow a_1 b_2 = a_2 b_1,$$

where $\qquad \mathbf{M}_1 = \begin{pmatrix} b_1 & a_1 \\ 0 & b_1 \end{pmatrix}, \quad \mathbf{M}_2 = \begin{pmatrix} b_2 & a_2 \\ 0 & b_2 \end{pmatrix}.$

Show that $\mathbf{R}$ is an equivalence relation.

For what values of a, b does the matrix $\begin{pmatrix} b & a \\ 0 & b \end{pmatrix}$ belong to the same equivalence class as $\begin{pmatrix} 3 & 2 \\ 0 & 3 \end{pmatrix}$?   [M.A.]

TWO PROBLEMS

These two problems arise from work by Mr W. Wynne Willson, of the School of Education of the University of Birmingham, and by Mr S. N. Collings, of the Faculty of Mathematics of the Open University. Each has been adapted to suit the present text; and each, the reader should note, can be developed much further as, indeed, these writers have done. I am most grateful for permission to use them,

1. From the work of Mr Wynne Willson

Let A, B, C, D be four points on a circle taken, for convenience, in that order round the circle (Figure 221). Denote by a, b, c, d, x, y lines AB, BC, CD, DA, AC, BD respectively, and consider the isometry **dcba** defined by the reflections **d, c, b, a** in turn. As in the text,

$$\mathbf{dc\,ba} = (\mathbf{dc})\,(\mathbf{ba}),$$

where **dc** is a rotation about D and **ba** is a rotation about B.

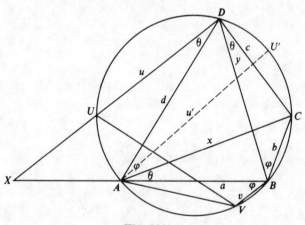

Fig. 221

Following standard procedure, let u be the line such that

$$\mathbf{uy} = \mathbf{dc}$$

and v the line such that

$$\mathbf{yv} = \mathbf{ba}.$$

Then $$\mathbf{dc\,ba} = (\mathbf{uy})(\mathbf{yv}) = \mathbf{uyyv} = \mathbf{uv}.$$

The resultant is a rotation if u, v intersect and a translation if u, v are parallel. We prove that the latter is, in fact, the case:

The line u passes through D; let it meet the circle again in U. The line v passes through B; let it meet the circle again in V. Then

$$\mathbf{uy} = \mathbf{dc} \Rightarrow \angle UDB = \angle ADC$$

and $$\mathbf{yv} = \mathbf{ba} \Rightarrow \angle DBV = \angle CBA$$

$$\Rightarrow \angle UDB + \angle DBV = \angle ADC + \angle CBA$$

$$= 2 \text{ right angles} \quad (ABCD \text{ cyclic})$$

$$\Rightarrow u \parallel v.$$

Hence $\mathbf{dc\,ba}$ is a *translation* in the direction perpendicular to u and v, in the sense from u to v, and of magnitude $2p$ where p is, for example, the length of the perpendicular from B to UD.

Exercise A

1. Prove that
$$\angle UDA = \angle BDC = \angle BAC,$$
$$\angle VBA = \angle DBC = \angle DAC$$

and that $$UA = BC, \quad VA = CD.$$

Deduce that $$UC \parallel AB, \quad VC \parallel AD.$$

2. Prove that the triangles UAV, BCD are congruent and that UV, DB are equal.

3. Prove that, if $X = DU \cap AB$, then the triangles XDB, ADC are similar and deduce that

$$DX = \frac{DA \cdot DB}{DC}.$$

4. By comparing the areas of the similar triangles XDB, ADC, or if you prefer, by trigonometry, prove that the length of the perpendicular from B to the line u can be expressed in terms of A, B, C, D in the form

$$\frac{2BD \cdot \triangle DCA}{DC \cdot DA}.$$

[For the area-ratio theorem for similar triangles, see Chapter 10, Exercise C, Question 8.]

Continuing the discussion, observe that $\mathbf{dcba}$ is defined by taking four of the lines joining A, B, C, D in the order DA, AB, BC, CD. Two other orders suggest themselves after some manipulations of the product:

$$\mathbf{dcba} = \mathbf{dcbx\,xa} \qquad (\mathbf{x^2 = I})$$
$$= \mathbf{d(cbx)\,xa}$$
$$= \mathbf{d(xbc)\,xa} \qquad (\mathbf{cbx = xbc}\ \text{for concurrent lines})$$
$$= \mathbf{dx\,bc\,xa}$$
$$= (\mathbf{dx\,by})(\mathbf{ycxa}) \quad (\mathbf{y^2 = I}).$$

We consider, then, the product $\mathbf{dxby}$ corresponding to DA, AC, CB, BD and $\mathbf{ycxa}$ corresponding to BD, DC, CA, AB.

Exercise B

Let the line through A parallel to u and v meet the circle again in U'. Call the line AU' by the name u'.

1. Prove that $\triangle U'AB = \triangle DAC$ and deduce that

$$\mathbf{dx = u'a}.$$

Prove also that $\qquad\qquad\mathbf{by = av}$

and deduce that $\qquad\qquad\mathbf{dx\,by = u'v}.$

2. Prove that $\qquad\qquad\mathbf{ycxa = uu'}.$

3. Deduce that $\qquad\qquad\mathbf{dc\,ba = (u'v)\,(uu')}.$

Since $\mathbf{uv, uu', u'v}$ are *parallel* translations with

$$\mathbf{uv = (u'v)\,(uu')},$$

it follows that

$$\mathbf{uv = (uu')\,(u'v)},$$

as expected, and that *the translation* $\mathbf{uv}$ *is the sum of the translations* $\mathbf{uu', u'v}$.

Exercise C

1. Using the method of Exercise A, Question 4, prove that the length of the perpendicular from A to the line u can be expressed in the form

$$\frac{2AD \cdot \triangle DCB}{DC \cdot DB}\,.$$

2. Prove similarly, by considering the triangles BAY, BCD, where $Y = AD \cap BV$, that the length of the perpendicular from A to the line v can be expressed in the form

$$\frac{2AB \cdot \triangle BCD}{BC \cdot BD}\,.$$

3. By considering the similar triangles ACN, BCM, where N, M are the feet of the perpendiculars from C to AD, AC respectively, prove that

$$\frac{\triangle CAD}{\triangle CBD} = \frac{CA.AD}{CB.BD}.$$

(An alternative proof by trigonometry is simple.)

4. From preceding work, deduce *the theorem of Ptolemy* (Chapter 11, Illustration 3) that, for the cyclic quadrilateral $ABCD$,

$$AB.CD + AD.BC = AC.BD.$$

2. From the work of Mr Collings

This problem is essentially directed towards properties of lines through the orthocentre of a triangle.

Let l be any line cutting the sides BC, CA, AB of a triangle ABC in points U, V, W respectively (Figure 222).

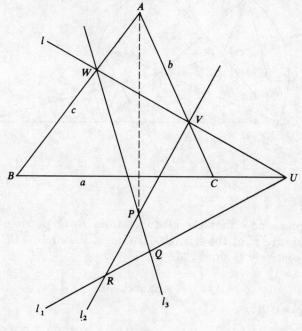

Fig. 222

Denote by l_1, l_2, l_3 the reflections of l in the lines BC, CA, AB (denoted by a, b, c) respectively, and write

$$P = l_2 \cap l_3, \quad Q = l_3 \cap l_1, \quad R = l_1 \cap l_2.$$

Then *there is a rotation about A that sends l_3 to l_2:*

In fact, $l_3\mathbf{cb} = (l_3\mathbf{c})\,\mathbf{b} = l\mathbf{b}$

$$= l_2,$$

and $\mathbf{cb}$ is the required rotation.

Exercise D

1. Deduce that A is equidistant from l_2, l_3 and that AP bisects an angle at P of the triangle PQR.

2. Prove that AP, BQ, CR meet in the in-centre, or in one of the escribed centres, of the triangle PQR. (In Figure 222, it is the in-centre.)

3. Prove that the counterclockwise angle from l_3 to l_2 is equal to $2\,\triangle BAC$.

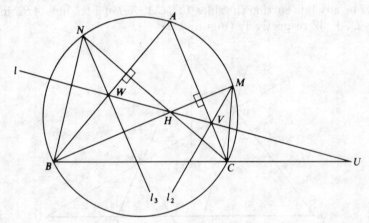

Fig. 223

Suppose now that the altitudes from B, C, passing through the orthocentre H of the triangle ABC meet the circle ABC again in M, N respectively (Figure 223).

Exercise E

1. Prove that

$$\angle BNH = \angle BAC = \angle BHN = \angle CHM = \angle CMH,$$

and deduce that M, N are the reflections of H in the lines CA, AB respectively.

2. A line l through H meets CA, AB in V, W respectively. Prove that the lines $l_2 = MV$ and $l_3 = NW$ are the reflections of l in CA, AB respectively.

3. Prove that $P = l_2 \cap l_3$ lies on the circle ABC.

4. Deduce that the points $Q = l_3 \cap l_1$, $R = l_1 \cap l_2$, defined previously, coincide with P, so that *the lines l_1, l_2, l_3 are concurrent at a point of the circumcircle.*

5. The altitudes AH, BH, CH of a triangle ABC meet the circle ABC in points L, M, N respectively. An arbitrary point K is taken on the circle (a convenient position is on the arc BC opposite to A) and KL meets BC in U. The line HU meets CA, AB in V, W respectively. Use the preceding work to show that MV, NW pass through K and deduce that the feet of the perpendiculars from K to BC, CA, AB are collinear, lying on the line 'half-way' between K and the line UVW. (This is the *Simson line* of K with respect to the triangle ABC; compare Chapter 11, Illustration 2.)

APPENDIX
Uniqueness of parallel

It was proved in Chapter 2, Section 3, that two parallel lines have no point in common. The converse, that *two lines with no point in common are parallel*, is less clear and its proof requires help from the later Chapter 10.

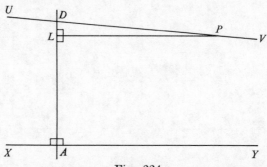

Fig. 224

Let XY, UV be two such lines. Take $D \in UV$ and draw DA perpendicular to XY. Take *any* point P on UV and draw PL perpendicular to DA. If L is at D, the result is proved, since then $DA \perp UV$ and $DA \perp XY$, so that $UV \parallel XY$.

If L is not at D, take the point Q on UV such that

$$\overrightarrow{DP}/\overrightarrow{DQ} = \overrightarrow{DL}/\overrightarrow{DA}.$$

Then, using the basic assumption at the end of Chapter 10, Section 2,

$$QA \parallel PL$$

and so

$$QA \perp DA.$$

Since YA, QA are both perpendicular to DA, they are the same line, and so UV, XY have the point Q in common – a contradiction.

Hence L must lie at D, and so the two lines are indeed parallel.

ANSWERS

Chapter 1

Ex. B   **1.** Concurrent.

Chapter 4

Ex. C   **7.** $PQRS$ becomes, in turn, $PSRQ$, $RQPS$, $RSPQ$, $RSPQ$, $RQPS$.

Ex. F   **3.** $R \notin UPQ \Leftrightarrow R\mathbf{n} \neq R\mathbf{lm}$. The case 2 is very special.

Ex. G   **2.** (i) $PQ \| u$;   (ii) $PQ \| u$ and length $PQ =$ twice distance from u to v;   (iii) take $PQ =$ twice distance from u to v.

Ex. H   **1.** Magnitude and direction $2\overrightarrow{BD}$.   **3.** On v.

Chapter 5

Ex. C   **1.** A, A, C, C'.   **3.** $B_2C_2 \| CA$.   **4.** $\frac{1}{3}\pi, \frac{1}{4}\pi, \frac{5}{12}\pi$ ($60°, 45°, 75°$).

Chapter 6

Ex. B   **2.** If points U, V, W are such that P is the middle point of AU, Q is the middle point of UV, and R is the middle point of VW, then S is the middle point of WA.

Chapter 7

Ex. A   **4.** (i) Parallel if C is right angle;   (ii) not coincident. **5.** A, C, A' collinear if $AB = AC$.

Chapter 8

Ex. H   Symmetry about (*a*) the following lines:

1. bisector of vertical angle;   **2.** bisectors of the angles;   **3.** lines through centre parallel to sides, and about diagonals;   **4.** mediators of the sides; **5.** mediators of the sides, and about diagonals;   **6.** none;   **7.** none;   **8.** diagonals;   **9.** diagonal joining intersections of the equal sides.

    (*b*) the following *points* (using 'centre' in obvious sense):

2. centre;   **3.** centre;   **5.** centre;   **7.** centre;   **8.** centre.

Chapter 9

Ex. A   **8.** The 8 lines all touch the circle described in the square (that is, touching all four sides). The centre of the circle is at the centre of the square, and the radius is equal to half a side. Use symmetry for the lines $A_2 B_1$, etc.

Ex. H   **12.** Let A be the centre of the first circle. Draw radii AU, AV so that $\angle UAV$ is the supplement of the given angle, and let the tangents at U, V meet at T. Draw the circle of centre A and radius AT. Similarly for the other circle. The two constructed circles intersect (if at all) in a point such as is required.

Ex. I   **1.** Rotate the smaller circle about O through a half-turn to meet the larger circle again in X. Then XO is the required line.

2. Draw a chord XY of U, passing through P, and let XA, YA meet V in X', Y'. Repeat for ZW. Then $PO_\theta = X'Y' \cap Z'W'$.

Chapter 11

Ex. D   **1.** Take any point on the first circle as A, and apply the transformation $A\{AC/AB, \alpha\}$ to the second. This meets the third circle in C.

Ex. G   **4.** $AC \cap BD$.

Chapter 12

Ex. B   **4.** (i) $2p_1 + p_2 - 2 = 0$;   (ii) $2p_1 - p_2 - 1 = 0$;   (iii) $3p_2 + 2p_1 - 1 = 0$.

Ex. C   **2.** (i) $\{k, 0\}$ for all k;   (ii) $\{0, k\}$ for all k;   (iii) $\{0, 0\}$.

Ex. D   **1.** For [1], all points of l itself; that is, $p_2 = p_1 \tan \alpha$. For $[O_\beta]$, origin only.

Ex. F   **9.** For example, (i) $\mathbf{a} = \begin{pmatrix} 0 & p \\ q & r \end{pmatrix}$, $\mathbf{b} = \begin{pmatrix} u & v \\ w & 0 \end{pmatrix}$;

(ii) $\mathbf{a} = \begin{pmatrix} q & 0 \\ 0 & p \end{pmatrix}$, $\mathbf{b} = \begin{pmatrix} 0 & v \\ w & 0 \end{pmatrix}$, where $q = p$.

Ex. I   **1.** (i) $\begin{pmatrix} 1 & 0 \\ -1 & 1 \end{pmatrix}$;   (ii) $\begin{pmatrix} 1 & 0 \\ 1 & -1 \end{pmatrix}$;   (iii) $\begin{pmatrix} 1 & 0 \\ \frac{4}{3} & \frac{1}{3} \end{pmatrix}$;   (iv) $\begin{pmatrix} 1 & 2 \\ 0 & -1 \end{pmatrix}$.

2. (i) $2p_1 - p_2 = 0$;   (ii) $p_1 + p_2 = 0$;   (iii) $2p_1 + p_2 = 0$.

6. (i) line $2p_1 + p_2 = 0$;   (ii) line $2p_1 - p_2 = 0$;   (iii) line $p_1 = 0$;   (iv) line $2p_1 + p_2 = 0$.

Ex. L   **2.** $k = 6; \lambda\{2, -3\}$.   **3.** $k = 1, \lambda\{2, -1\}; k = 7, \lambda\{4, 1\}$.   **4.** (i) $\lambda\{0, 1\}$;   (ii) $\{0, 0\}$;   (iii) $\{0, 0\}$;   (iv) $\lambda\{1, -1\}$;   (v) $\{0, 0\}$.

Chapter 13

Ex. C   3. $p = -2$, $k^2 = 5$.   **4.** None.   **7.** For example, $\mathbf{u} = \begin{Bmatrix} 3 & \frac{4}{5} \\ 1 & \frac{3}{5} \end{Bmatrix}$,

$\mathbf{v} = \begin{Bmatrix} 1 & 0 \\ -3 & 1 \end{Bmatrix}$. If $\mathbf{uv} = \mathbf{a}$ (orthogonal), then $\mathbf{u} = \mathbf{av}^{-1}$, so that $\mathbf{u}$ can be found for arbitrary non-singular $\mathbf{v}$ and arbitrary orthogonal $\mathbf{a}$.

Ex. D   6. (i) Reflection in line at $\frac{1}{8}\pi$ to OX_1;   (ii) rotation about origin through $-\frac{1}{4}\pi$;   (iii) rotation about origin through $\frac{1}{8}\pi$;   (iv) reflection in line at $\frac{1}{15}\pi$ to OX_1;   (v) reflection in line at $\frac{3}{4}\pi$ to OX_1;   (vi) reflection in OX_1.

Ex. E   2. (i) Stretch $\sqrt{2}$, reflection in line at $\frac{1}{8}\pi$ to OX_1;   (ii) stretch 2, rotation $\frac{1}{3}\pi$;   (iii) stretch 5, reflection in OX_1;   (iv) stretch 6, reflection in line at $\frac{1}{6}\pi$ to OX_1;   (v) stretch 4, reflection in line at $\frac{3}{4}\pi$ to OX_1.

Ex. F   3. The lines $l_2 p_2 + m = 0$ are self-corresponding.

Chapter 14

Ex. A   1. (i) -1, $\{1, -1\}$; 6, $\{3, 4\}$.   (ii) -1, $\{2, 3\}$; 6, $\{1, -2\}$.   (iii) 1, $\{1, -3\}$; 2, $\{0, 1\}$.   (iv) 0, $\{2, -3\}$; 7, $\{1, 2\}$.   (v) 2, $\{1, 1\}$; -4, $\{1, -5\}$. (vi) $7, \{1, 2\}$; $-5, \{5, -2\}$.   (vii) $3, \{1, 1\}$ only.   (viii) $1, \{1, 0\}$; $5, \{1, 2\}$.

3. (i) 1, $\{\cos\frac{1}{2}\theta, \sin\frac{1}{2}\theta\}$; -1, $\{\sin\frac{1}{2}\theta, -\cos\frac{1}{2}\theta\}$.   (ii) (complex numbers) $\cos\theta \pm i\sin\theta$, $\{1, \mp i\}$.   (iii) $\pm\sqrt{(a^2+b^2)}$, $\{a \pm \sqrt{(a^2+b^2)}, b\}$. Other forms are possible; e.g. $\{b, \pm(a^2+b^2)-a\}$.   (iv) 1, $\{1, 0\}$.

Miscellaneous Exercise

7. $\{3, 4\}$.

8. Reflection in BA followed by shear.

13. Construct $\triangle PBQ$ of required shape with $PQ = AB$.

14. $\triangle BPQ$ has constant shape, so BP as great as possible – diameter.

16. (i) Half-turn and stretch to $\{0, 0\}$, $\{-4, -2\}$, $\{-2, -4\}$;
   (ii) $\frac{1}{6}\pi$ rotation to $\{0, 0\}$, $\{\sqrt{3}-\frac{1}{2}, 1+\frac{1}{2}\sqrt{3}\}$, $\{\frac{1}{2}\sqrt{3}-1, \frac{1}{2}+\sqrt{3}\}$;
   (iii) shear to $\{0, 0\}$, $\{4, 1\}$, $\{5, 2\}$;
   (iv) let the line through a point M parallel to OP_2 meet OP_1 in U. Then the transform of M is M', where $\overrightarrow{UM'} = 3\overrightarrow{UM}$.

18. Reflected in OX_1 and dimensions doubled.

19. (i) Reflection in OX_1;   (ii) rotation through $\frac{1}{4}\pi$;   (iii) reflection in $p_1 + p_2 = 0$;   (iv) reflection in $p_1 + p_2 = 0$ and 'stretch' of $\frac{1}{3}$.

20. $\mathbf{a} = \begin{pmatrix} 0 & 1 \\ 1 & 0 \end{pmatrix}$, $\mathbf{b} = \begin{pmatrix} \frac{1}{2} & -\frac{1}{2}\sqrt{3} \\ \frac{1}{2}\sqrt{3} & \frac{1}{2} \end{pmatrix}$, $\mathbf{c} = \begin{pmatrix} -\frac{1}{2} & \frac{1}{2}\sqrt{3} \\ \frac{1}{2}\sqrt{3} & \frac{1}{2} \end{pmatrix}$.

$\mathbf{ab} = \begin{pmatrix} \frac{1}{2}\sqrt{3} & \frac{1}{2} \\ \frac{1}{2} & -\frac{1}{2}\sqrt{3} \end{pmatrix}$, $\mathbf{ba} = \begin{pmatrix} -\frac{1}{2}\sqrt{3} & \frac{1}{2} \\ \frac{1}{2} & \frac{1}{2}\sqrt{3} \end{pmatrix}$.

(i) *Parallelogram* $\{0,0\}, \{1,2\}, \{3,8\}, \{2,6\}$;
(ii) on *straight line* $p_2 = 3p_1$; matrix singular.

21. $\{-6,6\}, \{0,0\}, \{-8,8\}$.
Lines $p_1 + p_2 = 0$, $p_1 + 2p_2 = 0$. First line, reflected in origin and then stretched with factor 2; stretched factor 5. (The eigenvalues are -2 and 5.)
b is singular, so images are collinear.
c has no self-corresponding lines.

22. $\{-\frac{3}{2}, -\frac{3}{2}\}, \{\frac{3}{2}, -\frac{3}{2}\}, \{\frac{3}{2}, \frac{3}{2}\}, \{-\frac{3}{2}, \frac{3}{2}\}$.
Isometry – in fact, translation in the direction $p_1 = p_2$.

23. $p_1^2 + p_2^2 - 6p_1 + 18p_2 + 9 = 0$. Both $\{3, -9\}$.

24. $\{4,2\}, \{9,5\}, \{5,3\}, \{0,0\}$; $\{2,0\}, \{2,1\}, \{0,1\}, \{0,0\}$. $\mathbf{ab} = \mathbf{I}$.
Square $\rightarrow$ parallelogram $\rightarrow$ first square.

25. $\{0,1\}$.

26. (i) 2; (ii) OC; (iii) $\overrightarrow{CO}$.

27. Abelian.

28. No unit under addition.

30. Use, for example, $\mathbf{uv} = \mathbf{a} \Rightarrow \mathbf{u} = \mathbf{av}^{-1}$, where **a** gives an isometry.

33. **T** parallel to the axis of **M**.

34. Several ways; for example,
$$\rho_0 = \mu_1^2, \quad \rho_2 = \rho_1^2, \quad \mu_2 = \mu_1\rho_1, \quad \mu_3 = \rho_1\mu_1.$$
Not Abelian ($\mu_1\rho_1 \neq \rho_1\mu_1$).
Sub-groups $(\rho_0 \mu_1), (\rho_0 \mu_2), (\rho_0 \mu_3), (\rho_0 \rho_1 \rho_2)$.

35. (i) Let the line through any point M parallel to OP_1 meet OP_2 in U.
Then the transform of M is M', where $\overrightarrow{UM'} = 3\overrightarrow{UM}$;
  (ii) The transpose of a point M is the foot of the perpendicular from M to OP_2;
  (iii) Reflection in OP_2;
  (iv) Reflection in $p_1 + p_2 = 0$;
  (v) Similar to (i); (vi) similar to (ii).
  (a) take (i), (ii); (b) take (i), (iv); (c) take (ii), (vi).

36. Table direct.
Group of rotations of regular hexagon about centre.
Sub-groups $\{1, 6\}, \{1, 2, 4\}$.

37. Angle θ, where $\cos\theta = \frac{3}{5}$; $r = 5$.

Inverse $\dfrac{1}{25}\begin{pmatrix} 3 & 4 \\ -4 & 3 \end{pmatrix}$.

38. $\begin{pmatrix} 1 \\ 0 \end{pmatrix}$, $\begin{pmatrix} 1 & -1 \\ 0 & 1 \end{pmatrix}$.

39. (This is a very nice proof that the angle BOC at the centre is double the angle BAC at the circumference.)

40. $\mathbf{a} = \begin{pmatrix} 1 & 0 \\ 2 & 1 \end{pmatrix}$, $\mathbf{ab} = \begin{pmatrix} 1 & 2 \\ 0 & 1 \end{pmatrix}$,

so $\mathbf{ab}$ is like $\mathbf{a}$ with the roles of OX_1, OX_2 interchanged.

41. $\begin{pmatrix} \dfrac{3}{\sqrt{2}} & \dfrac{1}{\sqrt{2}} \\ \dfrac{1}{\sqrt{2}} & \dfrac{1}{\sqrt{2}} \end{pmatrix}$.

43. Area 4.

44. $\{7, 3\}$; $\{-7, 3\}$. $\begin{pmatrix} 0 & 1 \\ 1 & 0 \end{pmatrix}$; $\begin{pmatrix} 0 & -1 \\ 1 & 0 \end{pmatrix}$.

45. $k = 3$, $\lambda\{2, 1\}$; $k = -7$, $\lambda\{1, -2\}$.

46. Rotations about centre through $\frac{1}{2}\pi$, π, $\frac{3}{2}\pi$.
Reflections about diagonals and the lines through centre parallel to sides; not group.
Omit $\frac{1}{2}\pi$, $\frac{3}{2}\pi$.

48. $\begin{pmatrix} -1 & 0 \\ 0 & -1 \end{pmatrix}$. $\mathbf{b} = \begin{pmatrix} -\cos 2\theta & -\sin 2\theta \\ -\sin 2\theta & \cos 2\theta \end{pmatrix}$.
Reflection in the line through the origin perpendicular to the given line.

49. $k = 1$, $\lambda\{1, -1\}$; $k = 5$, $\lambda\{1, 3\}$.
Point on $p_1 + p_2 = 0$ unchanged; point on $3p_1 - p_2 = 0$ 'stretched by a multiple 5'.

50. Rotation through $120°$ about R, the third vertex of the triangle on PQ.

51. $a = 2\lambda$, $b = 3\lambda$.

INDEX